Maine Cottage
October
2001

Praise for *Walk on Water*

"A powerful, moving memoir and ode to fishing... Eloquent, raw, funny, this Hemingway has a voice all her own."

—*The New York Times Book Review*

"This is a brave, beautiful, and funny memoir by a woman who nearly drowns in the family legacy. Lorian Hemingway's famous grandfather would be proud to see how she casts a fly in fast water, but he'd be even more impressed by her toughness and talent as a writer."

—Carl Hiaasen

"Enchanting and excruciating, delicious and chilling, a memoir full of pain and courage—a drama of self-deception finally conquered by truthfulness... At its heart a book about life, fear, self, survival."

—*The Baltimore Sun*

"Ernest's granddaughter reels in memories of her troubled family, alcoholism and the happiness that can be found at the end of a fishing pole."

—*People*

"Unflinchingly candid but not unduly confessional, this is a primer on cultivating the luck required to connect with fish, as well as to survive one's own wounds and foolishness."

—*San Francisco Chronicle*

"Hemingway writes lyrically, without self-pity, and with a dry sense of humor of her harrowing and difficult life."

—*The Washington Post Book World*

"Lorian Hemingway tells terrific stories: stories about the fearless and curious child she was, about risks she has taken all her life from temperament and addiction, about the people she honors for their belief in her.... It is composed with honesty and wicked humor."

—*The Seattle Times/Post Intelligencer*

"*Walk on Water* is certainly the most harrowing of fishing books. But how heartening it is to see angling as part of the process of redemption when, as with Lorian Hemingway, the stakes are so mortally high and the struggle so moving."

—Thomas McGuane

"For this Hemingway, it's a love of fly-fishing, a weakness for drink, and a fine way with words." —*Time*

"The story of her recovery may be the most grueling one you've ever read. When she says the fishing saved her, when she uses it as a metaphor for salvation, it will strike readers as an idea organically arrived at rather than as a theatrical device. . . . A brutally honest story."

—*St. Petersburg Times*

"A great fishing book, more than a fishing book, *Walk on Water* is one of the most beautiful thank-you notes to unconditional compassion I've seen." —David James Duncan

"In this raw, to-hell-and-back memoir the enormously talented granddaughter of Ernest Hemingway describes, among other things, how she has fished some of the waters her grandfather loved, and battled the same self-destructive alcoholism that haunted him." —*Kirkus Reviews* (starred review)

"[Hemingway] tells this painful, ultimately triumphant tale with grace, wit and candor. . . . A work of sincerity, depth and power."

—*The Tampa Tribune-Times*

"This is a glorious book that's hard to put down. Of all the funny, sad, intriguing, beguiling characters, Hemingway is the biggest draw. Her honesty, her sense of humor, her total lack of guile—all are presented in that way with words that seems to run in families named Hemingway." —*Jackson Clarion-Ledger*

Walk on Water

Walk on Water

A MEMOIR

Lorian Hemingway

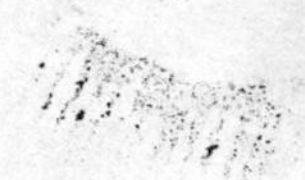

A Harvest Book
Harcourt Brace & Company
San Diego New York London

First published by Simon & Schuster.
Grateful acknowledgment is made for permission to reprint lyrics from "Suzanne" by Leonard Cohen. Copyright © 1967 Sony/ATV Songs LLC (Renewed). All rights administered by Sony/ATV Music Publishing, 8 Music Square West, Nashville, TN 37203. All rights reserved. Used by permission.

Library of Congress Cataloging-in-Publication Data
Hemingway, Lorian, 1951–
Walk on water: a memoir/Lorian Hemingway.—1st Harvest ed.
p. cm.—(A Harvest book)
ISBN 0-15-600709-6
1. Hemingway, Lorian, 1951– . 2. Women authors, American—20th century Biography. 3. Women fishers—United States Biography. 4. Fishing—United States. I. Title.
PS3558.E479127Z472 1999
813'.54—dc 99-15147
[B]

Designed by Leslie Phillips
Printed in the United States of America
First Harvest edition 1999
A C E F D B

Acknowledgments

FOR REMINDING ME that friends are as dear as family and a whole lot funnier, I want to thank the following people for their unfailing support: Holly Morris, Jessica Maxwell, Dolores Baer, Mitch Hale, Dr. James Plath, Carol Shaughnessy, Kate Hart, Joe Veler, Hubert Grissom, Mike Krause, Julie Rosten, Valerie Hemingway, Edward Hemingway, Randy Wayne White, Michael Whalton, Tom Martin, Rocky Flowers, Wendy Tucker, Rudy Prazen, Bob Bender, Tamará Mills for being so brave. And for *knowing* me, loving me, Jeffrey Dale Baker.

This book is for Dr. Howard Engle,

and for my fish-girl, Cristen

Jesus was a sailor when he walked upon the water
And he spent a long time watching from his
lonely wooden tower
And when he knew for certain only drowning men
could see him
He said all men shall be sailors then until the sea
shall free them
But he himself was broken long before the sky
would open
Forsaken, almost human, he sank beneath your
wisdom like a stone

LEONARD COHEN, "Suzanne"

Walk on Water

Chapter

ONE

I TAKE FISH personally, the way I have my life, like a sacrament. This is my body. Eat of it. This is my blood. Drink. I imagine this reverence is what they want of me. The alchemists made an eyewash (collyrium) of fish, believing it would bring omniscience. I've tried to envision the process: cooking the fish, as the alchemists instructed, until it "yellowed," mashing it into a crumbly pulp, mixing it with water, and then filling the eyes with this paste so one might gaze with as much dimension as trout in a clear stream. But as with all things in alchemy, it was the process that mattered, the final result never as important as the ritual preceding it.

Knowing fish is a process. I have been acquainting myself for forty years. To know fish you have to have been intimate, the way the alchemists were. One of the first fish I ever caught as a kid was a baby bass netted from a deep Mississippi ravine I lived in in summer. It was my refuge, that ravine, a place of discovery, revealer of miracles, its depth filled with a heavy current of reddish brown water during the spring floods, its red clay bottom dried to a pockmarking of deep holes by mid-July. I was tirelessly curious when I was young, bound inextricably to all natural mysteries behind four walls, nervous and jumpy if made to sit too long indoors, recalcitrant once sprung.

I'd watched this particular fish for days, trapped in a pothole in the ravine, swimming in a quick panic from one side to the other, instinctively seeking a tributary from its footwide prison. I empathized, imagined myself locked in my room for days, dizzy and breathless from claustrophobia, frantic enough to pull up the flooring with my bare hands. I understood feeling trapped, my life then nothing more than a crash course in how to escape. Escape meant steering past my mother, who sat limp at the kitchen table, stupid from vodka, or creeping past the time bomb that was my stepfather as he lay snoring, passed out in his recliner. I'd turn the handle quick on the front door and sink into the thick Mississippi heat, feeling, once I'd made it to the ravine, as if I had, by sleight of hand, through sheer caginess, become someone else. My head, which always seemed to buzz with a jumpy current whenever my mother raised a full glass to her lips, was clear.

Along the red clay of the ravine lip my bare feet moved with extraordinary balance, and I slid deep into the ravine bed without a sound, a small avalanche of pebbles falling in my wake. I stood then surrounded by wide canyon walls, a young girl ready to trap the very source of summer. I thought often it was the Cherokee in me that let me move like an animal, quiet, steady, aware. My great-grandfather had been a chief. His name was Golden for the strain of burnt-gold hair and green eyes that surfaced every few generations. My mother had the honey-colored hair, the green eyes. And then there was the dark strain. Mine.

After a few days the water in the pothole had diminished by half and grew so thick with ravine mud that the fish hung motionless in the ooze, its gills laboring for the oxygen it needed. On my knees I stared into the hole, goldfish net in hand, thinking it was evil, what I was about to do, snatch a living creature from its habitat and bring it, luckless, into my own. I remember the delicate thin striping on its flanks as I lifted it, unprotesting, from the muck, and how soft and filmy the skin felt as I stroked a finger along its length. I remember, too, how my heart raced as I dropped the fish into the jar, watched him sink quickly and then just as quickly take his first breath in a new world. Within moments he was moving through the jar as manically as he had the pothole days before. I had given resurrection in a pint of water, become God to a fish. Years later I would remember that moment as one of grace.

Fish became my fascination and began to appear in dreams, their shadows deep in dark water, cruising, fins breaking the surface from time to time, a teasing swirl of movement as I stood onshore with net or rod or hands poised to strike. In one dream I stood before a pool of monster fish with bare hands greedy, my fingertips singing the way a line does when it's pulled free from the spool. As I leaned forward, a shape would slide deliberately beneath my reach, and I would lunge into water that was dense and thick as oil, only to come up soaked and empty-handed.

I don't know now that the dreams had to do with catching fish, but rather with some unconscious, archetypal need. I have consulted Jung on this one for the obvious, loaded symbolism. I have even dreamt, in these later years, of Jung, standing atop the stone fortress of his tower at Bolligen, fly rod in hand, a wooden piscatorial carving dangling from his leader line. He smiles in the dream, proud of himself. He did say that water is the unconscious and that fish are a Christ symbol. I deduce, then, from these two boldly fitting pieces, that I am at times fishing for Jesus, or in some way, in recent dreams, dry-flying for Christ. I like the simplicity of it, the directness. I like that it speaks to Christian and hedonist alike.

But during those Mississippi summers that spanned my eighth to thirteenth years I paid little attention to dreams, mesmerized then by a world filled with fish, turtles, frogs, and lizards, anything remotely amphibian. Frogs were a class of fascination all their own, and I would capture them simply to feel the cool, crepey skin of their underbellies and watch the slow blink of their eyes. I progressed quickly from netting bass to catfishing with a bobber and worm, frittering away entire days on the banks of muddy lakes and rivers, certain, always, that the fish lived dead center, in the middle of the lake, assuming the notion that the truly elusive spend their time where we can never hope to reach them. To cast where they hid was my ambition. Eventually I understood that fish went wherever they damned well pleased, unimpressed by my clumsy form hurling hooks into their midst, immune to my need to know them. I had patience, the sort I suspect God has with people like me. It meant nothing to be skunked for days on end. I lived in perpetual hope of seeing that wayward shimmy of the bobber, then the quick dip and tug that signaled I had made contact with aliens. At that time in my life, *this* was my social interaction. I talked to the fish hidden deep in the ponds and streams I visited, trying to imagine what they saw beneath those mirrored surfaces, and reasoned it was hunger and not stupidity that made them take bait so crudely hitched to an obvious weapon. Compassion surfaced. I pictured scores of starving fish grubbing for worms, only to be duped into death by my slipshod cunning. When I'd haul them to shore I'd cry at what I'd done, at the sight of the hook swallowed to the hilt, at the flat, accusing eyes of the fish, and then I'd club them with a Coke bottle, the heavy green kind with the bottling company's name on the bottom. No one ever said there was another way to do it. In Mississippi, there was the hook, the worm, and the bobber, a holy trinity on a hot day in August—low-maintenance fishing I call it now. My guilt was usually pushed aside by their quick death beneath the bottle, and eating what I had caught seemed to remove the shame considerably.

My favorite fishing hole—I look back on it now as Mississippi's version of Mecca—was a place that to this day I am certain only one other knew of, the landowner who'd barbwired it off and posted a huge hand-painted sign along the fence—WARNING: SNAKES—a beacon to me. Yell "snake" and I ran not from, but *to* the source of panic, scooping the creature into my bare hands, trying to remember idly if red bands against yellow meant poisonous, or the other way around.

Roaming deep in a pine woods in rural Hinds County one summer afternoon, I came upon the pond, the edges of it rising in volcanic fashion from the otherwise flat land. I was accustomed only to ponds that were slipped like sinkholes into the surrounding pastureland, and as I made my way up the slight incline of earth, hands grasping the barbwire delicately, I beheld, not a rock quarry as I had expected, but instead a perfectly black pool of water, its dimensions no greater than those of an average swimming pool. At first I could not believe the color of the fish who were pushing to the surface, dozens of them, nosing one into another, their bodies opalescent as pearls, and huge, their lengths dissolving into the shadow of the pond. I had never seen albino catfish, had never seen *any* white fish, and thought for a brief, illogical moment that they had been segregated from their darker mates simply because of their color. In Mississippi then, it fit.

To have called this pond a fishing hole is misleading. I never actually fished its waters, too mesmerized by the cloudlike shapes that moved without sound through the deep pond, believing, beyond all fishing reason, that to catch them would bring the worst sort of luck. So I watched, alone in the woods with these mutants, some days prodding their lazy bodies with a hickory stick, which they rubbed against curiously, and on others merely counting the number of laps they made around the pond in an afternoon, hypnotized by the rhythm they made tracing one circle upon another.

The fish were as truly alien as my starkest imaginings, and I became convinced they were telepathic, reading my thoughts with such ease I had no need to speak to them. I called these journeys "visiting the fish gods," my treks to that mysterious water that had no business existing in a dry woods, and took into my life the memory of them, as if they were a talisman, granting me privileges and luck in the fishing world others could only dream of.

Chapter  TWO

IF I HAD been named Catfish, I might have moved through the world low to the ground and easy, without a moment given to self-doubt. It's a name that needs no last name, a name you can grow old with and that people speak with a peculiar respect. It has authority. It has a bebop, juke-joint, roadhouse sound to it, and you suspect people named Catfish can read palms, call forth spirits in boneyards at midnight, drink chicken blood, and whisper secrets you never knew you had. "What's your name?" I would imagine people asking, and in my fantasy I responded in a low drawl, "Catfish," hooking my thumbs into the pockets of my jeans, planting one foot a little ahead of the other, and leaning wa-ay back, a casual, self-assured pose, the kind you have when your name is Tex or Doc or Cisco, the sort you strike when your name *means* something.

I've known two women named Catfish, more than most will know in a lifetime. The first time I heard the name, before I saw the face that matched it, I got a picture real quick of reeds along a red clay slough, the dark water thick as soup with a smell like dirt after a rain.

She was a black woman who cooked at Mac's Cafe in Altheimer, Arkansas.

The cafe, a small, low, clapboard and tar paper structure that sat at the lip of Highway 79, right across from the railroad tracks and the little one-man depot that read ALTHEIMER, POP. 939, belonged to my stepgrandfather, a bleary-looking alcoholic, who one drunken night stepped on the head of my parakeet, Susie, killing her, an event that baffled us all until I recalled that Susie sleepwalked, like the old man, and had probably wandered out the open door of her cage for a stroll when she'd met the business end of a work boot. Murdering my bird was at the top of a long list of reasons why I couldn't stand the old man, his one unforgivable sin the fact that he was related to my stepfather, a lanky, shifty-eyed misogynist who had a talent for mathematics and a pathological disliking for me. Pa Mac, as I was commanded to call him, a cutesyism at which I invariably winced each time I choked it out, did a good business at Mac's, feeding the farmers, townsfolk, and the towering albino sheriff everyone called Pinky. I remember Pinky's gun and holster more than the man, the way it bulged at his hip when he settled his squishy-looking butt on one of the red leather stools at the lunch counter, and how, perhaps, if he shifted just right, his soft woman's hip might trip the trigger and drive a hole through one of his Cat's Paw work boots. Pinky talked a lot about fishing, how some weekend, when he had the time, he was going to catfish the way his daddy had done, with a trotline and some stink bait, catch enough fish to keep Mac's stocked for a week. I imagined Pinky's slick, poreless skin bubbling up and cracking beneath the hot sun, his absurd height a beacon to crows. I heard Pinky died a few years after we stopped going to Altheimer, smashed his car into one of the low bridges that spanned the bayous, and I always wondered if he'd died with that holster on and if he'd ever gotten his fishing weekend. That seemed the worst of it, to have died and never fished.

Each summer we'd desert the boiling heat of Jackson, crossing the wide, dark artery of the Mississippi at Vicksburg, its current slow as a drumbeat, the bluff that rose from its ribbon of shoreline dense in hardwoods, this same artery that bore the Union ironclads deep into the South. I loved the sound of its name, thought about how it had borne the bodies of the dead when Vicksburg had fallen, and took the smell of it in deep, the smell of history, of water and time. After Vicksburg came the bayou land of Louisiana, where cypress trees stood ghostlike in the green-and-brown water bogs and alligators slipped from beneath the murk, unseen. Then came the hell-blast heat of Arkansas, drier than Mississippi heat, hot and stinging with the grit from the cotton fields. I was born to this heat, wrapped in it tight like a straitjacket, and I knew its textures well. My mother, on the other hand, regarded heat as heat, and spent most of her life trying to slip by it. I have one clear picture of her from my youth, standing in the kitchen with an iced glass of vodka, the beads of moisture on it making rivulets down the frosty sides, her hair limp with sweat, her dark skin flushed a deep red, her whole body drenched-looking and tired.

"I can't take this heat," she'd say as I passed through the kitchen, always headed for my escape route, never stopping to chat, and she'd shoot me a pleading look as if I were the one who could put a pall on the sun, suck the humidity out of the air. On trips in her Country Squire station wagon, the kind with the fake wood trim that looked, from a distance, like a rolling casket, she, my stepfather, Bill, and I would tear across the narrow two-lane macadam from Jackson to Altheimer just so my mother could take in the breeze. At the end of a day on the road we were deaf from the wind beating at our ears, our faces gritty with dust, our moods foul. As we neared Altheimer I would watch the endless rows of cotton stutter by, trying, futilely, to count them, so many of them that the world, in summer, seemed made of cotton. Deep into the fields I could see black people picking the early bolls, their bodies bent low, their colored kerchiefs, reds and yellows, weaving and bowing in the shimmering heat, their half-full sacks dragging behind them, and I thought then, naively, that it must be a good life to work a field so close to a bayou where catfish swirled, waiting to be taken.

We left Jackson for Altheimer each summer vacation to visit Bill's parents, whom my mother hated, and to visit my mother's sister, Freda, in Pine Bluff, whom Bill feared. Really, we left

Jackson just to leave, for the sheer freedom of momentum, because once on the road we could pretend, for a short time, that we were not who we were. Pretend, say, that I was not a budding psychopath, a grubby tomboy of a girl who spent her days in the sour muck of the ravine, who punched boys in the face with a rock-reinforced fist, tore the moist, sweaty skin on their bare backs with ragged, dirt-caked claws, and quietly beat the shit out of anyone who crossed me. We could pretend alcohol wasn't plowing furrows into the smooth skin of my mother's face and that my stepfather was just a nice, normal guy, taking his family on vacation.

In his button-down shirts and sleek blue dress pants, horn-rimmed glasses accentuating the narrow planes of his face, he could pass for normal, but if you looked close at his eyes, paid special attention to the way the thin flesh at the corners puckered and the way the skin around his mouth grew tight, you could see the meanness. He'd been born to violence, schooled in it, and for short periods of time he could keep it locked down tight, so tight his muscles strained from it, until that one seemingly inconsequential thing—a look, a word misspoken, an invisible line trespassed—flipped the switch on him and he became, not that neatly dressed man behind the wheel of the family car, but a criminal who slammed my mother's head into the dishwasher until she was unconscious, hit her full in the face with his clenched fist, fracturing her jaw, belittled her until she wept, and two-timed her any chance he got. We could pretend, but I never bought it. The word "love" never passed between us, and never once, that I can remember, did we touch in a gesture of comfort. All I ever wanted was out of the car, my bare feet beating a path to the water, through a cotton field, anywhere but where they were, and I made a career, in those early years, of trying to run away. Each place we traveled I told myself, Here, here is where I leave them.

Because I was a dark child in both mood and appearance, adults did not coo over me or invite me to play ride-a-horsey on their laps, but instead regarded me as they would a rabid Chihuahua, warily, from a distance. When they asked what I wanted to be when I grew up, I would tell them, "A hermit," and stare them down until they looked away, nervously, never sure what to make of me. It confounded Pa Mac and his wife, the odious Ma Mac, as to what they should do to occupy me when I came visiting.

Ferrying ice water to the farmers at the booths and counters became my job during those two weeks in summer, the slick gold plastic glasses filled high with machine-crushed ice from a stainless steel bin with sliding doors. I had to lean in deep. I liked the wet, wintry feel of the ice bin and kept my head shoved in it as often as possible, while Catfish cooked in back in the grease-blackened kitchen.

It wasn't her birth name, but few people remembered what that was by the time I knew her, and Catfish was not the one to ask. Darker and far moodier than I, she rarely responded to direct questions, but instead gave out information randomly, apropos of nothing, as if she were picking up in the middle of a story she'd been telling all her life and you'd just happened by in the middle.

"Daddy sack fi'teen crawdad, two hour," she'd say, eyes steady on the burger she was flipping, feet spread wide apart in a steadying pose, and I'd wait patiently for more, shifting from foot to foot, my shoulder propped against the swinging door of the kitchen. After a ten-minute lapse I'd wander over to the grill and study her profile, check to see if her lips were moving and I was missing it. But it was all I got, that one choppy fragment, no matter if I asked, "So what did he do then? Hey, Catfish, what did he do then, your daddy?" Silence. Just the hiss of the burger as she pressed down hard. Two days later I'd hear, as I skidded into the kitchen for some clean glasses, "Sold 'em to market, get a good price." Four days later, "Bought some shoes." So at the end of two weeks I'd have pieced together the story of how her daddy caught a few crawdads, sold them, bought some shoes, hocked the shoes to buy a pint of liquor, had gotten drunk and gone to jail, shamed the family, and eventually accepted Jesus into his life. I look back now on Catfish's stories as my first introduction to cliff-hangers. It was the waiting to hear what happened next that killed you.

When she was a girl she'd spent her days dipping a cane pole into the slow, muddy waters of the Arkansas River, watching the homemade cork bobber roll in the current, waiting for it to shimmy and disappear. It was a trick she taught me later about bobbers, how you dare not breathe once the bobber began to twitch, and how you had to wait until it went all the way under, not just halfway, not just down quick and back up, but all the way down so all you saw was a deep swirl where the bobber had been. Then you yanked, hard and quick, to set the hook. No matter catfish swallowed the worm and hook whole, their mouths opening and closing in blind gluttony; no matter they'd have gone for a dirty sock or a fistful of ripe cat litter if you'd drifted either their way. This herking hard on the pole, feet braced, was a must-do.

"Catfish tricky," Catfish would say and nod, a woman who on any given day at the cafe might speak five words to me. She'd call, "*I*-ss wah-tah," in her scratchy-record voice if she were thirsty, and I'd shoulder open the swinging doors to the kitchen, pretending I was John Wayne in a kick-butt western, a full glass of crushed ice barely splashed with water held out at arm's length, an offering. If I stared too long while she drank the ice water in slow, easy draughts, it annoyed her. "Stop that," she'd snap if she caught me eyeing her, but I stole glimpses often enough to have one clear memory of her standing over the blackened griddle, her arms sinewy and hard looking in the sleeveless cotton print smock she always wore, her legs jutting like a couple of dark wood posts below the skirt line. She looked strong, not a hint of fat on her, and when I think of her now I'm reminded of a distance runner. Even her skin looked hard, drawn tight over high cheekbones, the Cherokee blood we shared evident in them, and when sweat bloomed on her forehead it wasn't that soppy, drenched-looking sweat, but neat, even beads of perspiration that stayed in place. She always looked cool and dry as a reed in standing water, and as she drank the ice water I imagined it hissing from her skin with a sound like a hot iron on damp cloth.

It might have been my grim, snaggle-toothed looks—I'd pried out all my front teeth, top and bottom, by the time I was six years old for the sheer fascination of watching the ragged enamel pull free from the gum—that made Catfish treat me a little better than most, better even than her husband, Winky, who came sniffing at the kitchen door after the lunch rush, looking for a handout.

"Go 'way!" she'd yell, trying to slam the heat-thickened door against him, and when it wouldn't close all the way she'd kick it hard with her foot, jamming it up tight, so later we'd both have to pull, our feet braced against the molding, until it popped free.

For my patience with her, for my indulgence of her lousy moods, or maybe simply because she knew I idolized her, she made me soggy hamburgers with extra pickles, rarely when I was hungry, only when it suited her, slamming the sandwich plate hard onto the raised counter that connected the kitchen and the front of the cafe.

"Sammich, missy," she'd call through the porthole, and when I'd look up from the ice bin she'd be glaring back at me from the dark kitchen, her eyes round and yellow as harvest moons.

I never asked if she liked me, suspicious that her attentions applied only to things she chose to do for me, little gestures like the burgers swimming in grease and pickles, and the handful of times she let me tag along with her to the river.

There was not one thing she liked better than catfishing, she told me once in a rare burst of speech. Not a man, not a child, not money in the bank. It was the way she put it, with great self-assurance, as if everyone else's allegiances were misplaced. When I knew her she'd been fishing fifty years, and it was still the first thing she did when she left the cafe each day, her pole propped outside the kitchen door, rigged and ready, so she didn't have to waste time going home. I saw her home once, a tar paper shack set deep in a cotton field where her husband sharecropped, and where she, in the early mornings before the cafe, worked the fields. I imagined Catfish picking cotton, her strong fingers dark against the bolls, her eyes fixed on the clods of earth that rose up in hard rows, one after the other, straight back as far as you could see, and how for every boll she picked she must have wished it had been a fish slick and fat in her hands.

When I was a kid I grew up knowing black people were poor,

all of them, without one single exception. On Sunday-to-meetings the women wore elaborate, flowered hats and gaudy flowered dresses, handmade, regal in their busy-looking clothes, but on Monday they worked for white people and traded the Sunday finery for a uniform. They did not wait on you in department stores, they did not serve your food, they were not mayors or bankers or lawyers, they were not even postmen. In Jackson they hauled our garbage onto a flatbed truck with slatted sides, waist deep in cantaloupe rinds, coffee grounds, steak bones with the meat still on. A woman named Gussie Mae did our wash, ironed my school clothes, and listened to my mother's ramblings patiently, standing beside the kitchen table in her starched white uniform. I wondered often at this disparity as I grew older, at the great distance, the gulf, put between the haves and have-nots by a thing as subtle, yet malignant, as color, and I became angrier than I ever remember being, believing for a time it wasn't Indian blood that ran in me, but blood black as Catfish's, the Niger River my people's first fishing hole.

Catfish never had a day off, but if she had she wouldn't have spent it at Mac's lunch counter eating a burger cooked by someone else. She could not even eat out back when the day was over. I knew because I'd asked her once to have lunch with me. "Not allowed," she'd said, her eyes intent on the griddle, her voice matter-of-fact.

She was easier by the river, softer looking. I never once went with her because she said, "Come on, child, and fish with me." No. I had to track her like a bloodhound, she was so quick out the door, pounding a path to the water, trying to shake me.

At the edge of the cotton fields the land gives way to river bluff, and beyond the bluff the Arkansas spreads out broad like a plain, its waters murky with red clay, its current deep and heavy. It has a smell as strong and powerful as the land, rich in minerals, saturated in heat, and in shady spots along the bank all you can smell is water. The scent rises up from the steaming fields and the river and hangs in the cottonwoods, thick as Spanish moss. Days after a fishing trip I would catch the aroma of it in my hair, on my clothes, and I have thought in recent years of bottling it, calling the concoction River, and making a billion bucks. Nervous, skittering trout rivers don't smell the same as Southern rivers. They are too shallow, move too quickly to grow anything worth smelling. When I came west I didn't trust water without an odor, imagining it barren, lifeless as a salt pond.

In Altheimer and Pine Bluff people spoke of the river with a curious respect and reverence, as if it were an unpredictable woman. "She lookin' tricky this season," I'd hear the sharecroppers say. "No tellin' what she do she get her belly fulla rain. Climb them banks like gettin' outta jail."

It happened. A strong spring rain, the kind where the sky ripped in half and water fell in sheets, could start the river rising like mercury in a thermometer. I remember standing along the ravine lip in Jackson one spring when the floods came, my potholed canyon transformed from benign sanctuary to a boiling hell, the rusty-looking water pushing along the crumbling edge where I stood, high above what had once been the ravine's bottom. Now it bore on its tide mangled car parts and tree trunks, and once, the body of a young girl. I saw her clearly, a girl my own age, dead, her eyes wide open to the sky as she floated high on the current, and in that instant of seeing her I understood the unchecked fury of water, how it could take you in, break you, and never once know who you'd been.

We settled in the thin shade of the cottonwoods along the bank, I with a six-cent bottle of Coca-Cola I refilled with river water when it was empty because I liked the taste of mud, craved it so much I'd dig the clay from the bank with my fingers and drop the globs of mud onto my tongue like gumdrops. Catfish never said a word about this peculiar practice and occasionally licked her own fingers clean of worm juice and clay, a reflective look on her face as if she'd just discovered the missing ingredient in a pot of underseasoned stew. She was laconic as usual, inscrutable, these ways of hers less disturbing by water because here is where the need to talk dropped away. I became comfortable just watching her tend to her gear as she looped a lengthy piece of line through the eye of her absurdly long cane pole, tied on a hefty hook, and spit twice on the line before she knotted it down tight. I loved watching her long, dark fingers, the quick, steady way they looped and pinched the line, not at all like my mother's trembling, fluttery hands, and I practiced holding my own hands still and straight before me, certain this was a skill worth having.

I flailed and fumbled with my own rod, one I'd filched from Pa Mac's gear, and whined when I discovered I was wormless. Catfish, unfazed by my pouting, gave me no sympathy, just a grunt and a pinched-off piece of meat from her own fat night crawler. She raised them herself in compost and sold them for five cents a dozen. I would watch carefully as she slid the bobber onto her line, a piece of pared-down cork with two tight metal loops equidistant from each other. I don't know if she couldn't afford the snazzy red-and-white plastic bobbers, or just preferred to make her own. It seemed impolite to ask. Bobbers were something I always had, stuffed into my pockets as I passed Pa Mac's tackle display in the little office adjoining the cafe. I liked the way they looked, like two-tone candy gum balls, and the slick way you could push down the plastic top and have the metal eye push free at the bottom, ready to hook on to a line, so neat and clean and secure. It had a professional feel to it, as if, for no other reason than the fact that I had fingers, I also had a Ph.D. in bobbers. And the way they floated, dipping in the soupy swells of the river, flashing red-and-white, riding high on the peaks, made me feel as if I had launched a searchlight onto those waters, a beacon that would draw all fish shoreward.

Catfish cast her line like a shotput, snapping the pole back high over her right shoulder and heaving with a big "ahh!" in the direction of the river. What I have come to realize is that I was watching a modified fly cast, the line unfurling and snapping clean with each motion, the power of Catfish's muscles traveling straight up the rod. The motion was impressive, strong and hard and purposeful. I imagined Catfish slinging full bale sacks over her whipcord shoulders, what concentration of strength this took, and understood why her husband, Winky, scrawny despite his field work, fled when she raised her voice. Half the time I expected to watch her sail into the water after her rig, she put that much of her body into the cast, or for the bobber and worm to fling free, but she always hit on the mark, her bobber landing daintily, light as a raindrop. I, on the other hand, had no finesse, no accuracy, no aim at all, and often snagged my line high in a cottonwood bough before I actually hit the water. Once I did, I could feel my heart quicken, my palms go slick. Every nerve in my body went on alert the moment I tapped into that other world, going haywire on me, burning off any calm I had felt watching Catfish rig her pole. For me fishing became, early on, that one exquisite, nerve-ripping source of adrenaline, the one pure contact sport, and the only thing I would pursue again and again throughout my life, relentlessly, with one exception.

As we sat a respectful distance from each other, our bobbers swaying in the current, the heat on us like a furnace blast, the river breaking wide around the bend where the cotton gin rose metallic against the sky, I could taste freedom, feel it sharp on my tongue like the bite of iron from the red clay I loved to eat. I ate it as I would a potion, expecting it to flush me with a sudden wisdom, prime my instincts so I would know, without ever having to think, how to move through the world. Catfish *lived* by instinct, the same way she fished, and I envied her this.

It was as if everything, eventually, would fit into the puzzle, the way her drawn-out stories did, one piece at a time, *chink,* falling into place, until you got the big picture. I tried to mimic her, but I did not yet understand the broad perimeters of instinct, the sharper taste of a different freedom.

Catfish eyed her bobber lazily for long stretches, nodding in the heat, her old hands loosening their grip on the pole butt, asleep almost, it seemed, when suddenly her eyes would open wide and sharpen, a quick instant before the bobber gave a dip, and I could tell by the look on her face, an expression of quiet sanctity, of knowing, that this was her calling, this one moment.

"Catfish!" she'd crow, her scrawny butt wiggling in anticipation, her bare feet doing a little dance in the mud, her drawn-back lips exposing a toothless cavern in a grin of pure delight. Watching her, I understood how she had gotten her name. In that electric, reason-shattering second of "fish on" she became a girl again, her ecstasy uncontainable, her grumpy facade torn to bits.

The fish was thick and eely, heavy as a sack of sand as she

dragged it to the bank, where it flopped and rolled lazily, its gills laboring, its whiskers distinct as a handlebar mustache. A slow pity rose in me as I watched the fish struggle, but rarely long enough to matter because it was all over too quick. With the heavy end of my Coke bottle Catfish smashed its flat head, and then with the razor edge of her pocketknife gutted it, anal opening to gills, neat and smooth and quick as a surgeon, the white underbelly ripping like silk.

I stood amazed before her talent, imagining myself as self-sufficient as she, my hands quick and steady with the knife, indifferent to the heart that lay, still beating, in the mud.

"What're you doing now," I'd ask, intent on the process as Catfish rinsed the guts into the river and ran her thumb deep along the spine to take out the blood vein.

"Gut him," she'd say, the terrific grin gone, all business now. "Gut him. Rinse him."

"Why?" I'd ask.

A roll of the eyes, an are-you-the-stupidest-child-on-earth look.

"You don't, missy, he *stink*."

"Huh," I'd say, absorbing this wisdom. "You can't eat him whole, then."

"Course not, fool."

I would spend hours, my eyes trained on my red-and-white plastic death buoy, while Catfish heaved in fish after fish, my head buzzing from the heat, my patience eroded.

"Got 'bout ten, fi'teen now, I'd say," Catfish would tell me in a judicial sort of tone, giving me a sidelong look, her eyes narrowed, trying to gauge, I suspect now, just when, exactly, I would blow.

Rub it in, I'd think to myself, just rub it in, you old witch, and I'd start to wonder just what I was doing with her, this sorceress who lured everything with fins from the river and laid the bounty at her feet just so she could gloat.

"How come I'm not catching fish?" I would finally ask after hours of standing scarecrow still, feet dug in the mud, eyes stinging with sweat from focusing too long on the water.

I remember Catfish turning on her heel in the mud and

drawing a bead on me with her dark eyes, hands on her hips in an I-know-everything pose.

"You edgy," she said matter-of-factly. "You wants fish too bad. They *knows* it."

If I had waited forty years on that same bank to hear gospel words on any given subject, those would have been the words. "You edgy. They *knows* it." I approached fishing with the heartbeat of a hummingbird, palms sweaty, eyes glazed, hands gripped so tight on the rod my fingers were white when I pulled them away. I was so shot through with adrenaline you could probably smell me the way you can ozone after a lightning bolt shears the sky. Fish sensed me, rigid as a post at the other end, my body putting off murder vibes. I tried loosening my grip, watching the water as if I were gazing out a window, calm as Catfish rocking back and forth on the bank.

When you take yourself out of the fish equation, when it becomes no longer a test of ego or skill whether you hook or do not hook in, when things are left to happen as odds would have them happen, something strange takes place. Overall, I did not consider myself a lucky girl, but it was with Catfish, on that Arkansas River bank, as I breathed deeply, taking in the scenery, my head repeating like a mantra that one distilled bit of wisdom—*you edgy, they knows it, you edgy, they knows it*—that fish luck, in all its quirky, ritual-bound habits, found me. My eyes glazed over. My grip loosened on the rod. I swayed with the river and didn't come to until the voice of a lunatic fractured the silence.

"Goddamn, child! Yank! Goddamn, yank that rod." The words hit me with a force like thunder. Who was edgy now?

"Pull hard, child! Get him up. That's it! Keep going, girl. Turn left, put some weight on him. You got him now. Yoo-hoo! You got him now. Swing round. All your weight this foot. *This* foot, I say. *This* goddamn foot! He heavy, ain't he? He a heavy one. Big supper. You got a big supper on that line, girl."

Her commands came quick and hard, and I stood stunned by them, my muscles suddenly rubber, my coordination lost. And "heavy"? The word did not touch what he was. I could feel the sheer anvil-like weight of him at the other end, submarining along, first left, then right, then in a beeline for the opposite shore. I lifted a hand from the rod butt to wipe the sweat off my forehead and pitched forward on one knee from the pull of him.

"Get up, fool," I heard Catfish yell. "Get your butt up. Ain't no time to pray."

My back ached, deep, like I'd taken a punch straight on, and my fingers around the rod butt were locked down tight. He pulled hard and I pulled harder, and then I yanked with my feet braced, gaining on him as I backed slowly up the bank, wondering to myself who had thought this up, this *zap-pow-bam* better than any earthbound tug-of-war. A genius, that's who. A goddamn genius. I stumbled along the shore now, toes digging in the clay, rod tip held high the way Catfish had said to do it, trying to acquaint him with a new direction.

"What you doin', fool," Catfish hollered, "take him down the next county? Come back wit dat fish."

I obeyed, moving up the bank toward her, the fish dragging like an anchor in the shallow water of the shoreline.

"Go get him, child," she told me, pointing to the catfish who rolled now along the bank, covered in red mud. "Don't fish much, do you?" she said, her voice softer now, a mild tone of pity to it.

I walked toward my prey, gathering up line in my fist, terrified now of what I might see, that somehow this one fish would be different from the scores I had watched Catfish take, a mutant fitted with outsized teeth, the one and only piranha the Arkansas would ever breed. But there he wallowed, no mutant but my first honest-to-God big fish, no flitty, filmy, flank-striped baby bass, no mere minnow, but a mother of a catfish, equal in size to the huge albinos I had seen cruising the periphery of the woods' pond, heavy in the gut, fat as a pig, his gaping mouth wide enough to hold my fist.

Without a doubt, this is why I had been born.

"He a hog," Catfish crowed. "He a big, fat hog, girl. What you think he weigh, fitty pound?" She winked at me then and I held back the urge to fling myself at her feet and wrap my arms around her ankles. My hands shook as I bent to unhook the fish, not calm and steady like Catfish's hands, but fluttering like butterflies above the monster, and I remember thinking there could be no feeling to match this one, this sense of self-sufficiency and pride at having snatched something edible from the wild. I regarded the river now as one giant, free-flowing fish market. From these waters, I was convinced, I could make my life.

I experimented with this objective in mind, eating acorns, wild onions, the bark of trees, pounds of red clay, road tar bubbled up thick in the heat of summer, and even the brittle shells of locusts, figuring that what didn't make me sick could maybe, in a pinch, help keep me alive. It was a thing with me when I was a kid, to learn to live by my own hand, because who knew, exactly, when I'd have to leave in the middle of the night, kerchief tied to my cane pole, the money I'd made waitressing at the cafe tucked in my jeans? I had a corny picture in my head, me as Huck Finn floating the swollen belly of a Southern river, no one to answer to, set loose in the world. It was always smart to be prepared, to know as much as you could about what you were up against; and now, as I knelt, struggling with the hook lodged deep in the fish's gut, I knew the formula: a pole, a worm, a hook, a bobber. Fishing meant freedom—not just idle fun, but a way to survive.

"Club him," I heard Catfish say as she handed me the Coke bottle. I liked the weight of it, the cool feel of the glass against my palm as I hefted it, aiming to strike. Murderer, my head said, but I did it anyway so Catfish would know I was just like her.

"Clean him," she told me when I finally got the hook free. The rust-pocked knife lay in her outstretched palm. I remember the particular pinkness of her palms, and how the lines ran deep in them, so deep they looked just like the cracks in the river mud on a hot day, and I wished again that my hands were like hers, not bitten up and swollen from gnawing on them when I was alone. It was a habit that followed me through childhood, biting at the skin on my hands until they bled and scabbed over, so people always asked about them, saying, "Child, is it eczema?" and I took to hiding them behind my back or in the pockets of my jeans. Later, when I read about the saints, I told myself they were stigmata, these cracks and lesions that wept even when

I let them alone for a day, and when I regard my hands now, the faint scars on them from years past, I think "stigmata" and laugh, remembering how, for a time, I had convinced myself I was holy, blessed.

I gutted the fish in ragged movements, slicing too far off center, jumpy at Catfish's breath on my neck as she leaned in tight to watch me. The guts were warm in my hands, slippery, and I could feel the heart pulse, erratically, against my own flesh, its scarlet sheath quivering as if it had been shocked. How long might it beat, I wondered, if I took it home in a jar? I'd seen the hearts from Catfish's catch strewn in the mud, pumping still, untethered. What was it that made them beat still? Was it like a chicken with the head cut off, the body unaware the brain was gone, or was it just this one heart clocking death? I let the heart slide from my palm into the dark water, reverent for a moment, horrified.

"Stop thinkin'," Catfish said, aware I was doing what no angler should do for too long, identify with the fish.

"Sure," I said, watching the heart slip beneath the murk.

"Skin him now," she told me, standing up straight, hands on her hips, delighted to be telling someone what to do.

This was a new one. All I'd ever seen her do was gut them and then pack them home at the end of a day.

Skinning catfish is like pulling Sheetrock off with your teeth. The skin, through some fluke of nature, is actually superglued to the flesh. No amount of normal pulling will free it. It has to be lashed to a backhoe before it will budge.

"Pliers," Catfish said as I knelt before the fish, tearing at it with my nails, sweat pouring off my nose and chin, soaking into the clay. She clamped her foot down squarely on the broad, flat head of the fish, slipped a pair of needle-noses from the pocket of her smock, and stripped the skin back with deft, even strokes.

"Better-a nail him up a tree," she said when she was done, and I understood then the best way to skin a catfish and the mystery of the cluster of catfish heads nailed to the trunk of a live oak that straddled one of the bayous on the way to the river.

I had become the gloating owner of a gutted and stripped catfish, its meat pink and firm as chicken, and when Catfish fried it up the next day at the cafe I took a full afternoon to finish it off, smelling the river in it as I ate, feeling the heat against my back again. I eyed the lunch crowd eating their burgers and felt smug, certain no morsel they could swallow would ever be as sweet as what lay on my plate. In my eyes I had become a certified big shot, a girl who could fish, and if you had told me there were other things to do, other things to be, I would not have listened.

Chapter  THREE

PINE BLUFF LAKE, in a dry season, is filled with the stumps of cut-down trees, eerie and dark as they poke above the muddy water line, lined up head to head like stones in a cemetery. At the edge of the stumps, leeches wallow in the rotting wood and vegetation, hungry for fresh pink skin, and offshore, sliding along the water like marbles on glass, cottonmouths patrol, their gauzy mouths opening and closing onto the hard shells of water beetles, the slick, oily fur of water rats.

On the ground, where I reasoned they belonged, I was partial to snakes, fascinated by their variety of color, the cool dryness of their skin against mine, but once waterborne they took on a sinister look, slipping up on you with no warning, their wide cottony mouths opened to strike. I had seen one shot once on a dock in Mississippi. A friend and I had walked across the dark wood planks, ready to dive into the lake at the end, when a cottonmouth had swum to a piling beneath and slithered up through the planks, its jaws unhinged wide so you could see the cobwebbing of its mouth, a memory that, forty years later, still comes in dreams. We'd yelled, "Snake!" and my friend's father had thrown wide the front door of the house, a pistol gripped tight in his hand as he'd run to the dock, screaming at us to get back, as we stood, our bare feet unmoving on the rough planks, stupefied with fear. He'd aimed, steady on his mark, and I remember the impassive look on his face as he squeezed the trigger once, twice, blowing the cottonmouth's head to flying bits of scale and foam.

We were sitting on the banks of Pine Bluff Lake, Freda and I, that summer of my eighth year, the same summer I had fished with Catfish. After visiting Pa and Ma Mac, my mother in a fit of boredom after the slow, lazy days at the cafe, we would drive the fourteen miles to Pine Bluff for a week with Freda. On this particular hot, windless afternoon in August I sat with my cane pole jammed upright in the mud and studied Freda's bow and arrow resting on one of the rotting stumps. Freda was my mother's sister, a fact few believed when they saw the two side by side, my mother a blonde, green-eyed beanpole of a girl, Freda raven haired, dark eyed, compact, and muscular as a gymnast.

At the age of thirty-five Freda had had a mastectomy. The bow and arrow was her therapy, to strengthen what was left of her chest muscles. Her body had been perfect, a sculptor's model, and she'd worn her summer shirts tied up high under her breasts, braless most of the time. She still wore her shirts knotted at the rib cage, but now they were men's cotton pajama tops, the material thicker so you could not see through; but often when she bent forward I could see the scarred bony place where the breast had been. I never knew if she was bitter for the loss, if she stared at the deformity in the mirror and wished for a time when she'd been whole. She never said. I never asked. She was not a woman martyred by tragedy, nor was she at all acquainted with self-pity. In fact I often wondered if she welcomed hardship merely for its challenge, she had had so much of it in her life, raised early on in stark, Depression-era poverty, and then in a Catholic orphanage when her mother, widowed, could no longer feed her. It was the nuns who ran the orphanage—"true bitches" she called them once—who would be the ultimate influence in her life.

Freda was a dazzle, a virtual watercolor of a woman whose moods and mannerisms were as electric as her wild black hair. Her grin alone, a flash of Ipana-white teeth, head tossed back, stopped men on sidewalks, delayed them in traffic, and threatened their wives so completely even the milkman was not allowed to deliver at Freda's house. It was her true talent, charming people, and she did so guilelessly, her jumpy Tennessee hills accent captivating in its girlishness. But beneath the pretty, jingling exterior, beneath her teasingly wicked eyes, lived a woman with unflinching nerve, a woman who, given the challenge, could murder.

She'd tried once to kill my stepfather, whom she'd always referred to by his first and last names, Bill McClain, the two words run together in her odd accent so it came out "Bimicain," sounding like a fungal cream. She hated Bill, he told me once, because he was taller than she, although when I asked Freda her reasons for firing a loaded revolver at him one hot night in the summer of my sixth year, she'd said there were certain people who just ought not live. The prospect of the man dead had cheered me greatly and I'd been disappointed when Freda had missed, the bullet slamming into the wall of the butler's kitchen in her home in Pine Bluff, a hair-splitting close call that sent Bill stumbling in a sweaty panic into the backyard, where he screamed, "Murderer! Murderer! Call the law!" The law came, all right, but left soon after Freda flashed her dazzle of a smile and smoothed the cops over with sweet talk, melting them where they stood, so they ended up leading Bill away in handcuffs for a night in jail.

I liked Freda's company, enjoyed the way she singled me out among her nieces and nephews and took me along on her outings. We had things in common, an eye for nature and blood so hot it boiled, she told me once. Through these things we both were bound, I her daughter by my own declaration, and she the mother who could never bear children of her own. I watched her all my life, enchanted by her and her singsong voice, her theatrical gestures, by the way she walked through a dry woods in autumn, toe to heel, barely disturbing the leaves so all you heard was a soft sound like wind, and by the way she shouldered a shotgun and took aim as deftly as any man—and most of all because she fled, as if her life depended on it, into the warm rich world of summer, exactly as I did, full of hope, anticipating secrets, intrigue, danger.

This day I fished Pine Bluff Lake while Freda shot at stumps, dipping my cane pole in a shallow, muddy pocket of the lake where baby catfish nestled like eels in the muck. I'd been delighted by their proximity and sheer numbers, never mind their puny size and the blindness with which they took my bait. All I had to do was give them a whiff of a worm and, bingo, I had a stumpy little fish, all whiskers, head, and mouth, and by midday a stringerful of these juveniles. Greed was my M.O. when it came to fish, and throwing back what I could not or would not eat wasn't yet part of my ritual.

Freda was serious about getting good with the bow, and I'd watch her from time to time as she drew it back tight against the string, her right arm quivering from the strain, and released the arrow in a quick snap. It was the look in her dark eyes that fascinated me, of concentration and purpose so complete she was unaware even when I stood beside her calling her name. Her eyes kept steady on the mark as she pulled another arrow from the quiver on her back, and each time she drew back, her biceps shiny looking in the heat, I held my breath until the arrow slammed into a rotten stump, shattering the pulpy wood. I pulled the arrows free when she called time-out, bracing with my sneakers against the soft wood, admiring the deadly-looking honed steel of the arrow point, thinking it a better weapon than a gun in Freda's hands, and wondered if she imagined Bill McClain's head propped on one of the stumps, if that's why she got so good so fast.

At midday the sun burned like a gas jet in the sky and I shed my clothes and dove from one of Freda's pulverized stumps at the lake's edge, into the opaque water, warm as the baths she drew for me in the evening. I could taste catfish in the lake, a taste like beets dug fresh from the ground, and rolled otterlike onto my back, the sun a blinding wash of sulphur above me, and kicked my way slowly opposite Freda, oblivious to her on shore as she called to me in a panic, "Snakes! They's snakes all over. Come back!"

You never truly know creatures who swim until you swim among them, try to match your stroke to theirs, breathe as they breathe, stare up at the quicksilver dome of water as if it were the very skin that contained you. I dove deep as I could go, my lungs filled with summer heat, ready to explode, trying to reach a cool spot beneath the warm blanket of the lake, a place the sun couldn't touch, and as I pulled myself down I imagined my body slick and finned, able to flick its tail and move twenty feet at a scoot. I would open my eyes every few minutes, expecting—what? Some water-world ballet in motion, or a laser blast of atomic light that would put the flash to every square inch of mystery this place had held for me these eight years of my life? What I got instead was a *Sea Hunt* peek at the murk, a thin shaft of light illuminating floating clots of algae and scum, and the faintest impression of water-bound bodies, fishlike, hanging in the near darkness.

I felt a smooth brushing against my legs and imagined it was catfish come to show me where they hid, where their big fat mama queen of a catfish lay in muck, belly so heavy with eggs all she could do was shift from side to side, her swimming days a memory. I'd take her then, slip my fingers alongside her gills and tow her back to shore, a catch that would put me on the front page of the *Pine Bluff Commercial.* Fish were news in Arkansas. A trophy-sized bass could shove a politician off the front page any day, and in idle moments I dreamt of locking on to a fish that would bring me fame. I'd heard of catfish in the Amazon, big as trucks, so big you had to tow them with a chain behind the boat. I felt the quick brush again and this time got spooked. Who knew what lived here, what this near-boiling water could nurture? I surfaced.

"Snake!" I heard Freda yell now. "Snake!"

I had a picture in my head before I saw him. He was twenty feet long and wide as a semi tire. I spun in the water, eyes searching, and it was on the second spin that I spotted him, body thick as my arm, s-curving his way in my direction, not thirty feet from where I dog-paddled. I felt suddenly dizzy, sick to my stomach.

"Cottonmouth!" Freda yelled, as if I needed to know.

It is an evil word when you come to know its meaning. Snakes in water, period, are evil. If the Garden of Eden had been a lake, I could have understood the wickedness of the serpent then, how he tempted. Had Eve seen him swimming toward her she'd have been so horrified she'd have eaten a bushel of apples just to placate him, to make him move again upon a surface that the laws of nature dictated he move upon, not in water like a sorcerer, no gills, no fins to propel him, just that weirdly undulating body his only locomotion, mouth open in a cottony wad, dripping venom.

On the ground you beat the grass with a stick to startle snakes and then stood perfectly still while they slid by. In water I had no clue what to do.

"Swim!" Freda was yelling. "Swim!" It worked for me. She was about as far away as the snake when I switched from a circling dog paddle to a windmilling crawl. I pushed back gallons of water with my arms, feet churning up the foam. I have never been a strong swimmer, and the snake would have taken the gold in any competition. I could see him sliding on the water, neck arced up curiously, and I remembered this was the posture cobras took before they struck, getting as much angle and arc as possible before they nailed you. Unthreatened, I might have thought it was exquisite, uncanny, the way he kept a bead on me, adjusting his movement with each stroke I made, the dead look in his eyes the exact dead look sharks have when they're feeding. There is a superstition that says if you do not look a snake in the eye he will not strike. I turned my gaze toward shore, maybe fifteen feet away now, at the precise moment Freda's arrow snapped clear from the bow.

I have reflected over the years on the likelihood of shooting an arrow clear through a waterborne snake. I figure the odds are right up there with my having a sex change. I have never expected to be believed when I have told this story, simply because it is so unlikely. For me it has become a staring-your-murderer-in-the-eyes sort of experience that creeps, decade after decade, menacing, into my fish dreams. I'll be casting into the round mirrored dream pool, the sky above me a cartoon wash of pinks and greens, when, *zap,* the rod I grip becomes a cottonmouth, the pole butt his dripping fangs. Jungians say this dream is something other than what I call it. I say, Ha! It is nothing more than stark, paralyzing fear revisited, the likelihood of reprieve, in life, infinitesimal. Who would have guessed Freda had gotten so good?

She had stood knee deep in the lake, my aunt, an off-hours Robin Hood, arm drawn back expertly, eyes trained dead at a point I could not see, did not want to see, directly behind me. There had been a sliver of a moment when that indivisible atom of doubt had clouded my thoughts; and I had feared, in that millisecond, that she aimed for me. And then there was the sound of murder, a stupid, silly sound—*bloop*—like ketchup being forced from a bottle. Then her strong hand dug deep into my muddy hair, pulling me the rest of the way to shore, yelling, "Hurry. Hurry up now!"

Onshore, my legs rubbery, brown water sheeting from my naked body, I turned to the hellhole from which she had snatched me to watch with her in silence. Ten feet from where we stood the cottonmouth swam in erratic circles, an arrow hanging limp in its midsection, its jaw opened so wide it looked as if it had come unhinged. Blood trailed in a circle, mixing with the dark water, and in a moment the snake went limp, sinking like a punctured inner tube.

I shivered in the heat, imagining the hollow fangs, leaking venom, driven deep into the soft tissue of my neck. It is a vision that to this day makes me want to scream. Freda turned from the lake, chucking her bow onto a stump, a dark look on her pretty face. I could see her trembling.

"Suppose I had had no weapon," she had said to me, her words measured, quizzical. "Suppose I had not taken up the art of archery. Suppose I had not been given any reason to. What then?" she'd asked. "Tell me, Lorian, what then?"

"What then" had never before existed in my repertoire of fears. "What then" belonged to adults, and in a kid's world I climbed high, dove deep, ate whatever looked interesting, never once considered that these had mortal consequences.

"Hmmm," I heard Freda saying while my mind and body occupied another planet, still spinning in the aftershock of fear. "Tell me, girl, what then?"

I thought about it long enough to grow uncomfortable, to understand how fate, snaking before your eyes, could bring a chill so deep, so penetrating, you had to spread your arms wide to the sun in reflex.

"I'd be dead," I said matter-of-factly, too stubborn to admit to fear. Still, gratitude flushed my body. She had saved my life.

Freda regarded me once, irritated, then turned her face to the sun, a righteous pose, and let loose.

"Not just *dead,*" she told me, stressing the evil word, her voice rising. She put her hands to her hips like Catfish and glared down at me. "Not just *dead* in the ordinary way, child—*fool*—but dead and fulla holes, poison in your body, bloating you up so you look like one of these soggy stumps, blown up after a rain, your face black, rotten with poison. Rotten, you understand? Dead like that. Not pleasant, you-go-to-sleep-on-your-pillow-and-everything's-cozy dead, but bad dead. Do you understand what I'm saying?"

I could see she was proud of herself; she always was any time she managed to scare the wits out of me. I got her point. I nodded. It wasn't enough.

"Pay attention when I talk to you. Hear? Hey!" She chucked me under the chin and I met her eyes. "Don't swim no more where they's snakes, you hear?"

I spoke the word "Yes" forcefully, a military response, and felt my skin crawling with the memory of what had brushed against me, hungry.

We took my stringer of runty catfish home, walking along the old brick streets of Pine Bluff, the hot wind blowing dust onto the sun-baked porches of frame homes, the mud from the lake drying itchy on my skin. Freda fried up all twenty of the tiny fish for supper, crusty-looking hush-puppy morsels that crackled when I bit into them and tasted like lake, like snake, like cottonmouth foam. I had to eat them all, she'd told me, because I had caught them. There was no okra on the side, no corn bread, just a plate full of headless lumps of bone and skin, barely any meat on them, and I wondered briefly at my incaution and my greed, what they had gotten me.

"More?" Freda asked, driving her point home as she reached into the sizzling skillet with a pair of tongs.

I shook my head no, remembering the day, how it had begun so brightly, so without threat, and how in the midst of rightness there had surfaced an evil so potent I might have, head beneath the water, deaf to Freda's cries, become its casualty. It made me wonder. It would be years before I would spend time with my aunt again, and I had no clue as I sat grinding at the cornmeal-battered fish that she would, at a given point in the future, put an arrow to the bow one more time and aim in my defense.

Chapter

FOUR

I REMEMBER the rivers in Africa, broad and dark as Southern rivers, snakes hanging from the trees that grew flush with the banks as we bathed in the warm liquid, my mother and I, the scent of brown water in my hair, rich as the smell of the Arkansas on those summer days with Catfish. My mother says we fly-fished. I do not remember, as she does, but I like to imagine her dividing the air with a fly rod, her slender body tipping forward as the line arced out, her muscles moving smoothly with the rhythm of the beat. It is a way I never knew her. It is a way I hope she was, balancing for that one moment in an act of grace so complete she forgot who she had been and knew, instinctively, who she could be.

My father, too, was in Africa, in those brief years before my mother divorced him and we moved back to the South; he was the same age my daughter is now, the spray of cinnamon-colored freckles that spanned his high cheekbones and the bridge of his nose matching my own. We looked alike, people always pointed out, and I have a handful of early memories of that look, his strong-featured face in silhouette in the darkness of the tent, chin pointed down, heavy eyelids half closed, his shoulders slumped forward, a posture of defeat. It is how I remember him, defeated, even in youth, even before I knew the uncommon strain of his pathology.

They had met in school, he and my mother, and I reason now that they knew instinctively what all sick people know, that things are easier with their own kind. They were not together long, not even in the history of brittle marriages, just long enough for me to walk, to talk, to show an inherent capacity for brooding. My mother picked up an English accent in Africa and left behind a husband. We took a plane back to the States and I turned six years old somewhere over the Atlantic. The stewardess gave me a cigar band for a ring and a pair of airline wings so, she said, I could fly.

Even after my mother married Bill McClain, we always lived near water. It is something I have come to know only in later years, how the smell and sound of it has marked decades, from the sweet salt scent of the Gulf in Louisiana to the mud and catfish tang of the Pearl in Jackson, and there was always the eerie sound of it rising in flood season, a sound that has no sound, an ear-against-the-seashell murmur, so you come to understand you are only one of a thousand vacuums it seeks to fill.

We came back to the South, after a quickie divorce in which my mother inherited one diamond bracelet and an undisclosed sum of money for my upkeep, and lived for a short time with my aunt Freda, in an apartment in the upstairs of the sprawling house. They went to the honky-tonks at night, the two beautiful sisters, the wild girls of the town, and sometimes packed me along, perching me on a stool in the corner of the dance floor so, as Freda said, "You can study the ritual, child." That was where my mother met Bill McClain, in a beer joint, and it seems, from the perspective of childhood, that they were married almost that same night, so quickly was he a part of our lives.

We traveled with him all over the South, the names of the towns we lived in—Dubach, Arkadelphia, Altheimer, Lake Charles—a litany of early poverty before Bill made it big as a businessman. But still there was water, my mother's one requirement for this penance of marriage (for this is what it became) that there be a "crick," as she called it, or some body of water nearby. In Jackson there had been the ravine, a tributary of the Pearl that raged in spring and dried to a scab in summer. After Jackson we moved to the outlying countryside of Nashville, where, across the road, the Cumberland River sprawled, and behind our house a bonus creek, its lazy trickle jammed with crawdads I'd bait with rancid chicken meat, snatching them angry from the water, their claws cutting the air. As fish substitutes they were passable, creepy-looking hors d'oeuvres I'd suck from the shell after dipping them in boiling water, their shells flushing the bright red of maple leaves in autumn.

With widemouthed Mason jars I dipped algae-flecked water from the creek and studied it under my microscope, an ocean of life in a teaspoon riding on the tide of my breath as I leaned in close over the slide, amazed and horrified at the teeming clot of life. I drank the water and imagined what lived in me then and if I would become amphibianlike, able to swim among them, water deep in my lungs, baptized. I regarded nature this way, believing that to take it in raw would give me power. I held hard to that one belief, for no other reason than that it was my own, that to eat what grew in earth, swam in water, and floated in air would, in a molecular exchange so potent, so volatile, somehow make me stronger, wiser, immune to the ordinary. Sometimes I knew, the way I knew the lunar pull on the tides of my own maturing body, that it was linked, in a way I could never hope to decipher, to the Indian in me. Struggling at the far edge of consciousness, where the fragments of dreams hover, was a knowing that this was what I was, this dirt, this air, this water. In my own solitary ceremonies I drank rainwater from the gutter spill, crouched on my knees in the wet grass beneath the darkness of a new moon—listening, waiting—and beneath the full, brightening moon I planted summer gardens, scored bloody furrows on my own arms with the point of an oak bow whittled sharp, packed my wounds in leaves wet from the ground with that pale light as witness, and heard the high-voltage-wire sound of cicadas give a voice to what I knew.

No matter where we moved my mother and her husband lived deep indoors, wrapped up tight with their bottles of bourbon and vodka, their limitless arguments, and I lived far beyond their walls. Neither of them ever quite comprehended me or the specific strain of my outdoor fever, my mother affixing the term "tomboy" to me and leaving it at that, my stepfather declaring me strange and eyeing me cautiously, as if, maybe, like Freda, I contemplated murder. Regarding my childhood now, across this expanse of years, I would say it was so, that few days passed during the decade I lived with the man that I did not think of killing him. And it was true, I *was* an odd tomboy of a girl, who used the hard torsos of Barbie dolls to hammer nails. Left alone to grub in the dirt and mud and water of the world, to spend dawn-to-dark days on the banks of creeks and rivers, I was oddly happy. It seems now no more than a process of distillation, happiness, the pure vapor rising in the glass globe, condensing, what might contaminate a remembrance left to settle in the bottom, unnoticed.

Water was more reassuring when it moved, when destination and purpose were obvious by its motion. A thing so full and heavy could not be made to stand still, was angrily intractable when it had the great pool of all waters beckoning, an ocean, a gulf, a sea. On an island low in the middle of the Cumberland River I contemplated the pilgrimage of water, with a young girl's eye to the dramatic, thinking, Were I to sail a bottle with a message from these shores, who would find it and where, and what, above all, would it say? It would have something to do with the free-floating rootless sense my life had taken on, the growing certainty that I fit in nowhere but in the wild world, my sensibilities too potent and crude for civilized people. Where, exactly, did a girl fit in who ate locust shells and fish guts, who thought of murder, whose curiosity had the hell-bent motion of the lethal? This message I would bind up tightly would be a plea, a shameless begging, for a perception kin to mine. I imagined my aunt Freda or Catfish bending to rinse their hands clean of fish in the Arkansas, how they would snatch the bottle by its neck as it floated by, unfold the damp message, and hear me across an expanse of waters.

In Nashville I fished the Cumberland as I had fished the Arkansas, but alone now, my cane pole and stash of bobbers cracked and weathered. On the island ringed in cottonwoods I made five-alarm bonfires, covering and uncovering the coals with an old blanket, choking out smoke signals deep into the night. I practiced heritage here, never calling it that, but feeling it, gauging wind direction by the slow drift of smoke, listening in the night for the quick rush of predators in the leaves, sniffing the air for signs of rain. I cooked what I had caught in the open fire—perch, crappie, catfish, hogfish, speared on a shaved bough—blackening the flesh until it fell warm into my open hands. In the clean air I ate the way you do after three days without a meal, greedily, casting the bones into the brush where possums and raccoons scavenged. This was what I knew of living. This was what I was born to, no matter that later fear and affliction drove me indoors, made me timid.

Those days on the Cumberland, stalking the river, feeling it warm and heavy against my back as I waded in deep, became my idyll, my quest, my one irreducible moment, and I imagined living like this on a slow journey across the country, moving from riverbank to riverbank, in summer sleeping in gauzy warmth beneath the trees, in winter digging a hole into the bank and nesting there. I studied a map of the United States, plotting it from coast to coast, letting my fingers trace the broad, solid trunk of the Mississippi, the filigreed veins of its tributaries. I drew a red star at my place on the map, a spot of land drifting on a thread of water, and thought, Unless I gave directions, you would never find me. I enjoyed the sense of isolation, tending it daily, making of my spot on the river a home stocked with supplies: cans of beans, matches, candles, my first Swiss army knife. It was on that island, while lying at night beneath a sky that stuttered with ancient light, that I realized how little, truly, I needed.

Sometimes I wonder, if I had left when the urge first hit me, if I had just slipped into the night and found my way blind along the banks of the Cumberland, what might have risen in my path to defy me. I wonder so often that sometimes I believe this imagined setting off into the wild was real. It has come to me in dreams, as fish have, this journey undone. It has defined, somehow, the fluid boundaries of my life. It has, decade after decade, in increments great, more often small, pushed me slowly across the map, so what I see when I look back at that time is a trail of bread crumbs leading straight to where I am.

Each time we moved, the houses in which we lived got bigger, fancier, and the creek that moved nearby a little smaller. By the time we made it to North Carolina, the creek was no more than a trickle on the south side of our lot. I was sixteen by then, expected to have other interests. The kids I went to school with skied on the glassy surfaces of reservoirs on the weekend, swam in the pastel chlorine of country club pools, and would have found it backward to drag a bait across the water on a sunny afternoon. I kept my fishing condition to myself, vaguely ashamed of it, and tried to fit into a world of saddle oxfords and high school cliques. I was not a success. Opinionated and defiant, I failed at socialization. In my tenth-grade year alone I was expelled twice, once for dumping a bucket of soapy water on the head of the driver's ed teacher, and another time for wearing a skirt so short that, as my chemistry teacher put it, "It ends at your neck."

At this time in my life I questioned everything, and my allegiance to my mother took the heaviest scrutiny. I wondered why she had kept me from my father all those years, from that brooding figure I remembered in the tent in Africa, his face so like my own, dark, inward looking, and why he had never written, called, come to visit. I assumed, ignorantly, that it had never been his wish to ignore me, not yet understanding the child's natural inclination to outfit the missing parent with qualities of sainthood. I thought of my father in this way, as my missing link to the natural world, his genetic ante the reason I walked around dumbfounded by stars and fish and birds. I wrote to him secretly and received a plane ticket to Miami in the mail, some cash, and eventually, when I told her what I had done, a proclamation from my mother that this was the biggest mistake I would ever make. It seemed she had been right about little in my life, but everyone has, at least once, an indelible moment of clarity.

Chapter

FIVE

I FISHED with my father just once, before I knew he liked to dress in women's clothes. The number of people who can say in perfect honesty that Dad is just a regular guy who prefers chiffon to a pair of chinos probably have a society going somewhere, and I don't want to know about it. The pope's a father, Christmas is a father, time is a father, but *my* father, bless his quirky sense of fashion, his possible indecision over the right shade of nail polish, is not what you would call a *serious* father. Not that he ever was, particularly, his days with me as a bona fide parent lean and few, spanning from my birth to the age of five years, of which time I recall only a random, muted image of his slumped-forward posture in the tent in Africa, his stiff form straddling the girth of an ostrich. I remember a rope used as a bridle as he rode the ostrich, dipping and balking into the sulfurous African sunset, his bowed legs curving perfectly around the bird's flanks. From ostrich riding to ostrich boas, my father embraced the mutability of manhood. The truth is, I never had a clue until my mother told me that he sometimes wore her girdle and painted his nails a bright, clean red. Not until, say, the change of life had become a foregone thing. I've seen pictures. He looks like Ethel Merman.

Around Mother's Day, in the Hallmark section, I am tortured. There are no greeting cards that read, "Thinking of you fondly, transvestite Dad." or, "On your special day, Whatsit."

I admit, though, a certain distance from the effects of my father's confusion over gender. I barely knew the man and fished with him only once in the purple waters of the Gulf Stream. It was during a time when he still clung desperately to manhood, or perhaps he merely paraded his remembrance of it for my benefit, so obviously was I seeking a father. And once was really enough.

• • •

THE CORAL atoll of Bimini rises like a sun-bleached carapace from the pastel seas of the Caribbean, its rocky surface dotted with scrub pines and coconut palms, the shallow waters of its shore rattling with the empty shells of queen conchs. Beneath the clear waters, schools of exotic fish flash like candles in the reflected sun as they torpedo along the flats, nose to tail, waves of them like giant sea fans tipping in the current. They surf in on the high tide—barracuda, jack crevalle, mutton snapper, ladyfish, sergeant major, snapper red as rubies—and skate out again, drawn by the moon. These gemlike waters that dazzle at first sight are a far cry from the bubbling opacity of Southern rivers. I watched them, spellbound, from the scratched window of an old seaplane as we flew in low over Bimini, and understood why they call such places paradise, for the dozen shades of aqua alone.

We did not know what to say to each other, my father and I, just occasional, painfully polite small talk as the plane's engine ground on and we dipped and bumped on the currents of wind. "Never a fatal accident on this airline," he said as he gazed out the window, never meeting my eyes. I was sixteen, and for a period of half a year had been uncharacteristically quiet and studious, a speed-of-light phase during which I tossed around the notion of becoming a nun, following my aunt Freda's lead. She had joined a not-so-uptight order and had become a nun in theory, if not in actual practice, wearing her habit around the house under her cotton pajama top, fingering her rosary and shooting me dark looks. I liked the spook effect it had and pictured myself sliding from room to candelit room, swathed in black. I wondered what my father would think of this, his kid, a nun.

I eyed him, sizing him up in off moments when he wasn't doing the same to me, catching glimpses out of the corner of his eye, probably studying, I realize now, the precise way I applied mascara. I didn't want to be too harsh, this being our first meeting in ten years, but I thought the man was a real pig. It was the first impression I'd had of him when I'd stepped off the plane and seen him standing at the gate, waving uncertainly. He was a short, oily, muscular man, his thinning hair slicked back in limp strands, and he smelled as if he hadn't bathed not just in days, but in months. This was a symptom of his illness, I would later learn, depressions so bludgeoning in their force that he would lock himself in a room for weeks at a time, and willingly commit himself for courses of electroshock therapy. When I met him, though, I knew nothing of his history, nothing of his future, only that we were flying to Bimini to fish, and that fish, even monstrous species I had never encountered, I could relate to.

• • •

CAPTAIN BOB was our guide, a broad, massive Bahamian who wore a gold shark's tooth around a neck the size of my waist, and gold rings on every finger. He called me "mon," which I took to be the Bahamian version of "ma'am," so I nodded to him politely each time. As we chugged out of Bimini harbor in the lengthy sportfisherman, my father manned the fighting chair and I took a curiously comfortable squatting position on deck, resisting the urge to sprint as I watched Bimini disappear on the horizon. My one encounter with boats, to date, had been on a leaky wooden craft on Pine Bluff Lake, a single oar my propeller, a stringer of catfish my anchor. This shiny white torpedo with an engine so powerful I was slammed into the cabin door as the boat gained speed was pure glory, a fishing machine cherried out in teak and brass, its elegant tuna tower rising toward the bright sky. This was a boat fish would leap into for the sheer luxury of the ride.

I did not have even a faint clue what we were doing. Now, having fished Gulf Stream waters many times for big game fish, I know, at least in a rudimentary way, the names for things, what you fish for and often where, but on this day in July over twenty-five years ago, our speed quickening as we left the channel and moved into open water, it all had a cartoon quality—the blue-white-green-blue tint of the water, the wash of purple sky, the gleaming white boat—and the shotgun-sized rods that flanked my father on either side of the fighting chair, and the double fist-sized reels that weighted them at the butt, were equipment I could never have dreamed, never imagined. A cane pole alongside this technology would be puny, pathetic, the bobber I would slip along the line useless in these peaked, churning waters.

And the water was pure Fellini. Behind us lay the calm pastels of shallow water. We floated now upon the purple ink of the Gulf Stream, waters deep as hell and as punitive, I imagined, as I watched the swells suck our boat into a trough and then perch it high atop a peak, a liquid undulation that, fortunately, has never bothered me. I have been told my time will come, that all who take to the sea in glorified bathtubs will eventually hurl their lunch starboard. Yet for days after a day at sea I cannot acquaint myself with the steadiness of earth, toppling along as if I am drunk, the ground rushing up to meet me at odd moments so that I've been forced on occasion to drop to all fours, too dizzy to stand. I've been told it's an affliction that comes from overcompensating in high seas, the inner ear adjusting to the roll and heave of moving territory so effectively it doesn't register when it's back on solid ground.

In no time I lost myself to the rocking, bucking motion of the boat, going with it, feet spread wide on the deck, my crouch position forsaken for the excitement of the ride, my toes gripped on the biggest surfboard ever. I stood to the right of the fighting chair while Captain Bob rigged the bait—split mullet—wiring it to grapple-sized hooks, rigging a couple of teasers in close off the stern, and then running the line to the outriggers that dipped, starboard and port, touching the water with their pointy fingers. It was exciting, all this preparation for a fish, and I got charged up just watching, the way I had when Catfish had slipped her homemade bobbers way up the line so the bait would ride deep.

And I watched the sky intently, a practice I'd taken up in Mississippi, surveying the southwest horizon daily for thunderheads and the strange black-green cast the light took on before a tornado struck. I feared them and the death they brought each spring, sucking up barns, houses, cows, people, and snapping them to matchsticks in their fury. Right after we'd left Jackson the worst tornado in Mississippi history had leveled our neighborhood, and after it had taken out the grocery story, the pharmacy, the houses, and the little hamburger joint where my friends and I hung out, it took the path of the ravine on into the next county. The mother of the boy I had had a crush on died. The pharmacist at the drugstore up the road died, and a dozen others, their bodies strewn in the cow pasture across the road. I'd wondered, too, what had happened to the baby bass as they'd been sucked high into the funnel of wind, the albino catfish, the frogs, snakes, and lizards. A friend had told me there had been nothing left as I had known it, that even the ravine was broken and oozing when the wind had died.

This day the southwest bloomed with thunderheads. I kept a close eye on them as I stood by my father, the baits skipping now, the engine at trolling speed so every dip and shift was heightened.

"You fish?" he asked me, a few of the handful of words he'd spoken since we'd met.

"Sure," I said, a little too eagerly, pleased he'd picked a subject I knew something about. "I did. I do. I just haven't much lately."

The boat rocked and groaned. The baits skipped wildly in the swelling seas. I turned my gaze again to the blackened sky, catching a glimpse of my father's oily, slicked-back hair, the peculiar pallor of his skin. He did not look well.

"What fish?" he asked, steadying himself in the chair.

"Pardon."

"What is it you fish for, exactly? The type of fish you go after, what are they?"

His accent, which I hadn't quite pinned yet, rattled me. I was usually good with accents, able to tell if you were from Virginia, North Carolina, Arkansas, Mississippi, or Texas right off the bat, but the way he spoke was like something out of an old movie, educated, upper crust, leagues removed from my nasal drawl—toney, intimidating, "What is it you fish for, *exactly*?" delivered with mild contempt. How would catfish trotlined with stink bait sound to Mr. Marlin?

"Catfish," I said, trying to sound like the cracker I was, drawing it out the way Freda would. *Kay-et-feesh*.

He made a face. I thought he might have caught a whiff of himself. He laughed a snobby little laugh. "Heh," he said, "heh-heh." I smiled, as if we'd shared a joke. "No," he continued, "not what we are going for here, catfish. Not at *all* what we are after."

So what the hell was it? I had seen no fish, and I'd been looking plenty. We'd been lurching in the water for a couple of hours, and the best I'd gotten was a frigate bird feeding the grass line.

"Marlin," my father said, the word spoken like a benediction. "We are going for the great blue marlin. Four hundred pounds, five hundred pounds, six hundred pounds in these waters. Monsters, huge, their bills like swords, their girth massive. You hook into one and they walk on water, trying to throw the hook. It takes hours to bring one to the boat. Hours."

I took in the reverential tone of this information, skeptical. Was this what he'd been doing all those years we'd been apart? I'd heard reports of his elephant hunting in Africa, how he'd killed just to watch them drop and how, when he'd come back to the States, he'd collapsed into an eight-year depression. If murder had been his hobby when he was on the upswing, I wondered what the dark days brought. At the time I didn't know that he was circling the funnel of that same depression, and that to have gotten out of bed that morning had probably taken everything he had.

I'd climbed the bridge to where Captain Bob sat at the helm, turned in the direction of the skipping bait, one massive gold-ringed hand idly steadying the wheel. Despite his overall Shaft-like appearance he had a generally benign, laid-back demeanor, and I felt comfortable around him. Years later I would run into him on Bimini again and he would nod in my direction and say, simply, "Ah. You de one."

This day he had some things to say about my father, and I had to listen close to his climb-the-scale dialect to catch it.

"He jus' tryin' to please, you know, mon. Nevah, hardly, he catch fish, I seen. I been out sometime, you know, wit him. He sick to de boat, how it rock, dis rock-king get him all de time, mon, *all* de time."

Captain Bob made a gagging reflex, a thick finger pointing at the back of his throat. I got the picture.

"You say he never catches fish," I asked, feeling vaguely ashamed, as if having blood ties to someone who lied about fish diminished me.

"No fish, mon, sure. I tell you right. Lucky charm what you be, on dis boat, mon. You see, he figger he burn de luck out. Mebbe. Mebbe no. Toss dah coin in, see, mon, we raise de fish. He yuh fa-thah, mon. Make nice. Bring de luck. Good."

It's the first I'd heard of offerings to King Neptune, of ways to bribe the fish gods.

"Into the water," I asked, studying the dimes bright in his outstretched palm. "I throw these in the water?"

"For de luck," he assured me.

I picked up the dimes one by one and held them a moment in my own sweaty fist, feeling the heat in them still from Captain Bob's hand. Leaning carefully over the edge of the flying bridge I flung them to the wind, watching them turn and spin, catching the sun as they fell, soundless, into the sea. And in that split second of tossing them I'd thought the word "luck" so loud and clear I'd have sworn I'd spoken it.

I believed in ritual even then, how a planned act, its roots deep in a subjective view of the world, held power. My aunt Freda had bizarre incantations for every occasion and would mumble them as she lit candles throughout the house before dawn, roaming through the cavernous rooms, trailing incense in her wake as she fingered her rosary, looking not beatific but slightly mad. The truth was, if dimes could bring this phantom fish to the surface, I was all for it, if for no other reason than to jolt some life into my father. It bothered me to think he never caught fish and that this day on the water had been packaged up just to make me think he was something he wasn't. A man. He wanted me to think he was a man. Still, early on I believed in the blessing of the fishes, that some had been given the goods and some hadn't, and that however the luck fell it was directly proportional to your worth as a human. I think he knew this, that I carried within me a ruthless need to judge, given nothing to go on but a few fine points, and that failing those he would be to me as he had been before—nothing. Not a man, not a father, not even a memory. Part of me hated him for all the years gone, and the rest felt pity and something vaguely like love. I wanted him to do well. I wanted him to show me the stuff *I* was made of.

"Twelve o'clock, mon!" It was Captain Bob's voice, loud, beside me. I jumped. Never had I heard the time of day announced with such urgency. I flicked my wrist over and checked my watch. Ten straight up.

"I say twelve *o'*clock, mon," Bob called again to my father, and then I saw it, straight out, high noon to the angler, the great bill rising up out of the water as if pulled by a crane, crashing down on the bait—*whack, smash*—spray flying, fifty feet out, and then he took it running, the line snapping free from the pin of the outrigger with a sound like a guitar string plucked once, up by the frets.

All of a sudden we were in a sci-fi movie with the water rolling purple in big peaks and the boat following it after the weirdest-looking animated mass I had ever seen. From the distance of the stern to the end of the line, maybe two hundred yards, the monster looked as if it had been armor plated and dipped in blue-and-silver sparkle dust, the red gash of its mouth open to cast off the hook.

I said, "Hey, what's happening?"

"Let him run dis time, mon," Captain Bob instructed as I

crashed down from the bridge, skidding into place beside my father. This was the be-all, end-all of deepwater-angling support, I would learn, to plant yourself solidly beside the one who'd been fish blessed and basically coach him through the labor.

"Ugh, what now?" is all I could manage as line screamed from the reel, spooling out so fast it blurred as I watched my father, futilely, try to slow it with his thumb.

"Let hem go! I say, let hem go, mon!" My father's thumb snapped away from the line as if he had touched fire.

The rod butt was wedged securely in the gimbal on the belt around my father's waist, his left hand white knuckled as it clutched the grip on the butt. I could see his biceps straining in a painful-looking knot beneath his pale skin. A fish so big you had to anchor him to your own body. I was impressed.

I looked at my father, at the pure fear that washed his face, and thought perhaps it was why I rarely remembered seeing him face forward, that to have stared at his terror, day in, day out, would have been too much. The panic in his eyes, the strong need to not screw up, was all over him like a rash. I could even smell it on him, the way animals who move in for the kill must smell their prey, sensing weakness in the fear they sniff, how one full-throated growl will put them over the edge. Boo! I thought of saying, but changed my mind.

The atmosphere on the boat had gone from lazy to electric, Captain Bob shouting orders—"Take a leetle up, mon, jus' a bit now, jus' a bit. Ah, no, mon, let hem go now, let hem go"—my father struggling awkwardly with the burden of the giant he had hooked fairly, his left arm tight as a bowstring, locked down hard, his right hand poised at the reel, shaking, ready.

You edgy, they knows it, you edgy, they knows it. I imagined scrawny old Catfish at my father's panicked side, hands on her washboard hips, scowling at him. The picture made me laugh, and my father turned quickly and gave me a searching look. "What?" he said, but I didn't answer.

A fraction of a league away, across the Jell-O roll of the Gulf Stream, I watched the marlin jump once, tearing himself from the heaving, darkening horizon in one muscular right-angle leap, massive prehistoric head thrashing, the bright gash of his mouth scarlet against the black backdrop of sky. Liquid spun from him like water from a shaken bough, threading into the air, suspended momentarily in the vacuum of his passage. I could see his colors, sidereal blue against pure silver, a living, breathing neon jeté caught in midair.

"Jesus H. Christ," I whispered. *"That's* a fish." Nothing had prepared me for his presence, for this was what it was, no ordinary flitty fish singing lightly electric on the end of a line, but a consciousness, pure and furious, an immense tail-walking giant who'd shot straight up into our element, rabidly pissed off, thrashing and lethal in his fury, pure wrath and survival intent. I wanted him for my own.

My father, sweating so hard now his shirt dripped at the sleeves, saw him, and in that one instant did what I knew, instinctively, he should never have done. Left hand frozen now like a claw to the rod butt, he yanked hard as the marlin descended in one great volume-displacing splash. The line snapped where moments before it had angled out taut across the stern, tethering the marlin to our boat, a direct cable line to the unbelievable. I knew the feeling of losing a fish through carelessness, but I could not comprehend having my lasso drawn tight on the Holy Father of All Fish only to have the rope snap.

"Damn it, mon. Damn it to hell," Captain Bob was muttering, ready, I was certain, to drive the gaff he'd held ready in his hand into my father's throat. How many times had it come to this, I wondered, my father stricken by fear in this same chair, the marlin sounding all the way to China as Captain Bob yelled, "Jus' let hem go, mon!" and then the inevitable, adrenaline-plummeting loss, the failure—*his* failure—huge and empty on the horizon? How did it feel, exactly, to keep losing?

If I had known my father, grown up with him, had ingrained in me that protective urge you sometimes feel for parents when you see them less than strong, I might have hugged him, patted his shoulder, something; but I stood there stiffly, left arm braced against the chair, uncertain what to do. The thunderheads had converged, lightning sheeting through them now as we rocked violently, white caps sloshing over the stern as Captain Bob climbed the ladder to the bridge wearily, gunned the motor, and turned the boat in the direction of Bimini.

My father looked broken. There is no other word for it. He sat crumpled in the chair, folded in on himself, his face an odd off-white, and I couldn't help myself. I reached out, touching my fingertips lightly to his forehead, a gesture, something to tie me to him this once.

"Sorry, Greg," I said.

He looked at me curiously, as if seeing me for the first time. I remember how his eyes were the exact color of my own, a brown so deep that even in the light of day they looked black. This was my father, the liquid, elusive half of my genetic pool, a man who for years had moved along the ragged contours of a plane opposite my own, lost to himself, to me, to my mother, stalking futilely the legend of his own father in these waters, on sun-blasted African plains, coming up short time and time again, so that it must have taken on the perfect look of a mirage, his life, the part he had played in it. I wondered how he and my mother had been, together, early on. I had seen pictures, the two of them on a California beach, impossibly young, both smiling, my mother's pants legs rolled up to the knees, her head thrown back, my father leaning toward her as if to catch her. Kids. My parents had been children together.

"You're a pretty girl," my father said slowly, touching his fingertips to the line of my jaw, regarding me as he would a portrait. "A very pretty girl. Call me 'Father,' would you?"

Such a simple request and such a simple word, almost like any other word but for the confusion it cost us both. And such an ungodly catch in my throat as I tried to speak it and could not.

He got sick over the side, pulling himself up wearily from the chair just in time. I noticed the nail polish then, a slash of it on two cracked and dirty nails, and remember the color of it well, a red bright as the inside of the marlin's hooked jaw. I followed behind, slipping my fingers through the belt loops of his pants to steady him, and watched the Gulf Stream rise up to meet us, the wind whipping it white and black, the spray running salty down the back of my throat. I thought of letting go, but did not. I thought of crying, but could not. It was a reflex that, for years, would elude me. I settled on an instant replay of the marlin, imagining how I might have handled him, how, when the line gave a little as he flamed into the air, I would have reeled a bit, no more, taking up the slack. I'd have let myself feel him so I would know what he was thinking, kept a lock on my fear so it would not strangle me. I'd have caught him, pulled him sleek and regal alongside the boat, I was sure of it.

My father and I parted stiffly, as we had met, neither of us mentioning again our day at sea.

"I will be in touch," he told me as he left me at the airport, the formal tone of his farewell sealing us off again, saving us.

"Good-bye," I said, thinking in my head, Father, but leaving the word unspoken. To this day I have never said it to him, have never once been compelled to give him the right to call me daughter. That sounds bitter, but it is not. It is simply that through fate or luck or the divine order of things, we have left the father-daughter path untrod, but for a few footfalls, and wisely so.

The next time I saw him was twenty years later, in a photo, a glossy eight-by-ten, and in that picture he is a woman, a stocky, bowlegged brute of a woman, but a woman nonetheless. His hair is frosted in a bouffant style, his nose bobbed and straightened, and he grins to show two even rows of capped teeth. It is his eyes, though, that capture, huge, dark, untrusting, the eyes of a bad boy, trapped.

Chapter

SIX

RECALLING my life, I often wince, thinking, No, I could not have done that, I could not have been that stupid, that desperate, that angry, that sick. It is why we grow older, I reason, to feel the full pain of embarrassment at having lived in dubious ways, and from that embarrassment comes something a little like wisdom, but cheaper. Call it acceptance.

I left home soon after I turned sixteen, and then, when I was eighteen, fled the South with nothing but a bail bond to my name. "A fugitive from justice" my mother called me, borrowing a phrase. I remember her voice on the telephone, and how by the very pitch of it, the dramatic, self-conscious way she gathered up her words, the way she stressed the syllables of my name—"Lore-*ee*-un"—as if it were an abomination, that she was deep into the drinking. She'd been drinking all the years I'd been her girl, and I knew, the way I knew from indelible memory the particular green of her eyes, that she was never going to quit.

The night before I left I called her from a pay phone in Charlotte, North Carolina. An electrical storm was turning the sky into a white-hot negative of veins and arteries, and as I told my mother my plans to leave the state, maybe the country, how I had dyed and cut my hair, gotten false ID, and had a job as a stripper waiting for me in Miami, I remember thinking, each time the lightning flashed and the inside of the phone booth was lit by an atomic sun, that maybe it would burn the image of me so clearly on the spot where I stood that someday, if I needed, I could find my way home.

This news, as far removed as it could be from any pretty hope my mother might have had for me, and by the simple, unadorned nature of its ugliness, threw her into a pathetic cerebral meltdown. In this state of near shock she blipped past vital chunks of information, like how I had used a personal pronoun and the word "stripper" in the same sentence. Rather than look this straight in the eye, rather than know in her gut what I had become, she said, with the sort of grave ceremony drunks are famous for, "You know, child, a fugitive from *justice* is what you'll be," the word "justice" emphasized as if it should have some sort of cosmic meaning. It did. At that time in my life I thought nothing fair, not even the weather. And I hadn't fished in two years. Hadn't thought once of fishing. My life was seriously wrong.

I had become, in the quick two years since I had fished with my father, a booze-sucking, pill-popping, dope-slamming druggie, a girl whose dark eyes now had darker circles and whose blue-veined arms now bore the ritual marks of the needle. I was a natural junkie, captivated by the daily rites, the coming off, the getting off, the pure fix of it, and I was in love with the points of needles, the way they broke the flesh with a fatal little *pop,* the way the blood, *my* blood, backed up into the syringe, turning it a cloudy, pale pink; but most of all I sought and stroked, as I would a lover, the slow, warm, vacant, weightless drop into purgatory. But you never knew it was purgatory. That was the trick of it. I went into it fast and hard, taking for my friends not the Izod-shirted, Weejun-shod preppies but, instead, the fringe-draped fringe, the dark den of bell-bottomed, rage-fed hippies to whom justice arrived, daily, in a bag full of pills, a bag full of powder. They were my people. They had seen the flip side.

We called ourselves the Family, after Charles Manson's lead, and pledged blood bonds to one another, cutting the thin flesh of our arms with razor blades as we sat in the dim yellow light of a circle of guttering candles. We had no furniture in the house we rented with drug money, just stained, sheetless mattresses, the occasional blanket, and plywood and cinder-block tables, where each night we cut and weighed the black bars of opium, the lids of dope that went then for five bucks a bag, and mind-splitting LSD we brought from the West Coast sealed in tennis-ball cans. We had connections, good ones, and to be safe kept our money in a drawer in the kitchen, in a utensil tray: fifties, twenties, hundred-dollar bills lined up neatly in the slots for spoons, knives, and forks. We trusted one another. And each day we got a little closer to death together. It meant something.

I turned eighteen in jail, locked up for sale and possession of an impressive pharmacy of illegal drugs. They busted me in a motel room, my unofficial sales headquarters. After two members of the Winston-Salem, North Carolina, vice squad knocked on my door and I politely let them in, they tore the pictures from the walls, the lining from my suitcase, and the ticking from the mattress. They dismantled the toilet, pulled up the carpet, unscrewed the p-trap from the sink drain, and stuck me with the bill. They even had a portable lab with them, analyzing what they found on the spot, and when they snapped the handcuffs on me—behind the back then, just like in the movies—they asked if I'd been turning tricks that night. I confess to certain moments of out-of-place naivete in my life, to lapses of pure innocence, and this was one of them. A drug addict on the run with a suitcase full of dope ought to know the meaning of the word "trick," in its street vernacular. Not I. Like the girl I had been who believed she could eat acorns and locust shells, wild onions and red clay, and be, somehow, infinitely wiser, I had become the street-tough teenager who thought tricks meant magic, women sawed in half onstage, rabbits pulled out of a hat. "No," I told the cops honestly. "I don't do any tricks."

It was Christmas. At police headquarters, in the vice squad's office, there was a scrawny Charlie Brown tree studded with little snowflakes of white paper, each with a name penned in the center of the flake, successful drug busts of that year, and the guy who had put the cuffs on me, a short, nervous, sweaty little man, added my name to the tree with exaggerated ceremony, asking me, "How does it feel to be famous, kid?" The question hit with a certain biting clarity. I knew my name would make the papers for what I'd done, but it wasn't that that bothered me as much as the irony of it. The last thought I had given to fame had been to make the front page of the *Pine Bluff Commercial* with a trophy-sized fish. I had come the incalculable distance from being in the blinding yellow heat of an Arkansas summer, my bobber riding high on the river current, to being very seriously indoors and locked down tight, in the span of a mere ten years. It was my worst fear, being bolted in.

Jail is maybe what you make it. I was in only a month, so I cannot speak with true authority, but know only that communities grow there, quickly, out of need, and that I fit in with alarming ease. My cell mates were a man killer, another drug addict, and a woman who fished. Her crime was theft, but we didn't talk about it much. She was black, young, although not as young as I, and I remember how she would offer a cigarette to me from her pack of Kools, opened from the bottom with the filterless end exposed so she wouldn't dirty the filter with her hands. It was a curious, delicate act of hygiene in an otherwise unhygienic place. Roaches would slide along the cell walls at night as I sat in the dark with my knees to my chest, sweating out the drugs, my muscles strung up tight and hot so that I could feel them burning through the skin, then so cold I thought they'd shatter, waves of nausea riding the back of my throat, so that any sound, any movement, any change in heat would send me buckling to the toilet that was riveted to the wall of the cell like bad Warhol art.

Someone at the jail called my mother to tell her I was sick, and she said, "Let her stay there. Maybe she'll learn." It took a week before I was cleaned out, and then I lay limp for hours on end, just feeling how it was to breathe. Sometimes I could feel the roaches on the pricked-up hair of my arms and would slap at them wildly with a candy bar one of the trusties had given me, saying as she slipped the chocolate through the bars,

"I'll fatten you up, girl," and I'd been reminded of the witch in "Hansel and Gretel," staring at her toothless smile, her simple face. She, too, had killed a man. Her husband. "Happier for it," she had said when I'd asked if it had been worth her freedom.

At night, when the banks of lights were shut down, and our cell, one in a block of four, grew dark, so dark I could barely make out the top rail of my bunk in the thin, slatted light from the street, the women would begin to talk or sing, a voice entering the silence like rain on water, and I would listen to them closely, amazed where I had landed, in this mother's nest of criminals, their lives no different, really, from any other, just harder, barely touched by luck or fortune or compassion, the edges more real for it.

"I'd be fishing," said the girl with the Kools from across the cell, the strong features of her face shiny in the darkness. "If I was outta here, I would. Night fishing be the best, out with the moon on the water and all them sounds like a ghost story, *woo, woo, crick, crick,* and the wind high in the trees, *woo, woo, crick, crick.*"

We giggled, listening to her making night sounds, and we made them back, filling the cell with catcalls and the shrill, jumpy tones of crickets, letting ourselves imagine the tribe of us loose on the night, what it would mean.

"What you going to catch at night," I asked the Kools girl, "besides wet feet? Besides a cold?"

"Anything you catch in daylight," she told me, grinning big in the dark so I could see the gold in her teeth. "Just huge."

I'd laughed, remembering it was true, how in Pine Bluff I'd snuck to the lake alone one night, cast my hook and bobber far out into the moonlit slick of water, and caught a catfish big as a baby. In the Cumberland, too, I had night-fished, unable at times to tell where land and water met, the evenness that darkness put on everything a test of instinct. In lightless territory the sense of smell becomes a way to see, and I would sniff my way along the bank like a dog, stopping where I was sure the scent of fish was strongest.

Confinement is an impetus to memory, allowing it open range while the body remains fixed in one place, cautious. I had time now to contemplate what, exactly, had brought me here and where I was headed once I jumped bail, because in my new rules of order only a fool would stick around for this. Southern courts were notorious then for slamming hippies in jail for drug offenses, often for years at a stretch, and I did not plan to be one of them. Anyone stupid enough to get caught, I reasoned, should be smart enough to fly.

There were probably easier kids for my mother to raise. Moody, sullen, quick to anger, I spent half my time running away and the other half plotting ways to escape. My allegiance belonged to the wild world, but somewhere along the way I had grown grimmer, darker in mood than I'd ever been, and had given up even that release, turning instead to the hopped-up religion of drugs, to late hours, to boys, to crime as a source of adrenaline, forgetting what it meant to sit on a riverbank and contemplate the movement of water, the life streaming beneath. I'd lost touch, and for years I did not comprehend what was missing. Dark rooms where junkies nodded and mumbled at nothing became a habit with me, and anything that moved beyond the vortex of that dismal place no longer had a name. I watched people die in those rooms. A boy we called Half-Breed. A boy named Mark. Kids.

During those years I danced with fate the way you dance after three pitchers of beer, out of control, slamming into walls, stomping on feet, never saying, "Oh, I'm sorry," but, "Get the fuck out of my way." I was institutionalized for drug addiction. I was raped and dumped in a backwoods in Georgia. I hot-wired and stole cars from police garages. I sold drugs for a living, stole to eat, slept under cars, felt the summer of love in my gut like a cancer, wore a peace symbol made from a tire iron, and rode with baby-eating bikers. They didn't, really, but who believed you when you said it wasn't so? One look at them was enough to make old ladies faint and guys in suits wet their pants.

Imagine, then, a madwoman, a lunatic straight out of the belly of the South, whose one sworn-to oath was to self-destruct. A girl whose anger, bitten back, had become deadly. To ask why is pointless, for I see no revelation in why, only a fleeting remembrance that I was this girl, this alien-to-the-real who tore her way through a decade and came out quiet, chastised for a time, not repentant, exactly, but curious again, the way I'd been in Mississippi, in that ravine.

I began to get curious in jail, wondering what running would do for my mood, whether the faster I ran, far, far from the South, the better I'd feel. I had the filament of an idea, listening to the Kools girl talk of fishing, a picture in my head of a farm with a creek running through, light playing on the water, the flash of fins beneath like candles in the sun. Some nights I went to sleep with that picture blazing behind my eyes as the women sang themselves into a deep comfort, gospel songs, plaintive. "Save me, Lord, save me," they sang, and I thought, Why not? While you're at it, save me, too.

Chapter

SEVEN

MY DAUGHTER is a Pisces, born with a gill slit beneath one ear. She is the fish I have borne on my own swelling tide, and in summer she floats for hours on her back in perfect rectangular pools of water, oblivious to everything but the rush of liquid in her ears. I imagine that she breathes it in through her one gill, that it is like oxygen to her, sweet and bubbly. Her father, too, was Piscean, a green-eyed cat man with the hands of a wand maker, magician's hands, his fingers long and finely shaped, the way he walked sleek and seductive and even. He was eating chocolate chip cookies and drinking orange juice when I met him, and I remembered he was the boy people I knew talked about, the smart one, the one who went to college when he was sixteen, the one who looked like Jesus, his eyes the thing you remembered about his looks, and about his manner it was his soft, bemused voice that remained in memory, and the way he turned his head to one side when he listened.

The night I met him we took a walk and looked at the North Carolina summer sky, at a meteor shower that rained into the darkness balls of molten glass that glowed green and white and left a trail in the ether. Jimmy pointed out the squared-off field of Ursa Major and the bright stars of Orion's belt, and I found a finger of a moon low on the horizon and thought of the Kools girl in jail with her night-fishing stories, and I thought, too, of how I never wanted to go back.

Jimmy left the state with me when I fled south to Florida. We stopped in South Carolina and stayed for a couple of weeks at an abandoned cabin on a lake, where I swam each day and where he tried to build a raft of logs, tethering the soggy, pulpy wood with vines. At dawn I would wake to see the fog over the lake like cotton gauze, and when we made love I thought of the texture of it, of water wrapped in cotton. It was there our daughter was conceived, by that lake, at dawn, and remembering it, I think of her water sign, of the odd gill and the fish girl she became.

We went south to Miami for a while, and then west as far as Jimmy's old blue Ford and a gas credit card would take us, slamming up against the foreign Northwest coast, where our accents made people snicker and where we decided, because we were flat dead broke, to stay.

We married, and I surfaced after all those years down deep, came alive to a hundred different things. There was motherhood now and college and a vital physical health that commanded I spend all my free time outdoors in this strange new place where everything was different, even the fish. They seemed, oddly, more cold blooded, and the very coldness of the water in which they swam, the rain that continually washed the streams and rivers, helped clean me out, too. I had been drug free for two years, reborn to solid, hippie, naturalist values. I ate soybeans and lentils, yogurt, no meat, and fish, but only if I caught it, and since there turned out to be only two trout in the entire state of Washington, I stayed busy.

I do not know where or when the ethic surfaced that to buy fish in a store was akin to buying air. It may have been that day on the Arkansas with Catfish, when I came to see fishing as a way to survive. The same logic held for the fishing license. To be expected to pay to fish was idiocy. It may have been the Indian in me, what I thought of as my birthright to these waters, but whatever it was, for years I did not shell out the cash for that little piece of paper that made me legal.

We lived in a little house in Seattle then, Jimmy, our daughter, Cristen, and I, a place that had belonged to a woman who had died in the bed in which I now sleep. She had had no surviving relatives to whom she could leave her estate, and for $34 a month the funeral parlor that had tended her body rented us her home. The coffeepot was still on the stove.

In the cobweb-choked basement I rummaged for goodies, finding an old bamboo spinning rod and open-faced Mitchell reel, gear that made the cane pole I had last used look barbaric. I'd seen spinning gear infrequently in my life, usually in the hands of white men outfitted in camouflage as they set out on the Arkansas for bass, snapping the bail back and flicking the line out over the water in one smooth motion. It was rich man's gear, this, and I felt rich just looking at it. I thought about the old woman who had died upstairs, and wondered if on a hot day she had tipped the rod over her shoulder and headed off for the lake near our new home. I hoped that with this rod she had caught a thousand fish. The rod eyes were crunched down, so I opened them up by sliding a pen back and forth until they bloomed round again. I wound sewing thread around the frayed and cracking stays to hold them secure, then painted the whole rod with fingernail polish to waterproof it. It was the one and only cherry red rod I had ever seen, an original. The Mitchell was a beauty, the spool casing black and sturdy, the bail strong and springy, locking into place with no give whatsoever, and there was line still on the spool. I bought some big honker hooks, the kind that look like mini gaffs, some pea-sized split shot, and dug up several dozen worms. I was set for Northwest fishing.

For years I'd been a junkyard fisherman, tackle something that always fell into my hands, that I never bought but merely borrowed, ripped off, or found. Hence I regarded it as something like a frozen dinner, prepared beforehand with all the necessary ingredients, rarely needing salt or pepper. For a long time I fished with the barest of necessities, never once replacing the line on the old Mitchell, watching it grow thinner and thinner over the years until the spool finally showed through like skin on a balding head. No matter the line was cracked and yellowed with age. No matter the top half of the pole sailed free when I cast, no matter the tip broke off. If this orphaned, patched-together outfit caught fish, I was satisfied.

Into the green, wet, fern-choked recesses of the Pacific Northwest I ventured with my new husband and daughter, figuring to raise my kid early in the habits of the wild. This land was a puzzle to me, and even though I had, at legal peril, taken it over my homeland, I was not comfortable here. The woods were all wrong, spongy with undergrowth, ferns, mushrooms, and moss, not open and airy like the pinewoods of the South, where the ground beneath the trees lay dry and solid. I learned later there is a reason little else grows in a pine forest—the trees are too acidic to allow anything to challenge them—and that their high water content makes them natural lightning rods. It's why you see so many pine trees blown to a pulp after a storm. The Northwest rivers, too, were suspicious. They ran fast and shallow, their beds rocky and dangerous looking, and most disturbing, they had no color. You could see clear through to the bottom, and I decided that what lived in these waters must feel as naked as a pet goldfish.

I remember the first time Jimmy and I knelt beside a Northwest river.

"Look at that," he'd said, poking a stick into the crystal water. "Have you ever seen anything like it. Have you ever?"

You'd have thought he'd discovered white bread. When we camped I drank this water without a second thought, disappointed, though, in the taste, or rather the distinct lack of it. It was tap water as far as I could tell, bland, no body to it, no floating flecks of unidentified mass to give it texture. Could fish live in water so pure?

"Pure," though, was my buzzword in the early seventies. The world seemed untainted and oddly pure, and I was as pure as I could get without having had the benefit of dialysis. After I'd had my daughter, certain her birth was a sign I should clean up my life, a reprieve of sorts that allowed me a glimpse at what normal was, I'd given up smoking, drugs, and had pretty much given up drinking with the exception of a tall glass of beer on ice in the evening, the ice to make it last longer, the tall glass because it would hold most of a sixteen-ouncer.

By the retractable yardstick I used to measure harmony, we lived ideally for a time, hand-to-mouth poor but occupied with something greater than ourselves, a hard-and-fast bond with the outdoors, my young husband a Daniel Boone in bell-bottoms and I the fledgling spin-cast wizard, armed now with true high-tech gear, ready to rip lips.

We hiked one weekend to a high mountain lake, back in the days when I thought being out of breath meant you were alive. Jimmy always busied himself roaming the woods, never a fisherman. In fact, in the six years we were married he did not fish once, a circumstance that secretly pleased me because sharing was something I did only when threatened. I took to the lake right away, packing along a small knapsack with my new whizz-bang hardware secured in several zippered pouches: the pea-sized split shot; a plasticine packet of 1-aught hooks, the bigger the better, and barbed; some shiny new golf-ball-size red-and-white bobbers; and a mayonnaise jar jammed with worms and dirt, air holes punched in the lid. The worms I'd dug from a backyard garden I'd started, squealing each time I uprooted a fat night crawler, imagining the very lure of its plumpness when presented to a Northwest fish. From what I could tell of Seattle and the lack of bait-and-tackle shops, no one had even considered fishing here, and so I reasoned that the rivers were, as a friend later put it, "sick with trout." Simply to give one another more room, the fish would murder for my bait.

With my cherry red rod aimed in the direction of the lake, the Mitchell screwed securely to the butt (I took pride in figuring out this simple mechanism), a giant hook tied on, a whole night crawler wriggling on its shank, I went hunting.

I had never seen a trout. Once or twice on a plate, headless, tailless, finless, battered and fried, but never in the wild. In the South trout were as scarce as catfish were abundant, and here in these clear waters I expected, out of sheer habit, to see catfish lazing below, their whiskers sharply defined, flat heads nosing in the rocks.

The lake was high alpine, the kind that to me means instant nosebleed, and cold as ice at the bottom of the world. To survive in this water catfish would need thermal underwear and down jackets, not to mention mud. This lake had never known mud. It sat like a giant pristine pothole, submerged in the surrounding hills, the side I chose a rock ledge from which I could gaze straight down into the unobstructed water. It gave me the creeps for a long time to be able to see so far, so clearly, into water. For years I had gotten a charge from simply guessing what lay beneath the slow, dark waters of the South, and sometimes I'd imagined it was a world identical to the one above, but washed over in a great flood and buried, its secrets limitless. And there were times I had imagined it was deep as outer space, that at the tip of a levee infinity began and that, if caught in its current, I'd be swept toward the stars. From what I could see as I peered, on my knees, into the lake, there was not one goddamned thing down there but rocks.

I flung my line in anyway, "flung" being the only way to describe how I cast with this new, unorthodox contraption. I had seen the bass fisherman on the Arkansas cast with spinning gear, but from a distance too great to study. Teacherless, I came up with my own technique, flipping the rod over so the reel sat bail up. Cocking the bail back I'd hold the line securely against the rod with my right thumb—pure control—draw back over my shoulder, and heave. The modified cane-pole cast. The sheer distance I achieved with this method was alarming, hook, worm, and bobber spinning free, threading out over the lake like a hummingbird, landing with a satisfying *whunk, splash* continents away. It was intoxicating, this naked sense of power. I spent a few hours just casting, reeling in the yards of line, driving into my memory banks this ass-backwards, bail-up method, so I was ruined for life to any other way, the same as it has been with my typing: I am self-taught, too, in this skill, so I can tap out 133 words a minute with four fingers. I hear there's a better way. I don't care.

After a few hours of practice casting I let the bobber rest undisturbed in the middle of the lake. Being unable to see that there was nothing to take my bait gave me a more hopeful feeling. It had been part of the mystique when I was a kid, never knowing your bait was being cruised until the bobber did its little wayward dance. It was like the wrapping on a present at Christmas, that dark water, concealing everything. I missed it.

Hours passed and the bobber rested more or less exactly where I had placed it, a big two-tone gum ball in foreign, frigid territory. The last water it had seen had been eighty degrees and red. I peeked beneath into the boringly clear water, expecting to see the same rocks I had studied till I was crosseyed, and spied instead, cruising in a locked pattern, two decent-sized trout. But I, redneck angler out of Mississippi, did not know they were trout. Sucker fish, my head said, garbage fish, but better than nothing. Who knew the fine distinction between a lowly bottom feeder and a mineral-water-sucking aesthete? Who cared at this point?

I reeled my line in and deftly laid the bobber in the general vicinity of the suckers, thinking here was my chance, suckers would eat anything. In time the trout nosed up to the bait and hung there motionless in the water, staring at it. They did not bite the goody and take off running; they did not even mouth it. My worst fear had been realized. These fish had never seen worms.

The depression that settled over me was as cold and wet as the Northwest air. Not only could I *see* the fish I was after; they had pointedly rejected my bait, either too stupid or too spooked to take it. In that one moment all the mysteries of fishing lay as exposed as those two quirky fish who eyed my bait as if it were a stick of dynamite, and don't think using dynamite didn't cross my mind. I dragged the bait back and forth through the water, teasing them, hoping if they saw prey on the run it would get their interest up. Nothing. These were some stupid Yankee fish.

So stupid I might even catch them with my bare hands. When you want a fish badly enough, body parts become weapons. I had heard stories about Indians hypnotizing fish with the movement of their hands, stroking along the fish's flanks, soothing it, until it gave itself over, limp and willing. I'd tried catching birds with a saltshaker once, a thoroughly bogus activity dreamed up by Bimicain to keep me busy in the yard, sneaking up as close as I could behind a jumpy sparrow and then shaking salt like a moron in the direction of its tail. Myth—for that is what it is, pure unadulterated—has it that if you can get the salt on the bird's tail, you can catch it. Well, sure. Any gourd can figure out that if you're close enough to shake salt on a bird's tail you're probably close enough to snatch it. But luring fish into my palms? Why not. I was Cherokee. I had a license.

I carefully eased my way down from the rock ledge into the water, stripped to the skin the way I'd done in Arkansas. Who knew it would be like flinging my entire body against a frozen pump handle, that the cold would be so cold my lips would peel all the way back to my teeth and my sinuses would feel as if I'd snorted sleet? It was an ice cream headache gone berserk. Every atom of my skin turned to stabbing pins and needles. I tried breathing through my locked-down-tight teeth. *EEE-eee,* my breath went. I discovered I could only breathe in. This looked like water, but my head said, *No way,* liquid nitrogen. I expected to raise an arm into the air and watch it crack and drop off. Where was that warm, baptizing, bathwater feel, that floating, bathed-in-the womb sensation?

After a while you go numb. It was a benefit I adapted to with ease. Fingers still work, I thought, wiggling them. Legs still work, eyes still move—I just can't *feel* them. I could have open-heart surgery straight out of the water.

My body dead as a rubber duck, I spied the fish, still hanging out by the worm. I'd left the bait in the water as a crafty diversion, just in case they had second thoughts. Lunging for them would not do. Even Northwest fish, I now know, after years of dissing them, have instincts. I took a deep breath and squatted beneath the lake surface, pygmylike, feet bouncing on the rock bed, cheeks puffed out like a guppy, and extended my outspread fingers, white and spongy looking as wet Havarti, slowly, ever so slowly, toward the suckers. The Blob, come ta getcha.

My head had retained some sensation, but went dead now in a stabbing wave, chin to forehead, and then, boom, I was the *Hindenberg,* all air and no skin. The fish, fake looking as my hands beneath the water, hung as if suspended from wires. I let my hands float closer, pretending they were clots of algae, innocuous, fish-friendly vegetation. I tried to communicate, telepathically, that I was a rock. Would they buy it?

Not a chance. My fingers mere inches from the fish, my breath held in so long I couldn't remember what sex I was, I reached out tenderly, ever so gently, to stroke the flank of one, and they shot off like twin Roman candles, leaving a vacuum where my hands still groped.

Back on the rock ledge, my skin the color of fresh-cut beets, I cursed this place to which I'd moved. Who could fish in conditions like this, water so cold it gave you a hernia, fish so few they were bored into staring at bait? It was not at all what I had had in mind when I'd envisioned this pure new world.

Chapter

EIGHT

I HAD KNOWN salmon only in the bastardized Southern form—the croquette—long before I came to the Northwest. The salmon came straight from a can then, pale and pink and riddled with heat-softened bones, looking vaguely like melted pencil erasers. It was one of those inedible edibles that fell into the category of mystery meats, like Spam, its very color alien. Once a year, in the midst of a down-home bonanza of pork chops and grits, black-eyed peas and boiled peanuts, my mother would, with strange glee, drag out her salmon croquette recipe, mix egg, onion, and bread crumbs with a can of salmon, and fry this hog-slop concoction to a road-apple shape and consistency. The taste, something like cabbage, a whole lot like Easter eggs left for a week in the sun, stimulated my gag reflex to the point that I invariably bolted from the supper table, hand covering my mouth, stomach muscles locked down in a fist. I took from this experience a distinct aversion to salmon, believing it to be the most odious fish ever to swim.

I now know a few things about salmon, among them that the

canned form has nothing to do with what swims upstream, this noble, struggling, tireless form I have seen in the rivers of Washington State, definite and true, leaping six feet in a ninety-degree trajectory to negotiate cascading water, spawning then like milk-heavy sows in the rocky beds of their birth. The integrity of salmon charms me, forces me to regard my own upstream existence, and invariably reveals new character flaws. Would I, for instance, abandon open acres of salt water for a certain standoff with death? Would I be impervious to my own rotting flesh to honor the simple act of procreation? I think not. I see salmon now as the metaphorical link to the definition of courage. But when I first came to the Northwest I saw them, of course, as catfish.

The people of Washington State love their salmon, keep a close eye on the population of the various salmon runs, build totems to the fish, sell tickets to alder-smoked salmon bakes, print T-shirts that read *Spawn or Die,* substitute salmon for turkey at Thanksgiving, and generally regard with a murderous eye anyone who is ignorant of the species.

In Seattle, a transplanted redneck, I made enemies immediately with my salmon ignorance. An employer, taking pity on me, I suspect, for my underfed look, offered me a fifteen-pound salmon as a gift, its flanks a bright silver, the exposed cavity meat a pearly pink. I took one look at the color, remembered the croquettes, and said, "No. Thanks. I'm not partial to salmon."

"What do you mean, 'not partial'?" she'd asked. "You don't *like* salmon?"

Her tone suggested sacrilege.

"No, ma'am. That's right. I don't like salmon."

"Don't be absurd," she told me. "Everyone likes salmon. Here. Take it."

She shoved the wet, heavy-as-a-baby fish at me, its cavity dripping pinkish white slime.

"I can't do that, ma'am," I told her.

Somewhere along the line I did taste the actual fresh variety, timidly at first, as if I were about to swallow Drano. What wonder. What surprise. What an absolute lie. This succulent, exquisite, unearthly meat had nothing to do with croquettes, did not resemble in any aspect the odious puck, but instead was a food of the gods. I wondered, idly, if they would bite on a worm.

• • •

THE UNIVERSITY of Washington Fisheries Department breeds salmon in large holding tanks on the school premises. When the young parr come of age, they are set loose in the fisheries pond, which connects via a salmon ladder with the freshwater of Lake Union, and then the open salt waters of Puget Sound. These young fish make their journey into the ocean, where they grow to spawning maturity, and then return to their home pond, at the Fisheries Department, to spawn and die.

In late October and early November, after the heavy rains, salmon fling themselves into the rushing water of the ladder, electric arcs of silver in the gray air. I used to take my daughter there when she was young, and we would sit close enough to what she called "the flying fish" to feel the spray from them as they leapt and flexed into the open mouth of falling water, their acrobatics so stunning Cristen would breathe the word "oh" out softly five times in a rush. After the ladder came calm water and a maze of shallow tanks through which the salmon swam before merging with their brethren in the waters of the pond.

I came upon the pond one day on a walk along Lake Union. Its dimensions and sinkhole appearance were nearly identical to the catfish pond from my youth where the albinos swam in wide, lazy circles, their pale bodies opalescent beneath the dark water. As I moved closer to the pond's edge I could see the heavy, mottled fish beneath the algae tinge, swimming in familiar laps along the pond's periphery. I knelt to get a better look. These were monsters, long as my arm from shoulder joint to fingertip, the jaws of many of them underslung and predatory, the bridges of their snouts hooked. These were the males in their swaggering, tough-guy, spawning disguise, but I, unaccustomed to the metamorphosis of salmon in their dying season, saw them merely as a sporting dinner, as so many giant sardines waiting for a cracker. Succulent. Tasty. *Free.* And being the predator *I* was, in all seasons, I wondered idly why no one was fishing this pond. It screamed, to my ears alone, Fish Me! Fish Me! and I watched across the water, along a grassy path, a couple stroll by, hand in hand, the two of them stopping from time to time to point at the fish.

This was new. Who in their right mind strolled by fish, pointed them out as if they were an interesting plant, then walked away as if they could come back anytime and not find the pond fished out? It was all I could do to keep from hurling my body, net-like, into the salmon's midst. My fingers itched for a pole. I imagined the happy sound the old Mitchell would make when one of these bruisers took off on a run. What opportunity. What sheer, unadulterated luck. I had discovered my own private, full-to-the-belly fishing hole.

I admit to indiscretions in my life, to sheer stupidity and ignorance, to a particular wantonness when it comes to fish, but only to a handful of people have I admitted that I was crazed enough to go, armed with honker night crawlers and spinning gear, to a fisheries pond to white-trash for salmon. Would that this were not true. I might offer a legacy to my grandchildren of a somewhat questionable fishing rep, but intact overall. As it stands there is this blight, this big fat *X* on my fishing past. I have been not a mere bank maggot, not a mere bait-and-tackle opportunist, but the most reviled, unsportsmanlike creature of all—a poacher. A salmon poacher. I have poached salmon, not in a little white wine and rosemary, but from their cozy home pond, where watercolors of Great-uncle Chinook hung, where they might have, in their safe nest, told big bad angler stories to scare the young fry, where they, quite simply, had returned literally to lay their burden down and die amongst their own. Into these sacred waters I flung my hook, worm, and bobber, and waited, like the criminal I was, in the bushes.

Did I suspect this was illegal? Vaguely, the way you suspect opening someone's mail is not a good idea. Still, I profess an ultimate innocence. There were certainly no signs that read: WARNING: THIS IS HIGHLY ILLEGAL WHAT YOU ARE ABOUT TO DO, AND STUPID.

Dressed head to toe in black, I arrived at the pond at 2 A.M. wearing polarized sunglasses to conceal my identity and so I might see the fish more clearly. It was a tip I'd picked up in a fishing magazine, which didn't point out that once the sun set you might as well poke a couple of sticks in your eyes. With the glasses on I had the depth perception of a possum.

An amphitheater of bushes sat several yards off one side of the pond. It was to this anonymous-looking cove I dragged my lawn chair, the long, fold-out, webbed kind, perfect for sunbathing and, as it turned out, reclining in the freezing drizzle. Outside the ring of bushes I cast dead center into the pond, ran back to the lawn chair, pole in hand, line feeding free, flung my bundled form down upon the chair, and cracked a beer. I call it relay fishing.

Alone in the frigid night, I watched my breath turn to sleet, my eyelids gather frost, and pondered the elusive salmon. Lights from the Fisheries Department illuminated the candy striping of the bobber and I watched it dip in the gentle swells of the pond, untouched. Were these salmon as stupid as the suckers?

I cast again, this time close in, where I had watched them swim in daylight. Through the dark windshield of my glasses I could still make out the bobber, and then, like a penny tossed into a well, it winked from sight—once, twice, then disappeared entirely.

Hint: a spawned-out king salmon is in no mood for a worm with a weapon. Once hooked, he is deeply pissed. Line screamed off my reel, an absurd Donald Duck sound that broke the cold, silent night. I slid slowly from the lawn chair yelling, "Ha! Bastard. Ha!" my heels dug into the wet grass, rod tip held righteously high as His Hugeness leapt and thrashed in three feet of water.

To date this was the biggest, meanest, hardest-fighting fish I'd ever had. I had expected the slow, lazy deadweight pull of a catfish and had instead locked on to a buzz saw. I took in line when the king leapt and lost it each time he hit the pond, displacing several gallons of water at a crash, then motorboating from one edge of the pond to the other, churning up a froth. I had a quick, nonsense image of the salmon, planning with a hard, armor-plated fist of fins and gills to knock me out cold on the grass.

I had skidded into the pond, ice water being the great equalizer, and my teeth came down on my tongue, hard, as I tried to gain on the bastard, intent on nothing but getting him in an oven. I had already planned how I would lay him out when he was gutted—a little onion and sour cream in the cavity, some lemon slices and parsley for decoration, arranging all this just so while muttering the words *"Croquettes, burn in hell."*

Deeds of treachery do not long go unnoticed. The Ralph Naders of the world patrol even the darkest, coldest night, waiting to yell, "Consumer fraud!"

"I don't believe it," came a voice from the shadows. "Look at him, fishing in the goddamned Fisheries pond."

"It's a her," came another voice. "It's not a him. It's a her. Look at the hair."

I regretted not having remained bald for the twenty years following my birth.

"Should we call the cops?"

There are those of us for whom the word "cops," spoken with no attending verb, uttered with the mildest of conviction, becomes the sine qua non to an attack of spontaneous diarrhea. A fugitive from justice, for instance, cannot appreciate the word. I had visions of myself, busted on a salmon rap, serving big time back in the state of North Carolina, where I was certain they would extradite me.

Fishing Rule #1: *You will risk jail not to lose this fish.*

I ignored the voices in the shadows. Go ahead, call the cops, I thought, this moldy, spawned-out, pathetic salmon is mine.

I fished with ten-pound test in those days because it happened to be what was on the reel when I found it. I didn't know then I could have given a sailfish a good run with such thick line, and that putting some pull behind the salmon was all I really needed to bring him to shore. I heaved and reeled and imagined blue lights flashing above the stirred-up waters of the pond, then the metallic flash of a badge as I held the struggling fish. I got the salmon within nabbing distance, his head and girth massive, his flanks a pure gun-metal gray, then slid my gloved fingers beneath his orchid-colored gills and ran.

I had never held a fish so big. Had never held a fish so big clasped to my breast while running in a dead heat for the car.

I'd parked on the grass because it is part of the poacher's creed to pack as many illegal activities as possible into an evening, and as I fumbled with the door with one hand while holding the flailing, gasping salmon with the other, managing, finally, to heave it into the backseat, where my cat, Mr. Cheese, lunged for it, hissing and spitting, doing for the poor fish what the Coke bottle would have done years before, I saw the university patrol car pull into the parking lot near the pond. I gunned the motor and fled, laying a tire trough twenty feet long before I hit dry pavement.

This is my salmon story. Not plugging for salmon in the gray, steely waters of Puget Sound, head to the wind, stoic, matching decades of tradition, but sitting on a lawn chair at a salmon fishery, worm dangling in the wading pool.

It is my abiding belief that you should always eat what you catch. Safely at home, the law off my trail, I inspected the king in the bright light of the kitchen. As I gutted and rinsed him in the sink I noticed the pathetic molting of his skin, how in his dying last days his flesh had actually begun to disintegrate. The fight he had given, for such an old guy, was impressive. To have died at my hands could not have been what he had anticipated as he swam circle upon circle, his flesh falling off in chunks, the time clock in his system ready to ring one final, explosive alarm. In the coming years, as I grew more attuned to the habits of salmon, to the habits of all things living, I felt overpowering shame at what I had done, remembering that I had poached not only this ragged daddy of a salmon, but others as well once I'd realized it was far easier to dip a net into the holding tanks and run, again, into the night.

I write this as a much-belated apology to those fish, to whom my ignorance could not have been more careless, more selfish, more deadly.

I served that first salmon, baked with sour cream and onions, to guests. Watched them chew and chew and chew on the old flesh, politely not mentioning how flavorless it was, how tough. It was a small payback from the fish gods, infinitely small.

Chapter NINE

IT IS DANGEROUS to speculate on luck, to believe it has no limit, that in its randomness it will twice act kindly. Around the time I caught my first Dolly Varden, my first marriage ended. The two events, like Mark Twain and Halley's comet, are forever linked in my memory. I see Jimmy rowing a boat across the muted blue of Patterson Lake in eastern Washington, my baited line trailing out behind the stern, and how he looked back over his shoulder to gauge the distance to shore as I kept the line taut, the wind catching his hair and blowing it into his eyes, and how he smiled at this, unannoyed. I remember studying his hands, the way they were locked around the oars, and thinking how certain they looked when he was doing something physical. I thought too of how we had talked a few nights before about how we couldn't stay together. It is odd I don't remember the reason why, but only that we were certain. As I watched him, regretting that this was not the lake early on, when we had first known each other, regretting that we would not be together to raise the daughter we had conceived by water, I understood in a moment so quick and precise that it remains in memory as a bright filament in my consciousness, that having known him and having loved him would be, always, a good thing. And linked to that one moment was the hard, distracting pull on my line, and what swam at the other end, a metaphor of sorts for what we'd had together, a full-bellied beauty, cream-and-crimson spots flushing its olive skin, mouth pink as the twilit sky, and then Jimmy's words as he smiled at the fish heavy in my hands, "You have all the luck. You always have all the luck."

After six years in the Northwest I was weary of the twenty-five-watt lightbulb Seattle calls the sun. I craved the metallic jangle of heat and glare, air thick enough to touch, white sand beaches, and water the temperature of a bath.

In the late seventies I returned to Bimini after selling my car, my sewing machine, my coin collection and living for a month on carrots to make the plane fare south. I had never forgotten the abortive marlin hunt with my father, or the nagging instinct that I was meant to do what he could not. I was also, like a few thousand others before me, on the hunt for Hemingway. In my late teens I had come up hard against the legend that had become my grandfather, forced then to read his works in school, forced to take a look, finally, at a heritage that, at first glance, looked suspiciously like a bummer. It was not a thing we talked of much when I was growing up, only that the man had been my grandfather and that if anyone asked if I were related I was, regardless of circumstance, to deny it. At the time I did not understand my mother was, in her curious, inconsistent way, protecting me from the prying, the nosy, but thought instead there must be some secret shame linked with the name, some darkness that, once spoken of, would taint me, too. When he murdered himself—for this was what it was, an act so violent I could never, in good conscience, refer to it euphemistically—I searched for some attribution to the process so I might know how this man I had never known, this blood of my blood, had come upon an alley so blind, so without illumination, that he had skipped town for good. There's the euphemism. It is hard to avoid.

I remember pictures of the man, in particular, the Karsh photo on the cover of *Life* magazine after his death. Looking at the picture disturbed me, knowing what he had done, how he had done it. More disturbing still was the inward focus of his eyes, the look of fearful communion with a thing so highly personal that you see, even at first glance, how it owns him. There is acquiescence in that look, defeat, a vague shame, and it is a look I have come to know not only in the eyes of others, but in my own as well.

It was not Ernest who gave me the fishing when I was young. People have suggested this, or blurted outright, "Oh. I see why you fish. Your name is Hemingway," as if this explained it. I must put this right. I barely remembered my name when I was young, so accustomed was I to denying it. In fact, for years I used my stepfather's name simply because it made things easier. No one asked then, no one assumed I'd had an insider's look at genius. To think the name Hemingway assured a fishing passion is stretching the limits of genetic theory. I fished long before I was aware of my grandfather's reputation for fish, long before I ever realized there were people out there who gave a damn. I did not tip through clear streams with a fly rod and creel, but went instead to redneck fishing school, priming the catfish sloughs of the South, eating mud and acorns and road tar to galvanize myself, refining my own tilt on how things worked. I did not grow up schooled by some kindly grandparent in the laws of nature but discovered them, randomly, on my own.

Still, legends get you where you live, seep into some unconscious strata and grab hold, forcing you eventually to define yourself in relation to others. Once I became aware of Hemingway's tie to fish, and of what seemed at times to be an undiscriminating desire to dominate species other than his own, I began to suspect a similar need coursed in me. Call it the Granddaughter Theory. And I was on the lookout for a man heroic enough to be my father, for the ultimate in fishing buddies. Dead men are always the safest bet.

As peculiar circumstance would have it, I had come to Bimini during the island's first-ever Hemingway Billfish Tournament. Although I was unaware at the time of the dubious honor, the tournament sponsor had been alerted to my visit and I became a designated Hemingway. A mild, local fame, the consequence of being related to this guy I wasn't supposed to say I was related to, became mine. People whom I would never care to know, whom I would not seek out even in a floating lifeboat cast off the *Titanic,* would do one of three things: ask me if I wanted a drink, ask if I wanted to fish, ask if I wanted to arm wrestle. I cannot say I disliked the attention, that after all the years of saying, "No, I'm not related," I was not now happy to fairly scream, "Yes, yes, by God, I am, and isn't it swell?" Still, there was always that vague sense of dirtiness associated with it and the knowledge that it was not I who had earned this attention, but someone who had come before me, a guy with bigger feet, bigger muscles, and a Nobel Prize. To say I was jealous of his accomplishments is accurate. To say that I fell into competition with his fishing feats may be taken as gospel. It is only in later years that I have come to understand the far reach of my competitiveness, and that in every sense it has been men—big, strapping, sweaty men—with whom I have competed.

People were always more than happy to have me on their boats, assuming, maybe, that I was taking a much-needed rest from big game safaris in Africa, bullfight watching in Spain. In this sense I took advantage of their expectations, never letting on that I was a dirt poor ex-hippie who would have begged for rides on their boats if they hadn't offered and probably would have beat a paying angler out of the fighting chair just for a shot at a fish.

I knew zip then about big-game fishing tournaments, unaware that they were basically scams to make the rich richer, weeklong fishing blowouts in which some very well-to-do people with hired guides, mates, and captains bet huge sums of money in illegal calcuttas against what were, at least on Bimini, the excellent odds of landing a trophy fish. But who was I to titter about morality when it came to fish? Still, it rattled me when I learned that these enormous, fatally elegant fish were caught and boated merely to be brought dockside and weighed, strung up for a few ego-charged pictures, and then dumped, dead and wasted, into the harbor for the barracuda to feed on. A five-hundred-pound marlin is a lot of barracuda feed.

The boat I landed on—the *Chanel,* named not after the perfume, but after someone who had been named after the perfume—became something of a floating family reunion. In the bar of the Compleat Angler that morning, as I had sat sipping my prefishing beer, a habit I'd slipped into in recent years, my great-uncle Les Hemingway had rolled in to order a plain Coca-Cola. It was the way he walked, rolling on the balls of his feet as if the ground were about to give. He bore a spooky resemblance to his older brother—wide jaw, salt-and-pepper beard, brown eyes that seemed to perceive something other than the obvious, and teeth that needed capping.

I had met him briefly, ten years before, when I had visited my father, and remembered with some alarm Les's peculiar exuberance and patently odd manner of speech. He was always raising his arms above his head, fists clenched, in a gesture resembling a ghetto salute, and proclaiming to anyone whose eye he caught, "What a *great,* great day this is! What a *great* day to be a human!" the word *"great"* delivered with the sincerity and power of a grenade. People would jump back when he spoke, sometimes flinch. His voice, too, was similar to his brother's: nasal, Midwestern, always delivered at high bellow, with singing stress given to adjectives and nouns. He called all men "Noble" or "Captain," and all women "Your Ladyship." It was a form of greeting he'd put the oil and polish to back during the years he'd been president of his own country, New Atlantis—a concept not exactly, but a little, like New Detroit, with water—a barge he'd anchored off the coast of Jamaica, and for which he had minted coins, printed stamps with his sister Sunny's picture on them, and had a flag stitched out of his daughter Hilary's diaper. My father had called Les crazy. I had found him fascinating. His screwy personality and sheer size had frightened me, though, and I hadn't spent much time getting acquainted during our first meeting. Now, as I sat in the dim Angler bar, I looked up to find him staring at me, his eyes wickedly alive.

"Good morning," I said, meeting his gaze, afraid not to.

"Your Ladyship!" he hollered, loud enough to make me brace my palms on the bar. "I'll have you know I have no intention of blowing out my tonsils anytime soon," and with that statement he downed his Coke and moved out of the bar with that rolling, side-to-side gait. I watched him for a long moment and decided, yes, the man walked like me. The bizarre comment had been so unadorned and had come so without warning that I had sat, stunned, trying to figure how his words could be even mildly reassuring, and I did not even guess then that this weird introduction would mark the beginning of ten years of understanding what it meant to know Les Hemingway. Like all things that never at first appear to be, having run into Les would become a blessing.

Onboard the *Chanel* I was surprised to find Les perched on the flying bridge. No one had said we'd be fishing together. He had a can of Coke in his hand, which he raised in a quick salute—he was diabetic and steadfastly claimed he used sugar for medicinal purposes—his daughter Hilary, seventeen at the time, at his side. These two, I would learn, were inseparable boating fanatics, given to patching up leaky, ocean-floor-bound heaps, and sailing off into the Miami sunset for parts unknown, a jar of peanut butter their only provision. Hilary had learned to walk on a boat and was just a baby when Les had made himself president of New Atlantis. To Les sovereignty was the one immutable key to integrity, and all his life he struggled to make that one distinguishable imprint that would declare him separate from his brother and, in his eyes, worthy of respect. Someone once wrote of Les that he was a fine writer who had been forced into the ring too early against a tough pro. One might have thought he would be jealous of his brother, but he was not. Instead he was the eternal good news guy, offering nothing but praise for his sibling, as well as respect and admiration.

He was also a card-carrying eccentric whose heart and passion, rather than his head, guided him in most matters. He had never been close to being the fishing junkie I was, but liked to be on a boat simply because the fever of the sea was in him. Up top with Les and Hilary was Les's best friend, Dr. Howard Engle, a sawed-off, neatly-buffed-looking Miami pediatrician who, I came to know after years of fishing with him, always wore pale blue Bermuda shorts held up by a brass whale belt buckle the size of my fist. He was the man who had helped Les get sober ten years before. He would become my fishing guru.

Our guide was a blue-black Bahamian named Bonefish George, the name reminding me of Catfish, and as I took my turn in the fighting chair—a ten-year wait to perch myself upon that cushy throne—I listened hard to Bonefish George's impenetrable Bahamian and had a quick memory of Catfish, imagining her on this boat with me, bigger than the shack she lived in, far from the muddy waters of the Arkansas, a massive cane pole in her hands, steel cable for line, dipping for marlin. What would she think of this and of her extra-pickles girl who had learned at her knee to wield a Coke bottle with deadly aim? What would she think of monsters who walked on water? I understood, thinking of her, how I had moved leagues away from my fish beginnings on the banks of the rivers of the South, and as I watched the heavy purple of the Gulf Stream rise in swells taller than any bank, any depot, any shack in Altheimer, crested at their peaks like exotic birds, I knew I was entering a territory that would take me captive and force me to look, eventually, at something ancient in myself. These waters were familiar.

To this day I do not know what Bonefish George, his skin darker than the water upon which we rode, his fingers exact as a surgeon's as he broke the spines on the bonefish and lashed them to huge hooks, told me about catching marlin. It might have been that you had to sacrifice a chicken in a boneyard beneath the full moon, drink its blood, swear off pork—I know it was a lot, and very long and involved, but his patois was as thick as the heat that scalded us, and I could make no sense of it. Sunglasses obscured the blank look in my eyes as he gestured in the direction of the outriggers, at the club-sized reels at my elbows, and out to sea, where his prized baits skipped in the trolling wake. Bonefish George was something of a legend in the marlin biz, and I will always regret that I carried away no wisdom from our meeting.

Clueless, feeling deep in idiot territory, I surveyed the gear, the fifty-pound test coiled on the massive Penn reels, strung up through the pins on the outriggers, yards of it dropping down and out behind the boat, the baits pierced and lashed at the hook end. I leaned back in the chair, felt the fighting belt lashed tight around my hips, the fresh-from-the-cooler beer in my hot palm, the spray from the wake bathing me in salty mist, and knew this was where I belonged. I lit a cigarette and, stupidly, held it dangerously close to the taut line. Bonefish George screamed a voodoo curse as he watched the hot end of my smoke brush the line. Whoops. He confiscated both smokes and lighter, slapping my hand. This time I understood him.

I'd read *The Old Man and the Sea* before coming to Bimini. Come on and get me, fish, I thought. Yeah, come on. I don't know what the fuck I'll do when I see you, but come on anyway.

For four days we trolled the Gulf Stream, diesel smoke rising in a low cloud above the water, the boat's engine sick sounding, the mate seasick over the stern until he was the color of squid, Les booming from the bridge what a *great* day it was to be alive, and for four days we raised nothing. Nada. Still, it had taken the Old Man eighty-plus days. This was a game of patience. It did not bother me. There would come a time. It was my initiation, this trip, with the people who were to become the core of my fishing family—Les, Hilary, Dr. Engle. I see it now as a jumping-off point into an arterial world formed by water, fed by water, undone by water, and in which we each had something vital at stake. And I would take it all on like nobody's business, it and the Old Man, too, and nearly die trying.

Chapter

TEN

I AM A CONVERT to the fish gospel according to Dr. Howard Engle, the man responsible for turning me from a redneck, backwater, bobber-packing heathen into a young woman who came to kneel at the altar of the great blue marlin. He is the man who lashed me to a fighting chair and commanded, *"Stay!"* as he would to a dog, the man who yelled, "I *knew* a little shit like you couldn't catch anything worth having," to make me boil just enough to keep on fighting, and the man who many times said, "Nothing like a cold beer in the morning when you're fishing," until he comprehended, painfully and profoundly, the depths of my alcoholism.

People pair up to fish as they do in life, drawn to each other by a common affliction, common waters; and as in any decent marriage, they keep fishing together because no one else quite comprehends the degree of their obsession and because no one else knows, exactly, what a good fishing day *smells* like. Together on a boat, their energies aligned, they are capable of fish miracles, of feats of strength and endurance wholly unnatural, and of a camaraderie that withstands even the vilest curses and recriminations. It is the true forge of friendship, fishing.

We rode aboard the *Kembé* that next summer off Bimini, Dr. Engle, Hilary, and I. Les had been hospitalized back in Miami for a blood clot in his leg and couldn't make it. He'd sent us off with this blessing: "Fish like the humans you are!"

I'd come to Bimini, broke as usual, seriously stalking now for Ernest, convinced in my more dramatic moments that we were somehow linked up telepathically—I through this deluded notion of him as the one man, even in death, who knew what the deal was with me, and he to me through this ancient water, this place of sorcery where he had raised from the deep the water-born twin of Merlin.

There had been a cocktail party the night before. It was the second night of the Hemingway Billfish Tournament, and a lot of the anglers and crew had been working on a decent, stabilizing drunk for several days. I had had my share of beer, enough to give me that false, fuzzy sense of security and a competitive edge that could turn belligerent. Yachting types crowded the bar, perched at the pool's edge. They were perfect-looking men and women, dressed in spotless sports clothes, and I would ease by them now and then, eavesdropping. They talked about marlin, occasionally Hemingway, and a whole lot about their suntans. My skin was dark but my clothes weren't perfect and I had a Band-Aid over my right eye—a testimonial to the rough and clumsy night before, when I had driven a toilet paper holder deep along the eye orbit. It was a talent I had when I drank, and I amassed dozens of minor injuries whose origins I could never quite place unless there'd been a witness. Later, in reading about Ernest, I would learn that he was "accident-prone," and thought to myself, Sure, I get it. He drank and fell down and got hurt. He drank and stood up under a skylight like a bozo, and got hurt.

Dr. Engle had sat with me at the party, regarding the scene impassively.

"You want to catch a marlin, don't you?" he'd asked, staring at me with a dead-on, no-bullshit look that forced me, over the years, to confess to many things, few of them good.

"I do," I told him, considering what this could mean in my life. I was fresh from reading *Islands in the Stream* and had taken on the manly ethics of the character, believing in Thomas Hudson's line *I know if he catches this fish he will have something in him for the rest of his life that will make everything else easier.* I was looking for that precise, exact promise, a test of endurance so altering, so exquisite in its brutality that all else in comparison would seem effortless.

But I wasn't entered in the tournament, and "gratis" was no longer a word associated with my visits to Bimini. I didn't own a boat and I couldn't afford to charter one. I would be the scruffy girl sitting on the dock with a warm Budweiser when the ships came in.

Dr. Engle has always taken my looking pathetic as a personal affront. He cornered a man named Marion Merritt at the party, pinned him up against a beer cooler for a good two hours, talked in that hard, fast, Miami way of his, and convinced the poor man, eventually, of my desperate need to fish. Merritt had been a fugitive from the Mau Mau rebellion in Kenya. I had met him the year before and liked his low, soft Georgia accent and had listened, rapt, to his stories about the ruthlessness of the Mau Mau. He had bought a boat and named it *Kembé* in honor of the Watusi tribal chief who had helped him escape.

"Young lady," Marion told me after Dr. Engle was done with him, "you are gonna catch a marlin you'll be proud of. But you're gonna do every goddamned bit of work yourself."

Those were the words I had been waiting to hear, and instead of choking me with fear, they burned the edge right off my beer stupor and charged me with an extravagant sense of hope.

• • •

I WAS READY to fish long before Bimini's dead-heat sun broke the horizon. It has always been that way. Mention a chance to fish and I'll stay up all night just to make sure you're not lying.

It was a *great* day for fishing. I could tell by the way I felt as I hurried to make it down to the boat. I didn't feel the usual beery stupor too much, but drank one while I was getting dressed just to make sure the night before wouldn't catch up with me. The hair of the dog had become a morning ritual.

"Nothing like a cold beer in the morning," Dr. Engle shouted as we converged on King's Highway, the two of us walking fast and stiff legged toward the dock, both of us smoking. He hated my brand of cigarettes and I hated his, but we still bummed them off each other.

"Give me one of those nasty little menthol things you've got," he'd say when he'd run out, and when I'd do the same I'd tell him, "Give me one of those things that make me wanna puke."

In all the years I have known him, no matter how early I get up, no matter if I never even bother to go to bed, he is always first at the dock and takes some sort of perverse glee in watching me streak by in ninety-degree heat thinking this will be the time I beat him.

Dr. Engle, with his salt-and-pepper beard and buffalo-hide face, looks like a rogues' gallery portrait, wicked handlebar mustache waxed to a point, eyes luminous and huge behind thick glasses, a pediatrician you might mistake for a mercenary, and I know he likes it.

Bimini's summer is a furnace blast. It must be avoided and resisted, and as I walked to Marion's boat that morning, the heat was suffocating. "Eight-thirty in the morning and it's ninety-one degrees," Dr. Engle said. There was a little breeze that would wilt before the day was over.

"Ready to catch a big one?" Marion called from the bobbing stern as we approached. It was a beautiful boat, a forty-seven-foot custom job with impressive woodwork and a flying bridge designed only for those surefooted enough to walk a plank in thirty-foot seas. Hilary was already on board. I said good morning to Tommy Sewell, a young Bahamian who had a reputation on the island as one of the best mates around.

Marion took me into the cabin and pulled a monstrous rod and reel from one of the overhead supports. Dr. Engle was on the sofa, having his fifth cup of coffee. You always knew how much coffee he'd had, how many cigarettes he'd smoked, what he'd had for breakfast, and what he was planning to have for lunch because he told you, all this information imparted with his official, boom-box-sounding voice, like a weather report. He watched, amused, as Marion began to drill me on the equipment. This time I would get a real lesson.

"You'll be using a rod like this. Fifty-pound test line, girl, so it'll be a little easier on your arms. It's harder to catch a big marlin on fifty pounds because you have to know what you're feeling when he pulls. Too much and it'll break. Too little and he swims to Cuba." He handed the rod to me. The weight of it was enough to send me off balance. I supported the butt in my right hand and kept my left on the grip.

"How's it feel?" Marion asked.

"Fine," I lied.

"Now, you're gonna be the only one that knows what's going on with that fish. I can only *guess.* Tommy can only guess. You gotta tell us so I know what the hell to do with that boat. We never want the fish to get under the boat. Do you understand me? Never."

Marion seemed to know a hell of a lot. With his white beard and perfectly round red cheeks he looked a little like a rogue Santa, Bloody Mary sloshing in his glass. And there was a certain kindness in his face that children wouldn't miss, but his voice was rough, all business, so he could get me straight on what I had to do.

He taught me all about the rod and reel, how to set the drag.

"Don't set the goddamned thing all the way up," he told me. "If you do you'll break the line. If you got a five-hundred-pound marlin on the end of this thing it'll snap like a stick unless you do everything right. You gotta let him run once you hook in. Are you hearing me, girl? Because I am *not* talking to hear myself. Just keep enough pressure on the line so you know he's there. You'll know it when you feel it. Trust what you feel."

I wasn't sure I would. The certainty that I would know what to do, the smug confidence that had washed over me when I had fished with my father years before, was gone. I was thinking about what I actually knew about marlin. Not much, but I had heard stories. A Bimini native had lost an eye to the needle-sharp bill of a marlin brought alongside the boat before the fight was out of it. Another was gouged in the side as the marlin took a final leap before the gaff reached it.

I had seen marlin dead on the docks and had seen them thrown, uncut and wasted, into the harbor. I had seen them mounted, one spanning the north wall of the Compleat Angler Hotel. And I had seen films of them jumping majestically, trying to throw the hook while great ribbons of scarlet streamed from their intestines.

"Look outside there," Marion demanded. "There's two flat lines, girl. There's a left rigger and a right rigger hooked up with them clothespin-lookin' things. When I yell, 'Flat line!' you go to that flat line and take the pole. When I yell right or left rigger, you take that pole and knock the line out of the pin if it's not knocked out already. Get in that chair, then, and Tommy will strap you down. *You* set the drag. *You* do it, girl. When I say, 'Let him go,' let him go, then you let the drag run. When I say, 'Hit him,' then set the drag. Here. Put this belt on, because if you get hit on a flat line, you'll need it before you can get to the chair."

He handed me a wide rubber and molded-plastic belt that hooked in back and had a gimbal in front to hold the pole. It was too wide and too loose, and the doctor helped me adjust it.

"You've got to rest it on the pubic bone," Dr. Engle said. "Otherwise you'll have internal injuries." What's the deal? I thought. Internal injuries. Ruptured kidney. Herniated disc. Stress fracture. I grabbed a beer from the cooler and poured it down my throat in one long stream. We were headed out of the harbor now and Tommy was setting the baits.

"OK," Marion yelled from the bridge a few minutes later as we were moving at half speed toward the Gulf Stream. "This is gonna be your drill. You get one drill and one drill only. The next time you hear it, it'll be for real. Get used to the pull of the bait on the rigger. It pulls hard, girl. But when you get a marlin on, you damn well better know the difference."

I was thinking about how maybe the Mau Mau had *asked* Marion to leave.

"Flat line! Flat line!" Marion yelled.

I ran to the right side of the stern. I grabbed the pole from its grip and tried to work it into the belt strapped around my waist.

"Let him go! Let him go!"

I set the drag down as low as it would go.

"Hit him!" Marion bellowed.

I set the drag up and pulled on the bait, a mullet as large as a good-sized trout.

"See how it feels, girl?" Marion asked. I told him I did. It took a lot of muscle just to pull the bait out of the wake.

We hadn't reached the Gulf Stream yet, but there was a light chop, and the sun, at 10 A.M., was a high-noon sun. The bank of purple clouds in the distance that had brought hard rains the night before showed in relief against waves that were green and aqua peaks, as if painted by a sea-struck van Gogh, all their madness and tranquillity taken into account. Fish swam along the corridors of reefs, their heads and tails flashing colors more brilliant than the light of the water.

"Right rigger. Right rigger!" Marion yelled now. I stumbled toward the right rigger and grabbed the rod.

"Knock it out!" he demanded. I slapped the pole to my left with all my weight, grinding the butt of the pole against my ribs, and managed to knock the line out of the pin. Then I jumped into the chair, set the drag, moved it to *strike,* and gave a big tug.

I was feeling proud of myself. A few calisthenics in the morning never hurt.

"The next time," Marion reminded me, "it'll be for real."

Dr. Engle helped me adjust the belt again, and I headed to the cooler for another beer. We were at sea now. Bimini's pastel waters and the watery symmetry of the coral reefs were lost to the purple shadow of the Gulf Stream passing just east of us.

I sat beside Dr. Engle near the fighting chair. He was waiting nervously, sipping apricot nectar from a can, studying the water.

"You're going to have to do this whole damned thing yourself, Lorian," he told me. "You know this, don't you?"

I looked at him once, nodded, and looked away. No problem, I thought. I'm ready. The smugness had returned.

This wasn't the easy time on a boat I had known before. Sure,

I had gotten my sea legs, learned how to climb the ladder to the bridge during a storm without falling into the Gulf Stream's warm, thick-looking waters. I knew how to tell a bad squall from an inconsequential one, and I knew where the flying fish would settle, but never had I known, nor had I ever conceived, the power and the unalterable raging beauty that a marlin at its fiercest and most loyal to its element would offer.

I was standing by the cabin door, smoking a cigarette, when the yell came. I thought they were kidding.

"*Ri-ite ree-guh!* Rrriii-iite ree-guh!"

Sure, I thought. Yeah, right.

"Right rigger!" Dr. Engle yelled with comparative calm.

I ran toward the rod, yanked it from the holder, and staggered toward the chair as if I were carrying a flag in one-hundred-knot winds. Tommy strapped me in. The boat came to a rocking halt in the water, and all except Marion, who was piloting the boat, rushed toward the stern.

"Let him go! Let him go!" It was Marion.

"He's five hundred pound, boss," Tommy said.

"Hit him!" I yanked back and felt the monster take hold.

"Jesus Christ," I whispered. "Jesus H. Christ."

I could feel the pain in my back as soon as I locked into him. Tommy had taken off the waist belt and was adjusting the straps on the harness. But it did not fit. I was pulling with all my weight just to keep myself in the chair. My muscles were cramping and I knew that I had to distribute my weight better or else lose that kidney.

I started the business of pulling back on the rod to get some slack and then slowly reeling as I leaned forward.

"You tell us how it feels," I heard Marion say. "You tell us how it damn well feels. Lorian! Where's he goin' now?"

"Take up the slack," Tommy said. He was at my left, ready to pound on me and keep up my strength as long as the fish stayed with me. I could feel the brutal pull on my left arm as the fish jerked the line out, steadily, against the drag.

"He's taking it out, Tommy," I told him, hoping there was a quick fix for this.

"Slow the boat, boss. He's taking too much." Marion inched

the boat back, and I felt a bit of slack on the line and began to reel it in.

Thirty minutes passed. I knew because, after each ten minutes, Dr. Engle would boom out the length of my fight. It was like hearing how long you had left to live.

A wet towel had been put on my head. Then a bucket of seawater.

"Give him hell, Lorian!" came the rough voice from the bridge.

Hilary kept rubbing my cramped back. My head ached. My fingers were numb. I wanted to see the asshole responsible for my pain. I wanted to see how he was holding up.

"Where the hell *is* he?" I asked, frustrated.

At that moment, on cue, the blue marlin tore himself from the water with a muscular leap. His bright mouth, open to cast off the hook, was a red gash.

I let out a yell that made no sense—"Whoo-whoo-whoo-whoo-wha?"—something to remind Marion of the Mau Mau. I screamed until I was hoarse, pounding my right fist against my leg as all the other voices came into chorus around me. Then I took up the slack on the line.

I fought him for fifty-seven minutes, the doctor told me, before the line broke. I had watched a weak, spliced section rushing out as the fish had sounded. But I'd hoped to God that it would keep.

I felt the weight of the fish release as quickly as I had felt it take hold.

I cried.

"That's one big baby you just labored over," I heard Dr. Engle say.

"I never cry," I told them all, forgetting then the bashed heads beneath the Coke bottle, how I had cried then.

I sat and brooded in the cool of the cabin.

"You didn't do a damn thing wrong," the doctor told me. "You handled the rig like a pro. Your grandfather would be proud of you."

Ah, him. That bastard with the history on me. That son of a bitch I wanted to outdo. I remembered a part of the reason I was on this boat, nearly sunstruck, sweat on me dried to a crust, so thirsty I could drink blood, out of luck now, tracking that ghost of the ghost of a man who supposedly knew how to do this right.

I didn't feel proud, but the fight had been enough. I couldn't imagine holding on to that raging weight for twelve hours, not for one single minute longer than I had. And I couldn't imagine losing him either. That was the unforgivable part. I began to hope the whole miserable day was over and that Marion would decide to head back to the dock.

Not a chance.

"The next one's going to be a tough one," Dr. Engle told me. "So get your strength back and be ready."

I laughed to myself and thought, Never again would I put myself through such agony. I remembered a man I had met several years before who had fought a marlin for just thirty minutes before his arm cramped into an indefinable shape. My left arm was still shaking, and my mouth still dry after two more beers. I needed to take a nap, to lose myself to the slow rock of the boat.

Still, curiosity gets the better of you. Who knew what might shoot like a geyser from the ocean? I peeked out the cabin door. The water lay flat as a lake, a mirror beneath the high sun.

"Maybe you don't need any more beer," Hilary suggested gently, timidly, treating me the way people frequently did in those days, as if I were poisonous.

"I sweated it all off out there," I told her, testy.

"It might make you weak if you drink any more," she suggested, and I could tell she was worried.

"You go out there and fight the goddamned fish," I said. "Beer won't hurt me. Pour it over my head. I'll take a sip when it runs into my mouth."

I was feeling tough now. The true fisherwoman. Out at sea. Never seasick. I was hard and tough and a lot of fun. I had to think that way to keep myself primed, but I hoped the test of it would not come. At 104 pounds, my body was not ready for another beating.

"Ri-ite rigger. Damn it, Tommy! Ri-ite rigger!" Tommy, Hilary, and I fought our way out of the cabin. Tommy let out a yell and then let out another one, louder.

I uprooted the rod in a panic and Tommy strapped me in again. I felt the same unerring two-ton pull when I hooked in as I had the last time. I listened hard to Marion's instructions and did exactly what he said until I was sure the fish was solid.

"He's hooked in the jaw, girl. He's hooked solid."

Then the work was mine. Bloody, wrenching, unrelenting work. My hands were blistered from the previous fight. I could see the pink skin bubbling into a gelatinous ooze I had seen only in science fiction movies.

"Get the gloves on her!" Tommy yelled.

The rod was jammed securely in the gimbal, and I was hooked to it. I could feel the deep, tidal pull of the fish as he took out the line, steadily, against my own weight.

"He's five times your size," Marion called down.

"What is it?" I hollered to no one in particular.

"It's a blue, baby," Dr. Engle called back.

Whatever was said after that bit of news I only vaguely remember. There was Tommy's steady talk at my left. A litany: "Reel. Pull. Just take an inch, no more. Save your strength. Half an inch is good. Get the belt under her! Don't give him any slack. She needs water. Hilary! Pour some water over her. Keep the tip up! Keep the tip *up!* Take up the drag."

"There is no drag, Tommy," I'd hear myself mumble. "He's pulling me in."

"Back her up, boss. Back her up! He's taking too much. Put that towel on her head. More water! She'll die out here in this calm, she don't have water. Get it in her eyes. Don't matter."

And so on. The talk was constant and assuring. Everyone was with me. Marion and Dr. Engle called me names to make me mad enough to hold on, and I called them names back.

"Reel, you goddamned wimp," Marion yelled.

"*Reel,* goddamnit," came Dr. Engle's voice.

"I *am* reeling."

"No, you're not, you little liar. You call *that* reeling? *Hah!"*

"Fuck you," I said. "Just fuck you. I have to pee. Come and take this goddamned thing while I pee."

"Go in the goddamned chair," came Dr. Engle's answer. "You won't be the first, honey."

"Lorian. Lorian! Are you OK?" It was Hilary, worried again.

Then a wince-inducing passage from *The Old Man and the Sea* found its way into my head, but I let it play, knowing it was true.

You are killing me, fish... But you have a right to. Never have I seen a greater, or more beautiful, or a calmer or more noble thing than you, brother. Come on and kill me. I do not care who kills who.

The fish had sounded four times. I had got him to the leader wire, which connects with the hook, three times, thinking that the molten pain in my arms and back would be over. But as soon as I'd get him in the clear he'd take off like a madman, sounding the line until I thought there would be nothing but a bare spot on the reel. It was eighty-pound test this time, and this marlin could pull harder than the first without breaking the line. Hilary and Tommy held me down in the chair at one point, my back bowed against the fish's unpredictable leaps and dives.

Everything that has been written about the fight is true. There is not another strength as holy and unrestrained as the strength of that one beautifully mad fish. Once it is hooked it will seek its freedom a thousand times before it gives up.

Before, I had thought there was not much to it, this man's business of fighting a fish. But I was wrong. There is luck and true skill involved in the testing of one life against another. And you *do* begin to love the fish because all the pain you must withstand to merely keep him on the line is equal to the pain he must feel in his attempts to lose the thing that has gripped him. Did he know who I was? Had he caught sight of me wilting in the chair? Did he care?

I was nearly delirious after an hour and a half in the chair. The sun was dead up and there were no clouds or even a faint breeze. The wet towel was still on my head and countless buckets of seawater from the Gulf Stream had been poured over me. The salt had dried white on my arms and I could taste the brine running down the parched back of my throat. I had a few sips of beer, a drag off a cigarette, and a Fig Newton that Hilary crammed into my mouth. My feet were locked into cramps and my toes bent back as I strained to reach the foot plates on the fighting chair.

I was trying to get a bead on the horizon and some sign of the blue marlin that Tommy said weighed five hundred pounds and was feeling heavier by the second. But I wasn't seeing too well. There were silver spots floating before me and my heart was skipping beats.

Heatstroke. Sunstroke, I thought. Maybe just a good old-fashioned stroke. I'll fall off this chair and never be able to walk again and then they'll be sorry for what they've put me through.

But please know, Thomas Hudson had said, *I would have stopped this long ago except that I know if he catches this fish he will have something in him for the rest of his life that will make everything else easier.*

I was stretched flat out in the chair, certain this was my last day living. The back was down and I strained to keep my hands around the rod. I could tell it was slipping, a sickening feeling, but I did not imagine once what that would mean.

Hilary poured a bucket of hot seawater over me. I was slathered in heat. Everything was heat, and I could feel the aortic slamming of my heart, clearly, in my fingertips.

"He's comin'! He's comin', boss. Comin' up!"

"Reel! Goddamnit, Lorian, *reel!* You priss, you lazy bitch, you lightweight, no-good little motherfucker, *reel!"*

"I can' reel."

"Yes, you can!"

If the yells hadn't been so thunderous, so vile, I would have passed into that calm, seductive vacuum I had already begun to dream about. I took up the slack, sitting forward in that huge chair built for a man or a large woman. I am neither.

And I saw him standing on his tail in the water, walking on it, moving that massive body that was all muscle and the same amount of fury. He was shot with purple streaks, and threw off sparks of green and spinning marbles of seawater, the tense sheath of his body as blue as jewel box silk as he stood in twisting power, his head thrown furiously, his mouth a gash of scarlet, and the hook in it wreathed in a mist of blood.

"Lorian!" Hilary was at my side. "Do you see him!"

"Oh, I do," I told her. "Yes, I do."

He was going down again, but Dr. Engle said it was almost over. I wasn't betting on it, though. I had seen what he was made of.

The cries grew around me, louder than the dull, incessant buzz in my head, louder than I ever remember any sound. My muscles were torn, but hearing their voices, this near-screeching primal sound, gave me the last edge of strength for the thing I had not finished.

"Reel! Pull! Reel! Pull!"

"Come on down, you bastards, I *am reeling!"*

I watched the line grow fatter on the reel. I had watched it run out five times and had lost my nerve each time. Now I was gaining on him and I could feel that he was tired.

When Hilary asked if I wanted to bring him on board or let him go, I told her I did not care. But when I reeled him to the leader wire, I knew what I would do.

I was twenty-seven years old when I caught my first and last marlin. It had been an eleven-year wait to prove to myself that I could do what my father could not. That I could do what my grandfather had done, and as well.

Someone helped me out of the chair. I think it was Dr. Engle. Bent like a palm tree in a gale, I moved against the deadweight of exhaustion to the spot where Tommy held tight to the wire. Three feet from his hand, just breaking the surface of the purple water, was the marlin, belly up, silver and huge. His length dissolving into the shadows so I could not see where he began or ended. Unbelievable, perfect of form, he had run himself to the pure edge of death, and in that moment of primal victory had surrendered. Only two confused fins on his belly twitched in the air to declare he was still alive.

"Will he live?" I asked.

"I think he's dead," Hilary said.

Marion and Tommy pulled the body back and forth in the water to resuscitate him, and I watched as he gave a half turn.

"Let him go," I said. "Let him go."

"That marlin's got your name on him, girl," Marion told me. "He's gonna give somebody else hell one of these days." Tommy reached over the side and separated the leader wire from the hook. The hook was left in the marlin's jaw, where it would dissolve in time.

Strength seemed to return to him slowly, and then instinct as he pushed his bill down and paddled slowly away. I cannot say that I did not ache for what I had done. I cannot say that it was enough that I did.

It wasn't the longest fight on record, but it was the one I'd gotten. Marion pulled the cork on some champagne, and we all spun one another around the small cabin of the boat. We shouted praise to the fish that had fought our trespass with such grace.

Marion flew the *Fish Caught—Released* flag when we headed into Bimini's harbor. He broadcast our day at sea over the radio to anyone who would listen.

"An average of eighteen days' fishing it takes to even get a look at a marlin," Dr. Engle said, "and you hook two in one day. And then you let it go. That's the way to fish, young lady."

"Yes," I told him, immediately proud, "yes, I did."

"Good girl. Good girl!" he'd said, grinning, and slapped me on the back so hard I'd winced.

I figured I could make a living at this, the rewards were so great, the ego stroked to a faultless purr.

And as I remembered the slow and perfect agony of the fight, days later, weeks and months later, I understood that I had now stepped into the gonzo world of fishing, where strength and courage and a whopping death wish were the banners of the true sportsman. I toted my newfound allegiance with Hemingway into that arena, pole held high, hooks shining.

Chapter

ELEVEN

I HAD VISITED my grandfather's grave in Ketchum the summer I had caught the marlin, arriving at the small hillside cemetery on a scalding July day, a half-finished fifth of vodka in one hand, a filter-tip cigar in the other. I'd made my way to the simple marble slab marked by a white cross, and stood swaying over the marker for a long time, expecting epiphany, resolution, a crashing, blinding flash of insight—something other than the searing summer heat at the back of my neck and the strangely resigned feeling I always experienced when I stood among the dead. I wanted to say something of value to the old man, perhaps that I had met a dare he had set forth by example, but nothing came. The neck of the vodka bottle grew hot in my hand. I tipped it to my mouth, taking a long swig, then poured the rest, a stream of booze, clear as Caribbean waters, at the head of the marker. "Here," I said, "have this," and walked away.

It was that summer I visited the grave that we went for swordfish off Cat Cay, a dead-of-night venture over the fathomless Gulf Stream, the weather that night violent, the seas as swollen and wild as hurricane seas. We were all together again, Les, Hilary,

Dr. Engle, and I, Les recovered from his surgery the summer before, ready to hitch a ride on any boat stupid enough to have us. I'd become, in the interim year, something of a local novelty, known now on Bimini as "the girl who catches marlin." Fishermen are a superstitious breed, willing to try anything once for luck, and I was, for one brief shining moment, a lucky charm of sorts, a woman blessed by Neptune. As long as the luck held I was welcomed aboard with a slap on the back and a cold beer. It was my career then, fishing bum, a position I had aspired to since those summers on the red, hot banks of the Arkansas.

We'd set off from Bimini at midnight on another fancy sportfisherman. I remember the eerie calm at 2 A.M. as the mates dropped Cyalume lanterns over the stern—the neon sign that in the dark depths of ocean flashes EAT AT JOE'S to swordfish. I watched the green-yellow glow of the lanterns disappear into the blackness, a faint phosphorescence like dolphins rising beneath the surface. On deck I watched the atomically bright flash of lightning to the west and knew it would catch us soon.

In the cabin Les and Hilary lay facedown on the indoor-outdoor carpet, asleep. Dr. Engle sat on a narrow window bench, sipping an imported beer, his eyes focused beyond the cabin door at the storm that was gaining on us.

"Ever been seasick?" he asked me. He knew full well the answer to this question, having asked it, without fail, each time we'd fished together.

"No way," I told him confidently, knowing deep in my gut this was not an affliction I would be victim to, ever. It was all a matter, I reasoned, of adapting yourself.

"Well. We're in for it tonight. There's no fish to be had in the kind of weather we're going to get. Mark my words. They go down deep and stay down. You just remember this, though. Everyone has their time. Being smug won't save you."

He winked at me.

"Yessir," I said.

We'd grown close, Dr. Engle and I. He and Les together were making up for my lack of an on-call father. Back on Bimini we'd sit on the porch of the Compleat Angler Hotel, eating conch fresh from the shell with lime juice squeezed on, or whip up a supper of fried potatoes and fresh grouper, Les raving in his window-rattling voice about how *great* everything was. The food, the company, this life, the weather, the locale—nothing escaped his praise. He was a man who had come back from the dead after his heart attack ten years before, and he did not miss one moment being keenly aware of the gift of this reprieve.

I eyed him stretched out full-length on the floor of the boat and laughed. This was a man who could sleep anywhere. We'd been staying on a cramped houseboat on Bimini, the tiny rooms like ovens in the heat, and at four in the morning speedboats docked at the end of the houseboat's long pier, dropped off bales of marijuana—"square grouper" they called it on Bimini and throughout the Caribbean—and woke us with the heavy thunk of the bales against the dock. One morning Hilary and I had found a drug boat overturned and riddled with bullet holes on Bimini's western shore. We'd spent the morning digging it out of the sand, expecting to find a body beneath, but instead found shell casings littering the sand nearby. It was always smart to stay awake on Bimini and catnap offshore.

On deck an angler was lashed to the fighting chair as the edge of the massive storm bore down on us. All around lightning popped now, charging the air. The boat began to rock—tightly at first, nothing too alarming—and I brightened at the thought of a little rock and roll at sea. I liked the giddy, stomach-floating sensation riding the waves gave me, but there was a serious, hard-fisted edge to it now. I perched in the open cabin door, keeping my distance from the lightning, waiting for the guy in the chair to hook a sword. I'd heard how they rammed boats, ran their long, hard bills right through the hulls. Lightning spiked the sky in a dagger pattern, illuminating the white-capped expanse of ocean, and the wind charged in a sudden, heaving gust, tossing the boat violently, starboard and port. I heard a frightening crash in the galley and turned to watch the cabinets and small refrigerator fly open.

"Secure everything!" I heard the captain call from the bridge, and the mate turned from his post at the fighting chair to indicate this duty was mine.

When the first huge wave hit I was dumbstruck. This was the

wall of water I'd seen in surfer movies, the "tube" curling up over us like a liquid fist and slamming the deck with the force of a freight train. The mate slipped a bright yellow slicker on the guy in the chair. I remember the absurdity of this, the man, wet as an otter, trying to stay dry. I was told later it was to shield him from the lightning, a rubber suit to prevent grounding. I had a quick picture of the guy melting like a hot tire in the chair.

Waves were smashing us nonstop now, the deck awash, and in the bright, lightning-lit moments I could see they were half as high as the bridge, a mad Fellini sea, frothed and hungry.

"Get your butt in here," I heard Dr. Engle yell. I stood and lurched ten feet straight into a wall, traversing Les's back in my stumble.

"Your Ladyship," I heard him groan, his voice thick with sleep. "*Great* massage."

The interior of the cabin tilted at right angles. It was like one of those pictures where the ceiling is the floor, furniture suspended above you like a chandelier. My inner ear went flooey and I sank, dizzy, to my knees, crawling on all fours down the stairs to the galley, lost in a sea of canned goods and spraying beer cans. Hilary had clawed her way past me, wide awake and deep green, and was now retching loudly in the head. Les lay sprawled facedown still, his fingertips white as he gripped the edge of the indoor-outdoor, his massive body looking like a human teeterboard.

Dr. Engle had crawled to the galley stairs and knelt with his hand outstretched, palm open. In it lay a little yellow pill.

"Take it!" he commanded.

"Whatsit?" I asked, trying to use as few syllables as possible. It was weird, but when I talked I could feel my voice tilting in my throat.

"Motion sickness medication. Take it." Doctors. They can't say "seasick pill" like the rest of us.

"No way," I told him, trying to back away, but instead landing spread-eagled across the head door.

"Go away!" Hilary croaked from the other side.

"Lorian," Dr. Engle said, his voice stern. "Take it. It won't hurt you."

I shook my head violently. "I don't need it. I won't take it."

Offer me a case of beer and I'd drink it in an afternoon. Offer me a pill and I'd accuse you of drug pushing. It was a skewed ethic with me—in my mind I had given up drugs years ago. I shook my head again, pushing his hand away.

"You'll be sorry," he said, crawling away.

There is definitely something *strange* about a doctor on all fours.

It was pointless trying to tidy the galley. I settled on bolting the cabinets and refrigerator shut, and was lying in the canned goods, drinking a spurting beer when I heard Les call.

"Your Ladyship," he said. "Do you think a tuna sandwich might be in order?"

I was watching the galley walls rush up to meet me as we tilted in the trough of a monster wave. Was he crazy? The weight of the canned goods was the only thing keeping me off the ceiling. Refusing Les Hemingway, though, was tough. It was like telling a kid who'd gotten all A's he couldn't have any ice cream.

"Sure," I yelled up from the galley floor. "I'm a goddamned martyr. White or wheat? Huh? Huh? White or wheat?"

"White," came the answer. I shook my head. Could he have missed the sarcasm?

I did understand Les's sudden appetite. When my own stomach started to crawl in motion with the sea, the first thing I wanted to do was eat. A full breakfast in the morning—five semiraw eggs, two thick slabs of buttered Bimini bread, oily mayonnaise, and tuna is an antidote to anyone expecting dry heaves.

So I flung myself—not deliberately—up and over the galley sink, can of tuna scrounged from the heap in hand. A large butcher knife lay on the floor and I snatched it up and plunged it quickly—again not deliberately—into a fat loaf of Bimini bread Hilary had bought that day. Our first stop on the island was always the Bimini Bakery, where the hot, yeasty loaves sat cooling on a wooden slab, twenty-five cents a loaf, the aroma of it thick in the humid air. It was the best bread I had ever eaten.

Sawing the bread was a cinch. All I had to do was lurch with the heaving of the boat and keep the knife away from my face. I was feeling more than adequate as a hostess, considering the conditions, a whiz with this automatic bread slicer, when the boat hit what felt like a two-thousand-foot air pocket and I sawed into my thumb. Blood ran freely into the tuna as I dug it straight out of the can with my fingers, undrained, and slapped the red goo on the bread, the oil mixing viscously with the blood, an honest-to-God hero sandwich.

I crammed my own sandwich in my mouth before I even made it up the stairs from the galley. Suddenly I had become ravenously, insanely hungry. I crawled my way to Les as the boat tipped, clutching the sandwich to my breast. When he took a look at the sawed-up bread, the dripping mess of tuna, oil, and blood, he said, predictably,

"Your ladyship, this is *great*. What a *great* sandwich. My compliments to the chef."

A lemon shark was caught that night, his pale, hibiscus-colored body luminescent beneath the surface of the roiling ocean. They cut him free when they saw he wasn't a sword. I could have told them if they had asked, long before they brought him up. Sharks all fight the same, deliberately, noses aimed straight ahead, the giant muscle that is their body boring through the water, intent on towing you to their territory. It's like fighting a submarine.

I watched a school of flying fish spill onto the deck from the crest of a two-story wave, their finny wings moving with the nervous speed of hummingbirds, their orientation ruined by this boat suddenly in their midst. One had a broken wing and I scooped it into my hands and felt the frantic beat of its panic, its fractured wing vibrating, useless, against my wet palm, reminding me of the smooth, jittery feel of baby bass in the ravine in Jackson. I slipped the flying fish gently into a bucket of seawater, watched it rise and fall with the swells of its miniature sea, and knew this was something I could not undo. A fish with a broken wing. Who could mend this?

The storm raged for hours and all on deck sought the comparative safety of the cabin. To lower the odds of my body becoming a missile, Les lashed me with rope to the window seat, and Dr. Engle hung on to me as anchor. When Les was done binding me, chuckling at the sight of me trussed and motionless, my eyes wide with fear, he flung himself facedown on the carpet once again, draping his strong arm over the dry-heaving Hilary, who lay limp on the rug beside him.

"Let me know when you feel sick, Lorian," Dr. Engle said as he gripped my ankles tightly and braced with his feet against the floor of the cabin. I looked up at him, taking in the idiocy of this.

"You gonna untie me when we get to port?" I asked, feeling suddenly like ballast, my body straining against the ropes as the boat bucked and rolled.

"Not a chance," he told me.

• • •

LES HEMINGWAY was a charmer, a man who could con you into doing anything once. He'd raise his great eyebrows, wiggle them up and down wickedly, and grin widely if he wanted to persuade you. The day after our hellish swordfish ride he wanted me to try sailing. It was a sport I'd always regarded with a certain degree of disdain, an activity for people who really wanted to stay clean. Still, when I heard of Les's plan to pirate a small sailboat from Bimini's Blue Water Marina, I was intrigued.

I had arrived at the dock armed with spinning gear and heavy, flashy saltwater spoons, figuring to catch a barracuda as we sped along the reef. Dr. Engle was already at the dock, hands on his hips, frowning up at Les as Les eyed a small sailboat that had seen better days. The paint on its flanks was buckled and peeled, and the woodwork on the deck bloated and cracked.

"You can't just take the goddamned boat, Les," I remember Engle saying as Les kicked a sneaker at the boat's hull, testing it.

"This vessel does not appear to be humanly occupied to me, Howie."

Engle shook his head. "It's not your boat, Les."

Les was already busy unlooping the ropes from their cleats, preparing to shove off as he waved me and Hilary aboard. Dr. Engle backed away, waving his hands in a dismissive gesture.

"You'll regret this," he said. "Mark my words."

The island was in the path of a tropical wave that was pushing up from Jamaica, the daddy of the storm we'd ridden out the night before. The wind was extraordinary—perfect sailing weather, Les said—and as I dipped my hand in the water and held it to the wind, it dried instantly. Les magically produced a key that had been hidden somewhere on board and we sputtered out of the harbor on the power of the boat's sick-sounding motor. Les negotiated the channel cautiously, his eyes trained on the coral bedrock that made the passage treacherously narrow.

Father and daughter were fond of cussing at each other when they were working a boat. It took a few times out with them to realize they would not make each other walk the plank.

"Goddamnit, Daddy!" Hilary hollered at her father. "You're going to run aground."

I watched the sharp, diamond-hard coral within feet of our hull and hoped that if something went wrong it would be now, before we entered the deep, hungry belly of the Gulf.

"Goddamnit yourself, Hil!" came Les's bellowed response. "I've been through this bloody channel *thirteen thousand* times, do you understand? *Thirteen thousand times. Thirteen thousand* goddamn times. Have a little faith."

"You're going to run aground, I tell you."

"I am *not.*"

"You are!"

"Am *not!"*

"Are!"

It was like sailing for the New World with two of the Stooges. Whatever confidence I'd had in their ability evaporated as quickly as the water on my finger.

Once we were safely through the cut they grew quiet and turned their attention to the glory of the wind-blasted water, the exquisite muted turquoise and jade that always made me feel as if I were riding atop a freshly painted canvas.

I rigged my gear and began trailing a bright silver spoon through the choppy water, attracting needlefish and then a large cuda, who smashed the lure with his serrated mouth and took off running. Like a pit bull on crack he sliced just beneath the surface of the water, ripping line off the reel with that maniacal sound that made my heart race and my palms go clammy.

"*Great,* Your Ladyship. *Great.* If he's under two pounds we can eat him."

Les rubbed his hands together and made hungry noises as the cuda continued to take out line, leaping in a vertical burst from the water once, twice, three times. He was a soft, gun-metal gray in the distance and his hard, bulletproof jaw seemed impervious to pain. After the marlin fight the cuda was no great burden, but feisty still and a hell of a dancer. I've always had a particular fondness for barracuda, never fearing them when we've come nose to nose underwater. The truth is, if you're not wearing flashy jewelry they pretty much leave you alone. It's their speed that amazes me, the way they can move from a holding pattern to a point a football field's length away in a matter of seconds. If you're a bait fish you haven't a prayer.

Why under two pounds? I'd asked Les, and was told that immature barracuda had not fed long enough on the toxin-soaked algae to be infested with microbes that, in humans, create ciguatera, a life-threatening poisoning of the system that can cause extensive nerve damage and, as a bonus, make hot things taste cold and vice versa. I would later hear the story of a man who had contracted ciguatera from tainted grouper and lived to tell about it, his only antidote the gallons of beer he poured through his system, relying on the bizarre instinct that this would cure him, which it did. I would also run across this same man, oddly enough, ten years later at a writers' conference in Birmingham, Alabama—the writer Jesse Hill Ford, who spun out his tale of poisoning and miraculous recovery as I sat with my mouth open, wondering what the odds were that the hero of a story I had been telling for years would one day be sitting next to me. Still, the thought of getting sick from a fish was vaguely sacrilegious.

"I don't want him," I said to Les, disappointed. "If I can't eat him, I don't want him."

Which was a lie when you got right down to it. The sheer buzz-saw power of the cuda on the end of my line was charge enough—never mind playing Russian roulette by eating him—

but as I gained a few feet on him he broke free, and my line, which had been tight as piano wire moments before, went limp now in the wind.

"Too bad," Les said. "I saw supper swimming at us."

We'd putted about a mile offshore when the boat's motor went *cuh-gah, cuh-gah* and died. I was not at all surprised.

"What luck," Les said. He was beaming. "Now we'll *have* to sail back!" Adversity had once more turned to knee-slapping fun for Les. I was grim. I eyed the wind-whipped acres of water before me, wondering if I could bodysurf back to shore. The night before had left me weak and off balance, and the thought of kidney bumping into the waves again did not appeal.

I surveyed the water. There was not another boat in sight. The faint hope I'd had of launching myself aboard anything seaworthy faded. Smart people had stayed ashore. Small-craft warnings had been issued, and not only had we stolen a boat, we were in direct defiance of the laws of nature. The wind picked up even more and the hull began to fill with water. There'd been a good reason no one had bothered to nab us at the dock. Sucking on seaweed would be our justice.

"We're taking on water," Hilary said as she pulled herself up from the boat's tiny cabin. I looked below. Two feet of liquid sloshed in the hold.

"Shit!" I said, scared spitless. "We're sinking. Goddamnit! We're sinking."

I looked around in panic. There was nowhere to bolt but into the frothing sea.

"Don't worry, Your Ladyship," Les said happily. "We have the power of the wind. Get the sails up, Hil!"

"Are you out of your goddamned mind?" she said. "We cannot *sail* in this wind."

"Hoist those motherfuckers! Now!"

Les had put me at the helm, a cardboard-cutout version of me, anyway, stiff with fear, one eyelid twitching, while he helped Hilary raise the sails. I told him in this screechy little voice I'd never heard that I could not sail.

"Yes you *can!* Don't think negatively. It's not the time."

I recall a distinct moment of clarity pushing through my terror, like a sunbeam boring through the gathering clouds, a profound and galvanizing comprehension that I was with incompetents, that my life was in the care of the absolutely witless. I gave the two of them the finger behind their backs and gripped my hand tight on the rudder.

Fortunately the wind was blowing in the direction of Bimini, otherwise we'd have made Cape Horn by sundown. Hilary and Les hoisted the sails with much bickering back and forth, and we shot full-blast on a zigzag tear toward the northern tip of the island, my sweating, shaking hand steering the boat.

"Nothing like a sail on a *great* day!" Les shouted over the wind, his fists raised above his head, joyous. We were breaking Mach 1 by now, our bottom-heavy *Titanic* born again on a jet stream of wind. I sank back from the helm, the blood drained from my palms, lips glued to my teeth, and let Les take over.

"Makes you glad to be alive," he crowed. "Feel that wind at your back."

It was like a jackhammer. And yes, we were moving. We shot by frigate birds, a school of porpoises, the wind-whipped spray, at the speed of light. The horizon of waves was a mere smear on the canvas, we were moving so fast. Hilary, truly worried now, tried to relax the sails, but they would not budge. The force of the wind had bent the runner, and we were moving with the grace and speed of an F-16, straight for the cut. You are gonna die, I told myself. This is the exact moment you will die, and these are the people who will kill you. So take it all in, baby. But things were streaking by too quick to register. I would die remembering a blur.

It was the patron saint of stolen boats who guided us through that channel. I'm sure of it. It could not have been that insanely happy man at the helm who kept yelling, *"Great! Great!"* against all reason. We streaked through the cut and into the harbor like a wild, waterlogged bird. Our slip at the dock was taken. Not that it mattered. We needed a concrete wall to break our speed. Les settled for a large yacht. I'd expected to blast on nonstop to Nassau when we crashed, nose first, into the massive boat. On impact the three of us fell back and I recall one pure moment of joy at being alive. I remember, too, the sick look of horror on the yacht owner's face as he stood on the deck of his pricey jewel, drink in hand, watching our unbroken course, realizing he was our port.

An outraged dockmaster stood screaming as I threw a line to him, smacking him in the face. We were lashed alongside, within inches still of the damaged yacht, but the boat still strained and bucked like a wild horse. The sails sucked up every ounce of wind on the planet and refused to be yanked down even when the three of us pulled together, even when Dr. Engle appeared on board, ominously silent, and helped.

"I've got it," Hilary said. "We'll hoist Lorian up the mast on a boatswain's chair."

Sure, I thought. A device of torture. I'll lay money on it.

"What the hell's a boatswain's chair?" I asked. Dr. Engle explained, ideally, what this might be, but for me it was a thin metal cable attached to a length of rope so I could slide myself through and then be run to the mast like a flag—thirty, thirty-five feet, say, the exact distance you need to fall to die. I also had to carry "tools" on my mission, to beat the runner senseless, exactly what I planned to do—get a target in my sights, start flailing, and never stop. Hilary stuck a wrench in my mouth, the heavy, crimestopper crescent type, lead, and I had an instant gag reflex, as I slipped my bikini-clad bottom into the loop of ass-cutting wire. Dr. Engle, Les, and Hilary grabbed hold of the rope then, their feet braced in an absurd tug-of-war position, and heaved. I shot up the mast like Greg Louganis in reverse. Along the way my right arm jammed between the runner and the mast. I screamed through the wrench, a muted *eew-eew* sound, and they took this as a signal to drop me down and heave again, ramming my head into the web of wires at the top. Once I'd reached a stable height—after six or seven yo-yoing dips and spurts, a hank of my hair yanked free along the way—I made the mistake of looking down. Below me Les stood on the deck, a mere pinpoint, arms raised in the air. My stomach rolled over. Here came that seasickness Dr. Engle had warned of. I bit it back, salivating on the wrench. Which would fall faster, a pound of vomit or a pound of feathers?

"Your Ladyship," Les hollered up, "be careful up there. We

don't want to lose a life. I want you to know this is a *great* thing you're doing. Just *great!*"

If I heard that word again I would gladly enter a French asylum. I bit down hard on the wrench and glared at him, then let go with my right hand and dropped it into my palm.

"Get your hands back on that motherfucking rope," I yelled, spit flying. "Now!"

I beat at the bent runner guides with the wrench, pounding them until sweat ran in sheets off my face, and they slipped free. I watched the sail balloon down in a soft, billowy lump.

Cheers rose up from the deck. The crowd that had gathered on the dock cheered. I waved at them all with my free hand, which still gripped the wrench, a Nazi salute. Then the three below, having lost their minds, let go of the rope and I plunged into a stomach-curdling dive.

"Whoops," Hilary said as I hit with a *whang-whack,* butt first. For days after I limped, my hips black-and-blue from the vise-like grip of the wire, my mouth still tasting wrench.

That night Les bought me a fried grouper sandwich for what he called my heroism. "Catch of the day," the waitress told me, and I thought, Yeah, the ciguatera special.

Chapter

TWELVE

DR. ENGLE and I had a fishing date that next April, an outing meant to erase my memory of our one bonefishing trip together, off south Bimini, when the only thing I caught was a sponge, which I kept for days until the rancid odor drove everyone in the houseboat senseless. I'd also kept a marlin bill infested with ants (that's the one and only way to clean out a game fish bill, Engle had told me), a ripe conch shell with the meat still inside, and a vodka bottle filled with Bimini sand. From every fishing trip we took together, I came away with trophies.

We were heading, this time, from Miami to Islamorada, Florida—"Purple Isle" the Spanish called it for the deep mottled purple and aqua of its waters. I'd lived in Islamorada, briefly, with a group of bikers years before and remembered the rural feel of the place and how I had consorted with bad boys then, thinking nothing of it, thinking this was what I was meant to do. Returning to the place in one piece had some meaning.

This was to be a new, exotic level of fishing, the guided trip, wherein you are literally escorted to the fish, told what bait to use, where to cast, how to angle, when to flex your knees, where your butt should be in relation to the pole, and for this stripping of identity and personal honor you pay lots of money. I balked at the idea at first, comfortable in my own eccentric ways, unwilling to hunt the waters with a stranger. The whole setup seemed wrong. But Dr. Engle tempted me, using the word "legend" to describe the man who would guide us, Jimmie Albright, "the best damn guide on the Florida Keys," as Ted Williams had once put it. We'd be fishing for tarpon, a fish I had yet to add to my life list. And fly-fishing was mentioned, so I told Engle, "Sure, why not, how hard could it be?"

I called Albright from Seattle to let him know I had never caught tarpon, had never done *any* saltwater fly-fishing, not to mention fly-fishing, period—to me it was right up there with sailing, a hairless sport. I was the bait-and-tackle girl, the redneck, hardware-toting, fish-slaying nightmare. I had caught marlin. Hey. I humbly said I hoped my lack of skill would not disappoint him.

"Naw," he'd said. "Nope. Don't worry."

But I did worry. Being decent with a rod and reel had become one of the few things I truly cared about, and the seventy-one-year-old Albright, from what I knew of his reputation, understood the hopeless fanatic. He'd fished with Hemingway off Bimini, with Zane Grey, Ted Williams, and Joe Brooks. He'd had a big part in introducing saltwater fly-fishing to the world simply because he'd decided to take a risk when others had thought the idea was absurd.

Dr. Engle and I camped at Cheeca Lodge when we arrived. It was the gathering place for the twenty-five backcountry guides who worked then out of Bud 'n' Mary's Marina. There was a trophy room where the guides' names were listed, along with a roster of recent catches. In the bar a large tarpon was mounted on the wall, the island's premier game fish.

We met Albright early the next morning at Bud 'n' Mary's. Coming eye to eye with a man who had made fishing history, who'd even had a knot named after him, unnerved me. My heroes had not achieved stature in the ordinary way, and since most had either caught fish or killed someone, I figured Albright fit right in. I had seen pictures of him posing with Ted Williams after an incredible tarpon catch off Islamorada, but these were old photos, and the only feature recognizable in the flesh-and-blood man was the chipmunklike grin, on a face that, even in youth, was sun scarred, and now scarred by skin cancer from years on the open water. Albright stood beside Cecil Keith, a guide who kept his skiff in a slip adjacent to Albright's. Keith had been a mate for Albright in the late forties, when he was just sixteen years old, and had started guiding on his own in 1954, a mere three years after my birth. His jaws were clamped down tight on a chewed-up-looking cigar, his pockmarked, weather-beaten face a rogues' gallery portrait. These were men who looked as if life had marched right over them with cleats on. Even Dr. Engle with his grizzled beard and sun-leathered face looked like an innocent in their company.

I headed toward the skiff with Albright and Dr. Engle, practicing my tough, I-can-roll-with-the-waves walk. I took a mental inventory of my body scars. Was I crusty enough to be with these two men, who in their combined hundred years or so of fishing had seen more drama on the water than God? Sure I was. Hard drinking was the greatest ager of them all.

Albright, born in Indiana in 1915, had lived in Detroit during the Depression. He had headed to Miami Beach for work—"to take what you could get"—and had hung around boats so he could get the feel of what fishing was all about. He'd been a mate for two years, earning a wage of $3.50 a day, and had gotten his captain's license in 1935 and fished off Bimini on his own thirty-foot Elco, the *Jam Bar.* This was where he'd met Hemingway and Michael Lerner, who were then baptizing the waters off Bimini with their extraordinary catches. Hemingway then had just become the first angler to bring a bluefin tuna to gaff off Bimini.

I had known only two men who had fished with Hemingway—lots had said they had, but when you got down to questioning them, the stories fell apart. One was Les, and the other, Dr. Engle. Engle, in his youth, had had a rowdy day at sea with Ernest off Cuba, indulging in activities he refuses to allow me to print. Now there was Albright, who mentioned offhand that he had fished with "Ernesto." It was the name Les often called his brother.

Albright piloted the skiff toward Caloosa Cove, where he picked up our bait for the day: black mullet that looked like a nest of eels in the bait well.

Albright swore aloud we would catch tarpon that day or the next. Engle agreed. This bit of bravado sent me into a spasm of superstition so strong I had to spit in the water five times and knock on the wood of the boat. Simultaneously.

Engle looked at me the way he always looks at me when I manage to embarrass him on a boat, exactly as if I had thrown up on his shoes.

"Quit it, Lorian," he'd said, slapping at my knee. "Don't be so goddamned superstitious."

But the superstition was real. Half an hour before the doctor and I had met Albright at the dock, a woman at the local grocery store had refused to sell me bananas.

"How come?" I'd asked her.

"You fishing today?"

"Yep."

"Then you can't have any bananas, not if you're going to take them on the boat. I can't allow that."

Turns out bananas at sea are the unholy nth in bad luck. In years after I have seen grown men freak when they've spied a banana on board twenty miles out. (Guess who was stupid enough to pack them along.) And if one had turned up within a hundred yards of the skiff that morning, I'd have refused to go.

We were off across the deeper, darker water that snakes through the flats of Florida Bay, past bridge number five, past Long Key, where Zane Grey established Long Key Fishing Camp in 1906. The camp was ruined in the hurricane of '35, taken out in a fist of wind and shattered all over the highway.

The wind this morning was goose-bump cold. I was used to the dead calm heat of July that can be broken only when a boat is moving. Albright asked a few times if I was warm enough, and I lied and said I was. I wouldn't be a woman who needed catering to, but still, I wanted the man's respect. It was a thing with me then, respect.

We settled southwest of Nine-Mile Bank after cutting through a lush mangrove channel. The boat's agility and Albright's skill with it amazed me. He would cut it away from a bank with split-second timing, driving full tilt across waters that were as familiar to him as a freeway to a daily commuter.

I asked about the name Nine-Mile Bank.

"I really don't know," he said. "Could be nine miles from the bank in town. People figure distance by water here."

We would be fishing with the mullet this morning on twenty-five-pound test, with a Day-Glo orange cork bobber attached. Hot damn. Bobber fishing for tarpon. When I had conceived the notion that there was one way and one way only to fish, had I been right, or what? There was no pretense made that I could learn to saltwater fly cast for tarpon in a day, and I was relieved and irked at the same time. But I wanted to watch Albright first so I could decide how I'd do it once I tried.

We had no luck this day, changing position frequently, anchoring in the relatively shallow water while Albright gave me instructions on how to hook a tarpon once the bait was taken.

He told me to keep an eye on the action of the mullet. When tarpon come nosing around, the mullet gets spooked and will do a scared little dance under the water, the cork bobbing like a belly dancer. This was my game. I took turns watching the cork and scanning the surface of the water farther out. I knew that tarpon might roll or leap if they were in the area, but having never seen one in its element, I wasn't sure what to look for.

"They look just like giant green cigars beneath the water," Dr. Engle said. "Just like green cigars."

I raised an eyebrow and studied him skeptically, said, "Sure they do," and kept on looking.

As I watched the horizon a gliderlike form lifted out of the water and into the air, a dappled leopard ray, propelled and carried high by the flapping of its prehistoric wings. It was a strange, galactic sight, its underbelly starkly white and smooth as muscle.

Albright mentioned how rays could leap into boats.

"That's right," Engle agreed. "A leopard ray out of nowhere, right by the boat. Wham!"

I shrank back and watched the water more carefully now. A

Portuguese man-of-war floated by, its deadly tentacles trailing five feet beneath the surface. We were sitting on hell's own watering hole.

"They can do some people in," Albright said as he and Dr. Engle watched the iridescent blob inch its way across the current. I have returned to these same waters during man-of-war birthing season and have watched the turquoise waters clotted thick with young men-of-war, so many of them that in choppy seas they slosh over the low boat transoms, a lutefisk nightmare.

I wasn't feeling so tough now. I said something about being allergic to shrimp, apropos of nothing, a comment that met with puzzled, manly silence.

We ate our lunch of fried chicken and talked and drifted in the wide open space of the flats. I reacquainted myself with the facilities on a boat that has no head, hanging over the side while gripping the outboard motor and listening to Dr. Engle yell, "When you have to go, Lorian, you have to go!"

I asked Albright about my grandfather, if he thought he was a good guy.

Albright looked puzzled. "Sure," he said. "He was a good guy. Everyone liked him."

He told me he had fished with him on the *Pilar.*

"It was a great fishing boat in those days," he said. "People might look at it now and call it a tug, but then it was top of the line."

The deadly-looking, black-painted *Pilar* was a serious fishing boat, and I liked thinking about it, how it would have been to have fished with him in the Stream, what I might have learned. In a way I envied this man who had fished with my grandfather, a witness to his quirky fishing habits. Albright laughed, and I wished I could have seen his eyes beneath the polarized glasses he wore.

"Ernesto used this twelve-aught Penn reel for deep-sea fishing. It had a star drag on it. He could never get that drag down tight enough, so he'd take a ball-peen hammer and hit the drag until it was as tight as it could go. Just take the hammer and bang the shit out of it."

Albright laughed again. Dr. Engle had a weird look on his face.

"So *that's* how those nicks got on the star drag," he said. "Les gave me that reel. Ernest gave it to him. I'll be damned. He used a hammer, did he? Son of a bitch. I figured somebody got mad and kicked it. I could never figure out how it got so banged up. Didn't make sense."

I had the leather waist belt Ernest had used on the *Pilar.* This, too, had been given to Les and then to me. A waist belt ruined by salt water and a reel with a banged-up star drag, this fishing legacy. Still, I liked it, liked even more that this towering, chipmunk-faced, cancer-pocked man had fished with a man of my own blood and was now fishing with me. It made a nice, neat little circle at the time. I was in the grip then of the illusion of heritage, full bore into the wind, drink locked tight in my fist, baited line bellying loose on the water. The daughter the old man never had. It's the way I saw myself then, an answer to a long-ago whispered prayer.

Albright poled the boat from the platform now. I asked about Zane Grey. Albright had been a mate aboard the *Floridora* in 1933 and fished with Grey then out of Miami Beach's Chamber of Commerce Docks.

"You know," he said about Grey, "he just didn't say much. Most of the day he just sat and read a book."

This amused me. I imagined Grey reading one of his own books after paying off anglers to stay out of his territory, the way he'd done when he'd fished for steelhead on the North Umpqua River.

Dr. Engle mentioned Al Pflueger, the namesake of Pflueger reels. Albright had a story. In the mid-seventies he was guiding Pflueger in the Gold Cup Tournament off Islamorada. They were leading on the third day and fishing off Nine-Mile Bank. Pflueger hooked into a 125- to 130-pound tarpon, and Albright gaffed it alongside the boat. But the fight wasn't out of the fish yet. It hauled Albright overboard—"I had no choice"—and pulled him under the boat and around to the other side, where Pflueger tried to gaff the fish once more and instead drove the gaff into Albright's calf and clean out the other side. They lost the fish.

Albright pulled up his left pants leg to show the scar. It looked as if a shark had made it with one powerful, deliberate bite.

We headed back in as the sun was setting in a pool of purple, the two old guys talking together about fishing days past, and I felt damned lucky to be with them, lucky that they understood what I was after out here, and not just that, but that they took me as an equal, and maybe even envied me a bit for the years I had on them.

In the morning I took grim notice of my sun-charred ears and bright crimson forearms, remembering Albright's cancered skin, and dressed in a long-sleeve black shirt, long pants, a hat, and knee socks.

This day—perfectly calm, sweltering—had me sweating the instant I stepped out the door. When Engle and I showed up at the dock, Albright had a different plan. We would fish off Sandy Key in water that varied from four to fifteen feet. On the long ride out we spotted a commotion on the surface of the water that looked as if two geologic plates were moving one against the other. Albright killed the motor. Two loggerhead turtles were mating and were spooked the instant we began to drift closer.

"It's springtime," Dr. Engle said, grinning.

We were miles now from any recognizable landmass, the shallow water absolutely calm, and the sun, even in early April, was treacherous. A school of dolphins moved up and down in the distance. A white heron, the largest I had ever seen, sailed overhead.

We stopped west of Sandy Key. The island reminded me of Bimini when you see it from a distance. It had the same carapace form, and the banks were pure white sand.

While Albright rigged the lines—here was a pampered first in my fishing experience—I got my first glimpse of a tarpon. North of us a school of them rolled on the surface, their armorlike scales flashing silver in the sun. They were not as big as marlin, but big enough. I watched in all directions now and saw tarpon leap straight up out of the water and crash back down, the spray from them reaching us in cool droplets, a quick shower before the long, hot day ahead.

We talked some about Albright's thoughts on taking fish.

"I don't like to kill fish," he said. He told me that the actual fish skin is no longer used for a mount, but a fish-sized fiberglass mold is used instead.

"It's a waste," he said. "People bring in fish so they can have pictures taken with the catch, and then they go home and talk about what heroes they are. It's the same way they did the elephants in Africa, nearly wiped them out. That's what's happening here."

I asked if he told people that fish were wasted unless they were brought in only for food.

"Sure," he said. "I try. But they don't listen. You quit talking after a while because you know it doesn't sink in."

So why was he a part of this slaughter for hire?

He stopped poling the boat, reached to remove the sunglasses that had obscured his eyes for so long that there were dents in his cheeks, and looked me dead in the eye.

"I make a living," he said. "I do what I can. You understand?"

I nodded, realizing I had trodden on touchy territory. Still, the irony was there. Why do something that forced you to hold people in contempt?

I asked the man what single thing annoyed him about guiding. More than once it had crossed my mind that this might not be a bad way to make a living, out on the water all day, no one to answer to.

"I don't like it when people complain," he told me. "There's a woman who brings a Porta Potti along. Nothing pleases her."

I scanned the small skiff, imagining a dour-faced woman sitting under a blanket on her Porta Potti.

"A lot of people will fish for an hour," Albright said, "and then give up. They want to know where the fish are and how come they're not catching any. It ruins a lot of vacations."

"You would think," Dr. Engle said, that dreamy look on his face that he gets whenever he's on the water, "that just being out here would be enough for anyone."

I agreed. We were in the strangest and most beautiful country I had ever seen. The water was literally evaporating on the surface from the powerful heat and lack of wind. A thick, impenetrable haze was the result. We could see dimly within our own territory, but not beyond it. It was the month and year Halley's comet would be visible directly south of Orion's belt in late evening, a celestial event I had planned for years to witness.

"Comet dust," I said to Engle and Albright, extending my hand into the murky air. "It's comet dust."

Dr. Engle laughed. "If you say so. If that's what you want it to be, that's what it is."

Once the baits were out, Albright drilled me again on how to set the hook in the tarpon's jaw. "Bow to him once, a how-do-you-do kind of bow, from the waist. Don't yank first, you'll pull the hook. It's the easiest way to lose him. Just bow, then pull and reel—pull once, twice, three times. Don't panic and he's yours."

I figured I would have a beer to calm myself. I remembered the marlin fight. This "just pull" business was never as easy as it sounded. "Just pull" on a five-hundred-pound slab of flesh. "Just say no" to pulling.

"Nothing like a cold six-pack in the morning, hey," Dr. Engle said, the look on his face when I drank now one of concern. He palpated my liver from time to time, checking for enlargement.

"Don't ever let me catch you with a swollen liver, young lady," he'd told me sternly.

"Sure," I'd said, wondering just how many beers it would take to do a liver in.

As soon as I had cracked the can, Albright pointed off the port side to a ruckus taking place in the water near my bait. The bright orange bobber skittered like a dime on glass, first one way, then another. Albright yanked the pole out of its gimbal and shoved it at me, and I threw the beer at Dr. Engle. I hit and reeled three times, the magic number.

The first hit felt like nothing, just air with a little bit of play. The second slam was more substantial, and the third hit took on weight. The test was twenty-five-pound, the lightest I had used on big fish.

The tarpon, which Albright estimated as *big* and then later at 115 to 125 pounds, shot from the water in a whiplashing frenzy, bent in half at the belly, head thrashing to throw the hook. He looked like a tank with fins, armor plated, with a mouth large enough to hold a bowling ball. For a brief, insane moment I forgot my job entirely and took one hand off the rod to point at the twisting fish.

"Look at that!" I yelled.

"Goddamnit, Lorian, pay attention!" It was Dr. Engle.

I pumped and reeled down, a task that takes the blood out of your hands, turns your knees to jelly, and socks you in the back like a fist. I ached, and the memory of that pain had a name. *Marlin.* But there had been a chair then, a big, fat cushy chair with a foot plate and armrests. It seemed like a luxury now as I edged and lurched my way around the small boat, following the rod tip and the fish's lead. I spied the beer cooler wedged against the poling platform. In a crunch, it would do. I asked if I could sit down.

"No way!" Dr. Engle said, but briefly he relented, long enough for Albright to strap the waist belt around me.

Something very odd happens when you hook into a big fish. Ordinary reality begins to slide away, replaced then by the hyperreal, and all you know is a dull pain and the lightning action of the fish, and your response to that action. I watched the tarpon leap ten times, maybe more. After the first leap I swore I was dreaming.

He was a rattling mass of silver off every side of the boat. I would follow his lead and he'd leap in a place I'd not expected. He took off on a long, line-screaming run, which was fine because all I had to do then was brace myself and wait until he was ready to make a turn home.

I thought of S. C. Clark's advice on tarpon fishing: "No man is strong enough to hold a large tarpum [*sic*] unless he is provided with a drag or buoy in the shape of an empty keg attached to the line."

I wanted a tank.

Dr. Engle's lucky fishing hat, which he had jammed down tight on my head in the heat of battle, had fallen off. Albright picked it up and tried to slap it back on but managed to shove the brim over my eyes, so I was now reeling blindly. I craned my neck, tilted my head back, moved my head up, then down, and still, all I could see was my feet.

"I can't see," I cried. "I can't see."

"That's funny," Dr. Engle said. "You could see this morning."

"Get this goddamned hat off my head."

Albright readjusted it and the tarpon dawned silver on the horizon.

Dr. Engle started up his chant.

"Come on, Lorian. *Reel. Pull. Reel. Pull!"*

But without a chorus of voices it wasn't the same.

I had gotten the tarpon closer now, but didn't have the height or strength to work him around the obstacle of the poling platform. I tried pulling him to the left, understanding then that his strength came from pure instinct and mine from a peculiar form of rage-induced adrenaline, the kind that blots out reason and allows mistakes to enter randomly.

The tarpon leaped in close to starboard, about six feet away, and I realized, for the first time, how dangerous this sport could be. An angry, green, fight-filled fish does not go gentle into that good boat, but instead lands like a chunk of skyscraper. If his leap had been just a little to the right he'd have slammed full bore into my chest. I tried to gauge his angle and reel at the same time. He'd been close twice before, within lunging distance, but too green to take my lead.

Albright scrambled to get his hand on the leader as I pulled the fish closer, straining the line. A wave of spine-burning pain crumpled me forward, and I asked, insanely, if I could let him go. I might as well have asked if I could shoot them both. *"No!"* saith the crusty duo. The two of them wanted the tarpon alongside for pictures and a perfect release.

I messed up. There is nothing more to it than that. As Albright grappled for the leader, I lost my strength again and struggled to the rear of the boat, the tarpon hauling me like deadweight.

The fish made a quick turn—I had heard how wily they could be, deciding anytime to do whatever they needed to do to break the line. On my end it felt as if a mad and contrary horse yanked the reins. He dove beneath the boat. For a quick moment I looked up to see if Albright would dive in after him. I could feel the line being pulled and raked on the underside. When I had an inch of slack I reeled it in and knew something was wrong.

I asked Albright what was the matter with the line, but I knew before I asked. It was frayed enough to snap, and it did. The six-foot tarpon that had been alongside the boat minutes before had found its freedom.

I had cried when I'd lost my first marlin, but I didn't now. The fish had to win once in a while, Dr. Engle kept telling me. Tarpon are strugglers who play with your wits and emotions, but the truth is they can pull free anytime they choose.

I remembered the tarpon's eyes—disks like twin harvest moons—taking in the foreign territory of capture and knowing, instinctively, what trick to pull to be free. I could not begrudge that instinct.

I was thinking about this while I sat at the front of the skiff, my back turned to them. They were smart enough to let me sulk.

"You lose a lot of fish?" I finally asked Albright.

"All the time," he said.

"When they're so close?"

"Thousands," he said.

"That'll do, I guess."

We spent the next five hours talking and watching the baits. Albright gave me a fly casting lesson.

At a distance of about sixty feet he lay the fly down perfectly near several rolling tarpon. I was sitting on the deck of the boat when he placed the fly, and then whispered in my direction, "Do you see them?"

I stood up and yelled, "Where!"

Dr. Engle winced, and Albright managed to say, "Hey, they spook easily."

"Well, I read—," I started to say.

"Don't read so much," Engle told me.

While we drifted Albright brought out his polished wooden box of flies. They were strung beautifully end to end, a magic box of Crayola-toned feathers tied to shiny, dagger-pointed hooks. I had seen the special "Albright's knot" diagrammed in a fly-fishing magazine and knew he designed and tied his own flies. It struck me as an aesthetically pleasing thing to do, and I had trouble matching this sun-wizened, gnarled-fingered man to the beauty in the box. I watched him tie the line to the fly, his thick fingers moving quickly and without apparent effort, every loop and twist a calm performance. I asked if he had names for the flies.

"Nah," he said. "I don't name them."

He pulled ten or twelve flies from the box. There were turquoise feathers the color of the water, speckled ones, orange-and-black; he placed them neatly on the deck while Dr. Engle and I watched.

The flies were a gift for Dr. Engle, who had promised he'd be back to fly-fish with Albright. Later Engle held the flies out to me, laid out in dazzling single file on his open palm.

"OK, Lorian," he'd said. "Which one do you want?" I told him I wanted the turquoise.

"Hah!" he'd said. "I figured as much. No way. You get the orange-and-black. When you catch your first fish on a fly, you get the turquoise."

Fair enough, I'd thought, but it would be a long time before I could rightly claim that one exquisite fly.

Chapter

THIRTEEN

GEOGRAPHICAL ends have their purpose, and in the early seventies I sought Key West, not on a lazy Sunday afternoon with the map of the States spread open on my lap, but desperately, the way you seek a fix for, say, your life. I had been with Jimmy then, our daughter conceived but not yet realized, and Key West was as far away as we could get in one unbroken run down the East Coast. The place was still a sun-washed fishing town, the atmosphere of tropical ruin as heavy as the humidity. Unpainted frame houses—called Conch houses after the name for the locals, who took their name from the once-plentiful saltwater mollusk—lined the rutted streets, giving it a French Quarter feel, but tourists were few and those who put down roots there, fewer. It was a private cove too quirky, too run down, too without pretense to give a damn, and people stayed away because of this, fearful of the unfamiliar, the sovereign.

Even in 1980 when Les, Hilary, Dr. Engle, my daughter, Cristen, and I came to Key West, wary now of Bimini and the steadily increasing drug traffic, random murders, and a general feel of danger on the island, Key West was still Key West, a little more glitzy, a little more sophisticated, but basically intact. We started a fishing tournament that year, a very small fishing tournament, Les's idea, the purpose of it that not just the rich be invited, but anyone with a fishing pole. There would be no betting, no boating a fish unless you planned to eat it, and sportsmanship was a requisite. Dr. Engle had a special sportsmanship trophy made up and Les, suitably, was to present it. The entry fee was nominal and the turnout the same. Cristen, six years old at the time, won the smallest-fish trophy for a grunt she'd caught on some worms we'd brought from Seattle.

It was that summer that Les's diabetes gained serious ground. The numbness and icy feeling in his feet and toes was a constant problem, and even in the oppressive heat he soaked them in hot water, trying to generate warmth. His doctors had talked of amputation and Les had repeatedly shouted them down.

My daughter and I stayed on for most of a year, living in a cottage on Little Torch Key, twenty-eight miles north of Key West, and Les and Hilary visited often. Hilary was worried about her father. We all were worried about her father. His mood, which had always bordered on the fatally optimistic, had changed radically. He still shouted, "What a *great* day to be alive," to those who approached him, but the words were hollow and the look in his eyes the same look I remembered in that picture of his brother. For brief periods he would seem himself again, the way he did when he took over the wheel while I drove from Little Torch to Key West, reaching across me and grabbing it in middrive, booming in that voice that was his and his alone, "Allow me to take the worry of the road from your hands, Your Ladyship," while I swatted at him, screaming, "Stop! You're gonna kill us," as we bumped and swerved along the narrow shoulder of the road. And he seemed himself when someone in Key West asked if he was related to Ernest and he looked them dead in the eye, saying, "Well, I do come from a long line of people." Still, these glimpses of the old Les were becoming more and more faint.

We fished in mangrove-lined Torch Channel, on the Gulf side, casting from the edge of the island into the green-and-turquoise waters, amazed that every cast brought a fish. In the pond that was fed by the channel a school of mangrove snapper swam, a muted red-gray beneath the clear water, and my daughter would study them for hours, watching them trace the periphery of the pond, the reverent look on her face maybe the reflection of my own so many years before.

Some days Les would join me out on the point of the island, sitting on a small bench that faced the water as he studied the breadth of the channel. The look that came over his face then was resigned, but there was peace in it, too, and I often wished as I watched him that I could bottle the whole goddamned ocean, have him drink it down in one healing gulp. These waters had been his life, the blue domain to which he woke each day, the one unerring heritage of his time that did not mock, did not disappoint, did not die, did not expect him to be something he was not. He loved them, and it was love wisely given.

We often talked about my life, where I was going with it, Les certain I was destined for something better than what I had known. It charmed me, this faith he had that I would not, ultimately, destroy myself. And I knew destruction was coming, could sense it, a vague guilt in me always that a black heart beat in me, that my true talent lay not in the doing of things, but in the undoing. But Les swore he could see ahead through some secret porthole where my future waited, shined up with all the good things. The advice he gave me often and without apology was that I write for myself. "Forget the goddamned muck suckers," he'd say. "The ones who'd have you do tricks. The ones who'd fuck you while you sleep. Believe in yourself, daughter, because if you don't, who else will? I can tell you *I* do. Does this help?"

And I would want to shout at him, "Yes," and I would want to tell him to hang on, to not give it up, because I did not want to know how things would look without him. The way he believed in me was good, but that is what Les Hemingway was about, offering people the world as this great, buoyant, brightening ball, and the notion that the most lethal form of treachery lived in the mind and heart, and that if you could cut a path through the jaded and the bitter, then you had half a chance at living well. And the funny thing is, he was right, and I did not know how right until he was gone.

Still, these were idyllic seasons, the ones we spent there. I rose in the morning to fish, and fished all day, tempting barracuda with a heavy string of pop gear I'd fling flashing into the bright water, retrieving it slowly, jerking the line a little to make the spinners dance. If a cuda were nearby it would strike every time, leaping far out into the channel once it was hooked, spending my six-pound test line, dancing for us all. I caught pinfish, more determined fighters than any trout, holding them firmly clamped at the midsection when I unhooked them, avoiding the sharp, dangerous spines that give them their name. They were as pretty as any of the grander fish, their blue and yellow stripes iridescent in the sun. They had been the staple of the old Conchs and Cubans in the Keys—grits and grunts—and I had a taste for the lowly fish myself, frying it up in cornmeal and flour and bathing it in lime juice.

Shrimp for bait caught anything in these waters, but for supper I drew a bead on the mangrove snapper who fed in close to the tide line, tight up under the mangroves, wary of anything artificial. Often, at the end of a day, I'd have a nice stringer of snapper, and every night we had fresh seafood. Along the weed-covered seawall Hilary and I hunted for lobster, waiting for their spiny tentacles to poke out like long, red spider legs. With our gloved hands we'd reach in quick and grab them by the tentacles, ease them out slowly, and shove them into netted bags tied at our waists. Sometimes I would tease blue crab from the water with a fresh chunk of pinfish, watching the greedy crab edge sideways beneath the clear water, then lash out with one strong, viselike claw, and hold on tight in sheer rage while I reeled him to the sandy grass above. On land the blue crab is a formidable enemy, snapping its claws like castanets and charging in a sidelong, crooked gait for anything it perceives as a threat. They would go for my ankles, the tips of my toes, my hand as I bent to capture them, continuing the charge as I fled, screaming, for the cottage. The only way I found to deal with a blue crab safely was to dump it with the bait still attached into a bucket of water, and then straight from the bucket into the boiling pot.

Often I used the cheaper, frozen-in-a-chunk pilchard for bait, my allergy to shrimp forcing me to deal prissily with them—gloves on, shrimp held at arm's length—a practice that took away from my tough-girl image. The pilchard we bought at the local convenience store on Marathon Key, a seven-mile-plus trip via the old seven-mile bridge, back before the new, streamlined version was built. The old bridge was a rickety, narrow, two-lane ride down death row, and in hurricane season, when people were evacuated in the Lower Keys, it was the only way out, the rising tide threatening its viability, the traffic backed up for forty miles. The first time I had crossed the bridge with Jimmy, years before, it felt as if I were on the one thing solid in a horizon-to-horizon expanse of glittering ocean. You felt as if you were truly at sea, out in the middle of the old bridge, and I miss it now, the pirate feel of it, the knowing that once you were on it there was no turning back. Les had helped build the original bridge, attaching old railroad ties for the sides, ties that had once been the track for the one and only overland passage to Key West, the Flagler railroad, running from Miami all the way down the crooked coral finger of the Keys. By the time we'd make it back across the bridge the pilchard would be thawed and reeking in its little Ziploc bag.

I cut the pilchard into chunks with my Swiss army knife, sliding the knife into the bait bag while I fished. A white heron, five feet tall if he was an inch, would show up in early afternoon, eyeing my catch, waiting for me to toss him a fish, which I never did, wary of his needle-sharp bill and remembering the story an old fisherman down on White Street Pier had told me, that herons will go for humans if provoked, drive their long bills through a skull in exactly the same manner they bore through an oyster shell, neck arced, bill striking with lightning speed and needle accuracy. I doubt it's true, but the point on the bill is impressive, the sheer height of the bird intimidating.

One hot afternoon the heron grew bored waiting for a handout and strutted right up to the bag of pilchard that lay maybe two feet from where I sat on the channel edge, shot his bill out with one deliberate jab, spearing the bag, complete with a forty-tool Swiss army knife, and sailed out across the channel.

Baitless, knifeless, I stood with my mouth open, staring as he disappeared somewhere over Big Pine Key.

After supper, at sunset, I would return to the dark channel, the western sky streaked wild with bright gashes of pink and purple, backlit in yellow. Sometimes the entire sky would go red and I would wonder at the natural extravagance and at the dangers of this place to which I'd come. Inside the cottage, scorpions roamed, climbing the walls at night, where Hilary and I would nail them with the butt end of beer bottles. But it was night fishing that was the challenge. It was then that sharks moved into the shallow channel to feed beneath the moon, and I would cast my wire-leadered line into the dark water, knowing sharks by the way they hit, with the weight of an anvil and a kick like a .45, and when they pulled it felt as if they could tow the ground on which I stood.

One weekend Hilary brought a rowboat down from Miami and we went cruising for sharks at night outside the channel, our only beacon a flashlight I pointed off the bow as Hilary rowed. We tied our anchor, a brick I had dug up from beneath the cottage, to a length of rope, looping the free end through the boat's single seat. I had upped the test on my reel to a sturdy fifteen pounds and had taken to fishing for sharks with a live pinfish, a slash cut in its side, a predator alert. Nothing draws sharks like bloody water. It was a moonless night with a fast incoming tide that dipped and bobbed our tiny boat. The flashlight cut the darkness for a pale six feet ahead and I cast blindly, hearing the pinfish land with a thunk and a splash somewhere far off the bow. There is a sense of being at the mouth of hell when you fish for sharks in the dark. Every push of the tide, every *slap-lap* of the water against the boat, every deep eddy that realigns the bow says shark. You know they're out there. You know there are hundreds of them out there, feeding where you can't see them, waiting.

"We're crazy," Hilary said as I swung the beam light past her, illuminating her face for a moment, its strangely giddy look of terror.

"You got that," I agreed.

There was no doubt what hit the pinfish a split second after my second cast. You cannot mistake a shark on the line. Nothing, with the questionable exception of a bonita or a jack crevalle, pulls like a shark, heavy, hard, determined, staying deep because deep is its territory. When he took hold I knew it was with a death wish. We took turns playing him, letting him tow the boat freely, and then all hell broke loose. The shark, satisfied for a few minutes to plow deep and steady, broke the surface of the water and made a turn in the direction of the boat. Something was not right. Later I realized that the fish's ordinarily acute sense of direction had somehow gone haywire. It was a hammerhead, the most hideously ugly, ungodly creature ever to swim, a relatively small one, no more than five feet, but deadly looking and hell-bent on getting to us, its eyes mounted on bizarre stalks, its down-turned, razor-packed mouth a gash on the white under-surface of its jaw.

"Cut it off! Cut it off!" I yelled, sick at the sight of the thing. It gave me the creeps as bad as spiders, and I wondered at the hellishness of water that could birth such a mutant.

"No," Hilary said, strangely placid, "we've got to fight him."

Hilary, who sought danger almost daily, would not let me live it down if I fluffed out on her. At the age of fifteen she and a friend had run a Boston Whaler from Miami to Key West, riding the boat hard and almost nonstop. She had raced speedboats, had learned how to walk on a boat, and could reassemble a boat motor from the ground up. There was no way she would let me cut the shark loose.

The hammerhead swam now in erratic circles around the boat, its compass pathetically off. I held the rod now and with each repeating lap the freak's circle grew tighter until it was mere feet from my hand, breaking the surface, rolling from side to side, its dead-looking eyes rotating in their stalks.

When it bumped the underside of the boat, the concussion like a fist rammed hard against a plywood door, Hilary said, "OK. Cut it off now."

"I can't," I told her. "That goddamned heron took my knife."

"So bite it off."

Biting through fifteen-pound test when your teeth aren't lined up right takes some doing. This failing, I raked the line against the rough brick anchor and kept an eye on the off-kilter shark. He looked insane. I have thought about it over the years, tried to put another name to it, but this is what it was, a predator whose fuses had popped, and we had been the ones who'd done this. I felt a vague pity while I worked at freeing the line. It finally frayed and I snapped it free. The shark continued to circle.

"Row!" I yelled, shining the flashlight away from the fish, thinking this might be the attraction. Hilary dipped the oars in deep and we moved off. The tide was helping to carry us now, deep into the mouth of the channel, in the direction of Little Torch.

"I think he's gone," I told Hilary as we neared shore.

Wrong. About thirty feet from shore he surfaced on the port side, just like *Jaws,* his mouth with the triple-edged dagger teeth open like some suckling demon, and when I hear how fakey people think the movie was, I think, No, you have no clue. They really *do* come after you. They really *are* assholes. I grabbed an oar and we paddled together now, the haywire hammerhead deluged in our wake. As we pushed ashore, safe now in the deep turtle grass, I looked back to see the pearl white of the shark's belly wink like a sliver of moon in the dark water and then disappear entirely.

"Close," was all Hilary said.

"And what have Your Ladyships done this evening?" Les asked as we walked into the cottage, wet, mumbling gibberish.

"Caught a hammerhead," Hilary said.

"Outran him," I put in.

Les raised his great eyebrows once and looked up, skeptical.

"Like *Jaws,"* he said, his eyes returning to the page he was reading.

"Really," Hilary said, sounding hurt.

"I swear," I told him.

"Quick," he said, pushing himself up from his chair, a look of urgency on his face, "Find the Bible. I feel an oath coming on."

"Well, it's true," we said, walking from the cottage into the starry, moonless night, grabbing our fishing poles where they stood propped against the house, looking at each other once and then moving quietly toward the waiting channel.

• • •

WE SPENT hurricane season on Little Torch and watched as hurricane David forced the water in the channel up over the seawall and into the sandy yard. The winds were a steady eighty miles per hour, and people up and down the keys held survival parties, boarding their windows up, stocking Styrofoam coolers with shrimp and beer, and keeping vigil by candlelight. The eye passed directly over Little Torch, and Cristen and I stood looking up in wonder as clear blue sky bloomed from a wall of gray horizontal rain. We met the shrimp boats at the dock in Key West and bought shrimp for a dollar a pound—there's nothing like a hurricane to drop seafood prices at the source—and Cristen ate shrimp for days after, stuffing them boiled and peeled into her pockets, ecstatic at this sudden bounty of her favorite food. We crossed the seven-mile bridge slowly, cautiously, feeling the ancient structure jolt with the sidelong wind, and I felt, briefly, as I had when I'd made my first journey to Key West across this same bridge, suspended above this great bowl of wind-hammered ocean, primally at its mercy. We crawled on through the wall of water to Miami Beach to ride out the rest of the storm at the old house on Biscayne Bay with Les, his wife, Doris, and Hilary. We had even brought our cat, Mr. Cheese.

Hilary met us at the door wearing fuzzy slippers—the temperature had dipped to a cool seventy degrees, a down-jacket alert in south Florida—carrying mugs of hot chocolate. The rainwater pushed in sheets through the great arched windows that fronted the bay, and we spent an afternoon covering them with plastic and following leaks with drip pans. We watched through the window at palm fronds sailing across the bay. I remember the distinct and uncommon feeling that we were safe in this stucco fortress, and that whatever damage the wind could do it could not reach us here. Together, it seemed, we might remain untouchable.

Les realized my attachment to the Keys, the way my days had become matched to the rhythm of these tides, and he talked about my moving with Cristen to south Florida permanently. He knew ways, he said, that a writer could live on next to nothing but wits. Selling balloons and popcorn at the nightly sunset worship on the dock in Key West was a start, and from something like this, he said, you could keep food on the table, you could keep your integrity. It didn't take much, he told me, just wanting it enough. He talked about helping me buy some land near the water, but we did not stay on.

That next year, back in Seattle, I opened a fortune cookie in a restaurant, smoothed out the crinkled paper inside, and read the fortune: *Do not go south this year.* It was not long after that I learned how truly ill Les was. The doctors were talking again of amputating his legs to stop the progressive gangrene caused by the diabetes. When I talked to Hilary she said I should not come south that summer, that her father was too sick and she wanted me to remember him the way he'd been. Not long after I received a letter from Les in which he focused once again on the importance of sovereignty for a writer. "Never write for *anyone* but yourself," he repeated. "This is advice hard-earned and true." And at the end of the letter he penned in his now-shaky hand, "I love you, and deeply, and this letter proves it."

I wondered for a time what he had meant by this, trying to read between the lines, and realized, finally, that the simple act of writing had been nearly impossible for him. He had retreated to a place where he would soon be unreachable. "A touch of sugar," as diabetes was once called, caused not only tissue degeneration but a darkening, numbing depression as well. Les's good cheer had been steamrolled by a blackness that he could not illuminate. Then, miraculously it seemed, a day before his release from the hospital in Miami where he had gone to have a vein in his leg replaced, Les's darkness seemed to clear. For a full week after, he seemed himself again. I know now it was because he was certain of his next move. I had read once that this was true in war, that when the enemy is in your sights, fear dissolves.

On the morning of September 13 he placed a gun to his temple and fired. Hilary and Doris found charred bits of manuscript in the fireplace. Days before, Les had told Dr. Engle that the words "would not come." To have his talent sacrificed seemed the cruelest blow. After his death I often wondered what it had been like for this man who had been so fond of the words *"great"* and "human," who never put the two together to describe himself, to have faced being crippled, to have been at the mercy of his body, and then to have had his mind turn savage, too. If this was the way he wanted to leave, then God speed him.

Newspaper reports, of course, made the too-obvious connections, and Les was labeled another Hemingway suicide, his remarkable life virtually ignored. This was a man who had snooped out Nazi U-boats in the Caribbean, a man who had conceived his own sovereign nation, a fine novelist in his own right, a seasoned journalist, loving husband and father, and the one man in my family who had called me "daughter." He was also a man who had, along with his wife, Doris, taken in the three abandoned children from my father's second marriage and raised them as his own. Now he was one thing: Hemingway's suicide brother. This enraged me, and my feelings about Ernest took a radical, merciless turn. His violent example of self-murder was responsible, in part, I believed then, for Les's death. But perhaps I know better now that death by one's own hand is, as F. Scott Fitzgerald once wrote, referring to something else entirely, "just personal."

My daughter and I returned to Miami that Christmas, to the old stucco mansion on Biscayne Bay where Les had lived and written on one of dozens of old Royal typewriters he'd collected over the years, his chair angled so he could look out the high arched windows that fronted the bay. This was his territory, this home that had an ancient, solid feel to it, a place of air and water and history, the Spanish influence of the architecture not just a builder's whim but the indelible mark of kinsmen. It was a house saturated in the smell of salt air, its open rooms filled with the breeze from the bay. I knew the moment I woke in that home what the weather was because it had bathed me while I slept. From the dock and the seawall on the bay I had fished for shark and gafftopsail catfish, watched Hilary give shooting lessons to Cristen and windsurfing lessons to her dog, and had contemplated the channel that led to the open sea, as Les so often had, needing all his life to be near this deep artery of water that met with the fathomless, darkening well of the *corpus maria*.

When I walked into his home that December night, three months after his death, everyone was asleep. I stood in the dark foyer, where Les had taken his life, and looked up the wrought-iron-railed stairs that led to the second floor, where I had so often seen him walk on the cool red tile, toes pointed out, the kind of walk that keeps you balanced in high seas. I looked hard for something he might have left behind, because that is what you do when you stand in a room where someone you love has died. On the foyer table sat a copy of the *Bimini Out-Island News*—Les's one-man enterprise—ALL THE NEWS THAT'S FIT TO PRINT in bold letters above the mag head, Les's cheerily ripped-off heading from *The New York Times.* "Let them sue me," he'd tell people when they pointed out the plagiarism. "It can only be good for business."

I moved through the open rooms of the downstairs, catching a glimpse of a portrait of Les, his smiling face tilted roguishly to one side, the guayabera shirt he always wore open at the throat. I stood in the dining room for a while, near the long table where Les always typed out the *Bimini News,* and where I often had a bowl of scrambled eggs at three in the morning, sleepless, needing to hear the water. There was a picture of Ernest facing the head of the table, the *Life*-cover Karsh photo, and I wished, for just an instant, to smash that picture. Death had hit too close to home to be a literary musing. And then I laughed out loud, knowing what Les would have thought of my solemn attitude and the bitterness that was rattling me.

We drove to Little Torch right after Christmas, Hilary, Cristen, and I, and fished the channel in memory of Les, landing a barracuda of edible size. Our plan had been to eat it, but I couldn't bring myself to cook the fish, and stuck it in the freezer instead. "Never waste what you catch," Les had always said, and as we left the next night we packed the cuda along, frozen solid.

There was a fine, full moon that night as we crossed the seven-mile bridge, the Gulf and Atlantic silver blue in the pale light. It was a night Les would have admired. He'd have called it *great*—no less, no more. We stopped the car midway across the bridge, grabbing the frozen barracuda from the cooler in back, and as we stood alone on the bridge, the three of us, our arms around one another, I gripped the cuda by the tail and flung it far and wide into the moonlit night. It turned head over tail, a spinning platinum sword, and we laughed as it landed with a solid splash somewhere out toward Cuba.

"There, Daddy," Hilary called out loud into the night. "We didn't waste it."

My daughter, eight years old at the time, began to cry. I remember thinking how acute were her perceptions for one so young. She spoke only a few words to explain her crying. "Don't you miss Les?" she said. "I do."

I did. Still do. So might we all.

Chapter

FOURTEEN

THERE SEEMS no end to murder once you start. It becomes as natural as sleep, as effortless as breathing, and you can suspend judgment of yourself until that time when conscience slips back into place, if it ever does, and you can forget who you are in all of it and focus clear and hard on the task at hand. It's easy, and those who say it isn't lie.

I once asked a writer I know why he had no pets. He said he liked animals too much to keep them captive. "But I have no empathy for fish," he said. "You can kill all the fish you want and I won't care." That's the trick. Selective murder. Carl Jung grouped fish among the "lesser" animals, as opposed to what he called the "proper" animals, like cats and dogs, who, he said, have souls. Well, who's to say? And by this definition did the sport I chose make me a murderer, or a mere opportunist? And did I care enough to ponder either way? Not anymore.

When Les died—and this is a lame excuse—the man who had once said, "Fish like the humans you are," died. The more I fished now, the less humanely I did it, the more immune I became to suffering. And when you drink a lot you become desensitized not only to blood sport but to life. William James called alcohol the great paralyzer of conscience, and by the mid-eighties I had become a bombastic, conscience-free, ego-driven alcoholic, immune to subtlety, grace, and personal perspective. And I do not flail myself unduly. That is the truth. I was, with the exception of having written anything I considered significant, pretty much a cardboard cutout of my grandfather during his last years. Here was the legacy, the heritage blindly given, and it was the alcohol, I now know, that ruined him, turned acuity to paranoia, burned synapses to a powder until, *pow,* he finally blew. A few misled scholars have debated me over this, gotten their shirts puffed when I've said I know, and they do not, what the deal was with this man who was my blood, because if there is one thing an alcoholic can spot, it is the tragedy of another.

Often, almost idly, I wondered if this were what lay ahead for me, the way he had gone, the way Les had gone, the way their father before them had gone, in a blast of light and shame and tissue shattered. I had already been asked once by a reporter if I planned to take my own life, in my book the most crass, unthinking question ever asked, to which I responded with a loud "Fuck you," terminating the interview. Besides, it was not my nature to take the quick way. What I knew best was slow torture, murder by degree. Still, I didn't spend much time worrying about it, only when I rose in the morning, shaking, sweating, lathered in fear.

I remember the panic that grew exponentially as consciousness claimed me and I realized with the jangled hyperclarity of a strychnine victim that I was dead cold sober. It is not a way you want to be when you haven't planned on it. The simplest task—even brushing my teeth—I could not face sober. Put six drinks in me, though—for this was what it took now to make me "right," to lock into what Tennessee Williams referred to as that "click"—and I could do anything. It just happened that I wanted to fish. Sort of.

The Keys were where I hunted now, and each summer season I added new fish to my quarry. Hilary and I fished together for bonita and black-tip shark off Key West. I remember the skipper of the small boat we were on chumming the bonita to the surface. I realized quickly that to let them take even an inch of line was a mistake—once down, they wanted to stay down, a buzz-sawing weight that pulled heavy as a moving anchor on the end of my line. The instant the feeding fish would surface I'd cast my bait among them, and the split second they struck I'd heave hard on the rod, ripping them from the surface of the water. Why waste energy fighting them, I figured, when in the time it took to take one, you could take ten? In fact, why bother at all? When I hooked into a black-tip shark I grew bored with the fight right away, tired of the predictable depth to which he dove, the way he refused to let me fight him. I caught dolphin and king mackerel with the same so-what attitude. Dr. Engle had seen me once or twice on these trips and said I needed something to shake me back to normal. "You're jaded," he told me, and I think he still hoped one last fishing trip might cure me.

The last trip we took together while I was still drinking was off the Everglades in the Ten Thousand Islands, with Engle's old friend and guide Glenn Smallwood, a man every bit as ancient and water wise as Jimmie Albright, but less worldly. He'd been raised in backwater cracker country and his smile was perpetually shy and self-effacing. He called me "ma'am" so often I thought he mistook me for an adult.

We put in on the Barron River, a brackish, mosquito-choked channel that feeds into the Gulf of Mexico. The thick clusters of islands that ring the open Gulf are mangrove-covered oyster shell mounds, built up by Indians around the time of Christ, high ground from the storms and hurricanes that can turn low ground into no ground at all. Once we were out beyond the river channel the mosquitoes lifted like a midday fog and the dark green lushness of the islands bloomed on the water like a fisherman's picture of Eden. West of where we first put down anchor was an island known as Dismal Key, where some years before there had lived a man who came to be known as the hermit of Dismal Key. A raging alcoholic who couldn't trust himself in ordinary civilization, he had opened a map one day, closed his eyes, and jabbed his finger at a spot, swearing to himself that wherever his finger landed, this place would become his exile. Once a month he'd ride his boat over to Everglades City, cash a government check, drink up all the check while he was in town, and then head back to Dismal Key for the sober balance of the month. I liked the story. I understood his reasoning.

Despite the damage the alcohol was doing—my liver was now severely inflamed and about the size of a large pompano—this day was one of the best I'd had on the water in a long time. It had all the earmarks of a farewell bash. Dr. Engle was relaxed and at ease with the relic Smallwood, who had been guiding Engle then for some forty years, the two of them comfortable enough with each other to be quiet, to just fish and drift. The feeling this brought on in me was vaguely placid, so I could sense my own love of the sport taking a deep breath, settling in.

That day we caught ninety-seven sea trout—"spotted weakfish" was the correct name, Engle told me—keeping enough for ourselves and for Smallwood, the silvery, trout-sized fish waiting in line for our bait. I caught ladyfish that leapt and spun like shimmering ballerinas high above the bright surface of the water, amazing me with their agility. "Poor man's tarpon," Engle would say each time I hooked a ladyfish, but I thought secretly that they were much more fun, less serious than their plodding, armor-plated cousins. I caught jack crevalle that pulled like tugboats, their ugly, blunt bodies disappointing when I reeled them in. We would take short breaks just to rest our arms, drifting in the low shelter of the islands, not talking much, just looking.

There was a rookery—just another oyster-shell island, but with birds—and we watched great white herons perch creakily atop the sturdy mangroves, and spied a rare flock of white pelicans and some roseate spoonbills sailing low with their storklike legs behind them.

It was a day with a little bit of breeze to cool us, but not enough to ruffle the fishing. I caught a prehistoric puffer fish, who bloated up like a soccer ball when I brought him to the surface; watched sharks and rays cruise beneath the clear water; thought of Les and what he would have called this day; and felt, for those few hours at sea with Glenn and Dr. Engle, that early, imperturbable fascination I had once had with nature. It *was* a *great* day.

When we got back to Miami, Engle invited me into his cool, low-to-the-ground icebox house, the place Les said had the best air-conditioning in Miami, and the place we would all gather sometimes after a good day fishing. I remembered how Les had looked sitting on Engle's low sofa in the cool dimness of the living room, his big hands resting limply on the sofa, his head tipped back. He could sleep anywhere.

We walked into the kitchen and Engle pulled out a chair for me at the table.

"Sit," he'd said, and did not look at me.

It was in this kitchen where he had cooked for me the bounty of our catch—stone crab bathed in butter and lemon juice, poached sea trout, pan-fried yellowtail, smoked sailfish—fresh, exquisite meals that have left a particular memory of their own. When Hilary and Cristen and I had driven to Little Torch after Les's death, Engle had packed us a bag of smoked sailfish, and we'd fed one another along the way, digging greedily into the corners of the bag for the last firm shred of meat.

"Uncle Howie sure can pack a picnic," Hilary had said when we were done.

"So, are you sitting down?" Engle asked me, his back to me still as he stood over the kitchen sink, washing his hands. For a fisherman he always had the cleanest fingernails.

"Yeah, I'm sitting," I told him. "You said to. So I'm sitting."

"You want a beer?" he asked, back still to me.

"Sure," I told him. I was wondering when he'd get to it. I'd always waited for him to ask, but he'd sure taken his time. And when had I ever turned down a beer?

He usually kept a six-pack of Old Milwaukee in the vegetable bin—the horse piss of beers, I'd teased him, but I would drink it if there were nothing else. The truth was I would crack a can of antifreeze if there were nothing else.

"I thought so," he said. There was something wrong with the way he sounded. Weary. I looked at him, saw him looking back.

"What?" I said, like I was supposed to have another answer for him.

"I thought that's what you'd say," he told me. "Well, I hate to disappoint you, but you're not going to get one."

Just deny me that one thing and I started getting angry. I looked away, afraid of what was coming.

He stood by the refrigerator, hands on his hips, his face as serious looking as I'd ever seen it. I remember thinking how old he looked, and I studied his eyes for some hint of teasing, the bloom of a smile, the old hah-I-had-you-going-didn't-I look. Nothing. He pulled up a chair and faced me across the table.

"Look at me," he said. I raised my eyes, saw the thin, soap-bubble reflection of my face in his glasses.

"Yeah?" I said, wary.

"You are going to die, Lorian," he told me, his voice strained, his words the very timbre of breaking glass. "Do you know that? You are going to *die.*" I looked away.

"Look at me, young lady. Look at me, damnit! You look me in the eye, or I'll make you do it." His voice rose. "I will not watch this again. I will not do it, do you understand me? If you do not stop drinking you will die. Your liver's going. You've lost forty pounds, you're yellow, your eyes are yellow, and you are going to die."

Something broke loose in me, something like shame, but with a harder, meaner edge, and I started to cry. He ignored it.

"And if you can't stop for yourself, do it for your daughter. Look at me! And you will never, ever drink another beer in my house. *Do you understand* me?"

Did I? And what was dying? A bad hangover, that was close to dying. Waking up sick and wretched and blown full of holes. *That* was dying. Shaking so bad I couldn't get the bottle to my mouth. That, too. But what he was talking about seemed easy—dying like there was nothing to it, dying as smooth as letting out a breath—and I was as close to doing it as I'd ever been, that night I'd walked in his door. He knew it. He knew me. My friend, my old fishing buddy. The man who'd yelled at me to make me mad enough to fight. Would it work now? I wouldn't lay him odds.

I nodded to him, an affirmation. Yes, I understood. I could feel my eyes filling with tears again and watched them splash down onto the bright tabletop. I wanted him to wipe them away. I wanted him to say he was sorry.

"You quit or you die," he repeated, no pity, no bullshit, no compassion in his words. Not an ounce. He stood then, turned his back to me, and walked away.

"I love you," I heard him say from the darkness of the hall, a whisper, but I heard it.

Chapter

FIFTEEN

WHEN THE leaves have fallen in the Upper Peninsula of Michigan, the long spit of land, flanked by Lakes Michigan and Superior, becomes a palely iridescent etching. At night white-and-pale-pink sand dunes and bare white birch trees glow like marble in a cathedral. Green hemlock, cedar, and pine shed their rough bark, exposing the red wood beneath. And the fine, light-reflecting mist blows off Lake Superior and settles in caches along the mouth of the Big Two-Hearted River.

It was an occupational hazard with me throughout the 1980s, traveling to where Hemingway had fished, trying to get a piece of what the guy had already done, and then writing about it. I had typecast myself, afraid to venture beyond the familiar. For years I had pointed my finger at editors, accusing them of wanting from me only stories about Hemingway and fishing. The truth is, it was as much my doing as theirs.

I'd had a call from an editor who wanted me to fish the Big Two-Hearted in the dead of winter, camp as Nick Adams had, hunt for grasshoppers in a barren land. No matter Hemingway had merely used the name Big Two-Hearted because he liked it, and had fished instead the nearby, trout-prolific Fox. I was expected to recreate a fictional fishing history. I remember reflecting on the absurdity of this as I packed my bags in Seattle, and also on the absurd notion that I would be going anywhere short of a hospital. This was—with all dramatic overtones intended—the eve of my darkest hour.

No longer able to hide my alcoholism, I was now addicted to the tune of thirty-two beers a day, ascribing to the failed F. Scott Fitzgerald logic that drinking beer instead of the hard stuff kept you safely among the ranks of social drinkers. I was social all right, a walking beer fest. To manage the five-hour flight to Michigan I packed along a couple of six-packs for maintenance, and I recall, through the haze that borders all my memories of those times, a stewardess yelling at me as I stood in the aisle of the plane before takeoff, pouring a nice, warm foaming one into the black mug I always carried.

In Michigan I met up with Jeffrey Cardenas, Key West fishing guide, photographer, and writer, who'd been hired by the magazine to photograph me on the river. I'd known Jeffrey for about seven years then, and he had never seen me in such bad shape. I remember knowing there would be no way to keep him from seeing what I was, and I feared he would lose respect for me. It had been important once.

We had breakfast together the first morning out—two raw eggs for me, the only thing I could stomach now after a night of drinking—and Jeffrey had pancakes, which he wrapped in a napkin to take with him on the river. He mentioned how Nick Adams had wrapped his breakfast of campfire-cooked flapjacks in oiled paper when he was leaving camp to fish the Big Two-Hearted, and I mentioned something snotty about taking yourself too seriously. My edge was starting to show.

After breakfast we drove to the river, following an intricate artery of paved, gravel, and finally dirt roads. The last leg was a wide, sandy swath that snaked through hardwood forest and then logging areas, where the forest had been leveled. It was disturbing, this contrast of the living and the dead.

We reached the mouth of the Big Two-Hearted well before

noon. I stood for a long time, scanning the territory, thinking of what Dr. Engle had said back in Miami and feeling uncommonly alone, up against the wall now and knowing nothing but its dimensions, how cold it felt, and how I had ridden myself hard and wet for years. If it was time to stop, I didn't have it in me.

Along the trail we took to the river, tiny blue-and-white finches dove down to eat the pale blue moths that were thick as gnats in summer. The Indians of the peninsula had called them spirit moths and believed they held the souls of ancestors borne on the air. They looked like blue four-leaf clovers, held aloft on an updraft of wind, then taken in flight by the finches.

Jack pines grew along the edge of the tea-colored river, becoming denser upstream. No tropical wind blew here, no sun beat hard against my back. I saw a goose with a broken wing standing on the thin, frozen lip of the river, frost covering it. It was cold and still as death here, and I put a flask of brandy to my mouth and swallowed, felt the artificial heat burn me alive.

I heard it before I saw it, a sound low and full bellowed, like a heartbeat turned up a hundred notches. I asked Jeffrey, who was annoyingly energetic, already tromping around looking for things to photograph, what he thought it was. He did a double take—like, how come I didn't know?—and said, "Why, it's the lake." He told me that if I walked across the narrow swinging bridge that spanned the river to the beach side, I would see it.

The swinging bridge then was of wooden planks lashed by rope, a relic of the past that swayed with my weight and the wind as I crossed slowly to the north bank of the river. On the other side I stood with my mouth open for a long breath. I could see beyond the wind-scarred bluff to the ocean swell of Lake Superior, no common fishing hole with park benches scattered along the shore, but a body of water startling in its breadth, its tides drawn as steadily and rhythmically by the moon as those of any sea. Here were *Hiawatha*'s shores of Gitche Gumee, the shining deep-sea waters of Nokomis, daughter of the moon. And here was the monster who had swallowed ships whole. I was impressed. The sky was overcast that morning, threatening snow, but the water still shone a clear blue-green.

I was happy to stay in this spot for the rest of the day, beer and brandy in my knapsack, a full pack of cigarettes in the pocket of one of the two down vests I wore, a trove of colored rocks and agates at my feet, the wind that blew off the lake hypnotic in its voice, but at Jeffrey's call I walked back to the river, dragging my feet, dreading the day ahead.

The fishing gear I'd packed along was a bastardized version of the real deal. I still couldn't fly-fish, but had brought along a fly rod anyway, and a mismatched spinning rod. In the stupor that clouded all my trip preparations these days, I had, before I left Seattle, packed two incompatible sections of rod, half of the old Mitchell, half of a steelhead rod. The result was a cockeyed, bulging contraption that I had to bind together with strips of masking tape and that had absolutely no balance. It reminded me of a rod I'd taped together at the joint when I was a kid.

The line on my spinning reel was a mess, still caked with salt from the Ten Thousand Islands trip. I thought again of Dr. Engle, how he'd always told me to take my rod in the shower with me.

"Easy for you to say," I'd told him.

"Just lather up," he'd said, "and hose the rod down with you. You've got to take care of your gear, Lorian. Show some pride."

Still, I figured it would catch fish. If there was one thing that hadn't deserted me yet, it was fish luck.

I was wearing a down vest, down jacket, a ten-ton fly-fishing vest—all my gear and about twenty rocks I'd cadged from Superior's shore were crammed in my vest—rubber outerwear, and whatever other heavy clothing I had spied that morning. I looked like one of those sand-weighted plastic clown punching bags.

All through the story "Big Two-Hearted River," Hemingway notes how happy Nick Adams is on the river. Sure. He was a fictional character. I felt cold and miserable. I cracked a beer, which was about the same temperature as the frozen air, and felt pissy as I watched my lure catch on some roots on the other side of the river.

There was traffic on the swinging bridge, and I looked up to see Jeffrey walking behind an old, white-bearded guy who wore a red stocking cap. The man was full in the belly and walked like Les, rolling with the bridge, his feet splayed like a duck's. And he was laughing as I watched him near. I did not want company. I looked up wearily as Jeffrey introduced the man as Travlin' Gravlin. Uh-huh, I thought, people with names like this always have a story.

The old guy squatted down beside me, his breath a white cloud in the cold air. He looked into my bloodshot, road-mapped eyes, then down at my shaking hands and the steelhead rig I was using, a length of lead stuffed inside some surgical tubing with a hook strung about six inches up the line.

"You need help," he said simply, his tone betraying nothing but an honest, matter-of-fact appraisal.

There is something I have come to know as well as my own name, and that is that one drunk—especially one who has given up the stuff—can spot another drunk in a crowd, with or without a sniff test. "You need help," he'd said, and in that one brief, calculating moment I had been sized up by some hobo who'd come walking off the river. I knew it and he knew it, and neither of us said.

"You mean my gear," I said, flustered.

"Sure," he said, winking at me. "I mean your gear."

He told me the rig I was using for steelhead was all wrong, and tied up a simple one for me—a bit of split shot on the line that I pinched down with my teeth.

"You're lucky," Travlin' said. "I used to bite shot like that." He grinned, exposing a bank of missing teeth. He tied on a trout hook and jammed a netted bag of salmon roe onto it. "Hey. There's no way you won't catch a steelie on this."

I reached into my knapsack and pulled out the brandy flask, unscrewed the cap, and offered it to him.

He looked into my eyes again, ignoring the flask. "Nah," he said. "I quit. Long time ago, I quit."

"I didn't," I told him, taking a swig.

"I already knew that."

The guy was starting to bug me.

He suggested we take a couple of boats up the river to fish. "If Harry's up for it," he said, referring to his fishing buddy.

"Sure," I told him, thinking, What could it hurt? I'd get a story, be done with it.

Back at the mouth of the river we found Harry, a skinny, grizzled guy who wore horn-rimmed glasses lashed to his head with a thick rubber strap, and a Day-Glo orange outdoor suit, the brightest spot on the landscape. I climbed wearily into his flat-bottomed boat, tired of the cold, thinking this guy was a poor excuse for Dr. Engle. He said we'd head upriver for about forty-five minutes to some good fishing holes. Behind, Jeffrey and Travlin' followed in the old man's canoe.

We did not see another boat as we paddled slowly upriver. This place was still, by modern definition, a pristine wilderness. Along the banks that rose and fell with the level of the river, pines grew thick in the sandy soil. Harry pointed out beaver homes burrowed into the banks and sharp-pointed aspen cuttings the beavers had felled. "When you see tag alders," he said, pointing to the blood red tree saplings along the bank, "you'll see a beaver home nearby."

"Now there's a beaver home," he'd say, and I'd nod my head and think, Yep, there's a beaver home, and who gives a shit? I was cold. I was tired. I wanted another drink. I looked over at Harry as he rowed, wearing that insane orange suit so bright it hurt to look at it, and thought he was probably a pretty nice guy, and I felt a little sorry for him, having me along.

"Right around this bend," he said, "is a hole with a fourteen-pound steelhead in it. I know. I had him on the other day. He busted up my gear and I lost him, but he's still here. Now I want you to cast to the right of that brush area, next to the log."

I wasn't in the mood, but I cast anyway, was short on the cast, and reeled back in. I cast once more and tangled my line in the log.

"Goddamnit!" I said. "Goddamnit!"

"There you go," Harry said when I finally pulled the line free. "No need to get upset. There's another big hole up here a ways. And we can stop at a coffee shop, warm up a bit."

Seriously, I scanned the pine-thick banks ahead. The guy had to be lying.

"Do they have beer?" I asked, thinking maybe what he'd said was true, that a beer-and-bait joint would float up like a mirage off the misty water.

"We can ask," he told me.

When we reached another bend in the river, Harry said, "This is the coffee shop," and opened his thermos and poured himself a cup of coal black coffee, the aroma of it sickening to me. He yelled over to Travlin' and Jeffrey, who'd just caught up with us, "Hey, I told her we'd stop at a coffee shop. She believed me!"

I reached into the knapsack for my dwindling stash of beer, angry at having been tricked.

We were along the north edge of the bank now, maybe a mile from where we'd started. Harry pointed to a deep pool flanked on one side by thick brush. He told me to cast a couple of feet to the left of it and let the bait drift down.

"Now, I *know* there's a steelhead in there," he said.

I cast and let the bait settle, then sat on the rickety lawn chair Harry'd set up, and waited. I let the line out a bit and watched it circle the brush. Right then I really didn't care if I ever saw another fish again.

When there was a quick tug on the line I was quiet for a long moment, gauging my fish pulse. I felt the tug again, stronger now, someone rapping at my chamber door, then that one insistent, unmistakable yank. I pulled the rod back, stood up, and hollered, "I've got one!"

Not dead yet.

I was surprised at the fight in the fish as I maneuvered him out of the hole. He pulled out line right off so it whizzed and screeched the way I remembered line being stripped by the marlin. My palms turned slick with sweat and I realized that, no matter where I was or how I felt, that one screaming sound was the fish equivalent of "Amazing Grace."

I could see the trout in the clear brown water, pulling left, then right, then diving in a frenzied zigzag for the cover of his hole.

Harry began the litany, with variations: "Easy now. Don't lose him. Don't let him under the boat. Don't keep *too* much pressure on him."

Don't. Don't. Don't. When had I ever fished when that word wasn't the first one out of someone's mouth?

"I've *got* him," I told Harry. "Quit worrying and get the net ready."

The pole was bent double. I pumped and reeled hard, gaining on him. Who'd have thought a trout could fight like this? After he made another haywire dash at the hole I pulled him back out slowly, steadily, and felt my hands start to freeze up on the rod butt. I could see the silver flash of him beneath the water, precious metal drifting in a liquid beam of light, and eased him up carefully, holding my breath, trying to keep steady, until I got him alongside the boat. I looked to Harry, who held the net, ready. He scooped the struggling fish up then and raised it high for Jeffrey and Travlin' to see.

He was grinning wildly, proud of his new angler. "When this girl gets a fish on," he said, "it's like you stuck a hot needle in her butt." Harry said it was about a four-pound trout, but we decided to lie and call it seven.

I looked at the beautiful steelhead bleeding on the floor of the boat, its rainbow colors bright again after being in the freshwater of the river, and I did what I hadn't done for years. I cried. Not a gentle little sniffle, but full-throated sobs that came in waves and wouldn't quit. Harry stood embarrassed at my side. I had no words for him. I was cracking up. What was there to say?

We moved upriver. I told the guys I wanted to see them catch fish now. I had the one trout, my first steelhead. It was enough this time.

Jeffrey and I switched boats. "The only rule on this canoe," Travlin' said as I stepped in, "is don't stand up." I surveyed the narrow, curved hull, imagined what it would be like to die in ice water. I noticed the sides were painted different colors and I asked him about it.

"Someone sees me from the green side, I'm that guy in the green canoe. They see me from the blue side, I'm the guy in the blue canoe. Just something to keep people guessing."

He laughed then and told me about the time he'd stood up in the canoe and fallen into the river's icy water. He'd looked up from beneath—"the way a fish would"—and realized, clearly, that he might die.

"That cured me," he said. "I don't take many chances on the water now. Did I tell you I used to be a deacon? You believe in death by water when you're a deacon. Some churches will baptize you till you drown."

A few T. S. Eliot lines surfaced: *Fear death by water. The drowned Phoenician sailor. Those are pearls that were his eyes.*

I sat perfectly still in the bow of the canoe, my back to the old man, watching the deep current of tannin-stained water. It was odd how you could see through such dark water. The contrast where it met with Lake Superior, the almost-black water merging with the blue, had looked like that of good and evil.

"You like strawberry ice cream, or chocolate?" I heard Travlin' ask.

The old man was odd, asking about ice cream when the air temp was twenty degrees. Then I decided it might be one of those trick questions rigged to reveal something criminal about me. The truth was I never thought about sugar. A rack and a half of beer a day took care of that.

"Strawberry," I said, to humor him.

"Huh," he said. "Now that's really funny."

"How's that?"

"Well. Most alcoholics like chocolate."

The way he'd said it, so lightly, but like he *knew,* hit me like a sucker punch. Two old guys in less than six months' time had my number. I didn't like the odds.

"Truth hurt?" he asked gently.

It took me a long time to answer. A very long time. I think we'd done a mile of the river before I got the nerve to say.

"Maybe," I said finally, my back still to him. I laughed a little, nervously, trying not to upset the balance of the canoe. Suddenly, I was shaking all over.

Travlin' told me about the alcoholism that had claimed him and forced him to live on the streets of Chicago. He had quit in 1968, near death by then, and spent a lot of his time now helping other alcoholics. He told me all this like I had a card-carrying right to know. He held meetings at the campground, he said, when there were people around.

"Sometime, when you're back here again, you might want to come."

I was silent. I was wondering how it was for him, living on the streets.

The thing that meant the most to him now, he told me, was being sober and the way it was fishing the river alone or with a good friend. He said the river was capable of "healing a soul." I thought that it felt as if I had poured every last drop of me straight into it, all these years on the water, and now here I sat with it washing past me again. I dipped my hand into it, felt the pull of the current and the bone-aching cold, thought, Go ahead, heal me. I dare you.

As we paddled downriver, my face to the wind, I concentrated on how I would die from hypothermia before we reached camp.

"You worry too much," Travlin' said from behind.

I turned around carefully on the canoe seat and looked at him now. He grinned widely, the missing front teeth making him look harmless, oddly wise.

"So you read minds now?" I asked.

"When I'm on this river I do. You're Indian, aren't you? You should know these things. This river has a spirit. So does the lake. Same with the woods."

I turned back around and watched the bare beauty of the river, the poetry that came not only from its name, but from the way it worked its way deliberately, inexhaustible, to the deep body of the lake.

"Now you know what you have to do. I can't tell you."

I heard his voice behind me, sounding like Les. I tried to think of what he'd say to me now, but nothing came.

"Why not?" I asked Travlin'.

"It doesn't work that way. It has to come from you. You can feel it when you're on the river. It's coming to you right now. Wait. You'll see."

The only sound was the oars pushing through the water. I identified beaver dwellings to myself as we passed them. I thought about trout hovering in pools along the bank. I thought about my own life, broken. This man was trying to trick me, like his pal Harry. What I might have learned from any river I should have learned years ago.

The wind came up then in a hard, persistent rush, flattening the spindly tag alders low along the river. A high cluster of pines on the north bank bent and spun fiercely with the force of the wind. Mist from Lake Superior blew fast into the canyon of the river, filling it, and through it I could see Travlin' watching me, studying my face. I could feel the skin on my arms rising up in points, the hair on the back of my neck prickle.

"Daughter," I heard Travlin' say, "those pines are talking to you."

I snapped my head around and looked at his white-bearded face, at the ridiculous Santa Claus hat, and then at his eyes. They held a calm, almost beatific expression, and he just nodded his head. "They're talking to you."

Who but Les had called me "daughter"?

So I listened and thought of one who had come before me on this river, in these woods, having an experience of youth that would change him forever. It had not been Mississippi for him, but Michigan. I imagined how he might laugh at me, fishing the edge of winter, trying to recreate a story that was his and his alone. Throughout his life he had wanted to return to the trout streams he had known as a boy, but he never quite made it back, the experience as elusive as grasshoppers in November. I knew, profoundly, that wish to return to the sanctity of youth, to spin back in time to a place where you did not know so much, and where you had been capable of falling, without fear, into the broad, widening heat of a summer day. Was it possible to take on a new life the way a river, over time, took on new territory?

"We're going to name that fishing spot after you," Travlin' told me when we reached his campsite. "Just remember that. Each year the story we tell about you and that fish will get bigger and better. By the time you're fifty that trout will be twenty pounds, the biggest ever taken from the Big Two-Hearted."

"People know there aren't twenty-pound trout in that river," I said.

"Don't matter. They'll listen anyway. What the hell do you think we do around here, recite the newspaper? We tell *stories.* You'll be the star for a while. The seed grows and the next time it will be bigger. Pretty soon you won't recognize it."

We fixed the trout that night over a campfire, its firm, pale flesh wrapped in bacon, the smell of it rich in the cold air.

Late the next afternoon Jeffrey went fishing without me, fed up by now with my nasty mood and the way I'd cover my face whenever he tried to take my picture, and I waited on the bank for Travlin' to return from the river.

He pulled up in his blue pickup—I snuck a look at the other side to see if it was green, but it wasn't—wearing the same hat, the same gapped grin. He said the luck had been lousy that day.

He told me he wanted to show me something, and we took the truck to the edge of an incline, got out, and walked along a wide, sandy road to a ridge over the Big Two-Hearted. There was an old campsite circled by pines and hardwoods. At the edge of the high bluff stood a wooden bench for cleaning fish and cutting bait, and beyond was a clear view of the Big Two-Hearted, a hundred feet below. A pine-covered island broke the current of the river into riffles, the water catching and fracturing the light of the sun that had dawned bright that morning. It seemed a perfect place to camp.

"I said a powerful prayer for you last night," Travlin' told me as he looked out at the river. He reminded me of Les again, the way he watched the water. "And my prayers do not go unheard. *That* I can promise."

For a moment, all the doubts I woke to each morning were suspended and I was willing to believe him as once more the wind pushed hard through the trees, a cold, breath-catching blast of it that blew in under my coat and flattened the riffles on the water, caught and lifted Travlin's red stocking cap, and sent it flying. The almost-evening light took on a bright gray tint, not unlike the false dawn that comes an hour before the sun rises.

"I wish you kids could stay," Travlin' told me as we made our way back to the truck. "I get tired of talking to Harry all the time. We tell the same stories over and over."

"Well," I said, "like you say, you have a new one to tell now."

"That I do," he agreed. "That I do." He smiled at me warmly, patting me on the shoulder.

As we sat in the cab of the truck, Travlin' reached to pull free a little booklet that hung from his rearview mirror.

"I've had this since I got sober," he told me, holding it out to me. "I want you to have it now."

I took the slim sheaf of pages from his outstretched hand, noticed how the palm was callused and rough, and shoved the gift in the pocket of my fishing vest without looking. I said, "Thank you," with my head turned away. Almost two years later I would pull the booklet from the vest, the pages stained yellow by damp cigarette butts, the edges curled up, and read in bold letters on its cover one word: ACCEPTANCE.

Chapter SIXTEEN

IN THE FLAT delta land of Arkansas, after cotton harvest, the bare fields lay hard and brown in the autumn light, the even rows of tilled earth littered with stray bolls that clung to the brittle plants. I remember how that land had looked right before harvest, so thick with white the air was hung with the dust of it. Cotton blown high into the heavy limbs of sweet gum and live oak, snagged on the splintery boards of bleached-out fences. Clots of cotton turning like tumbleweed down the rutted streets of Altheimer, caught in the quick, violent spin of dust devils that swept through the gullies and out into the fields, gathering up more cotton until it stopped them dead with the weight of it, and then it rained cotton. Cotton clogged in the fine mesh of screen porch doors, floating like bruised lilies on stagnant catfish ponds. It made me think of impermanence, all that cotton loose on the wind.

I drove my aunt Freda's '56 Chevy down the potholed arrow of Highway 79, the late September light still bright and metallic, past the freshly picked cotton fields that stood empty now, a flat, rich ocean of earth reaped and resown a thousand times, and on into Altheimer, population still less than a thousand.

I'd come home to see Freda before she died. She was sixty-seven years old now, her body sheared to seventy pounds by the pancreatic cancer that had torn through her. I was thirty-five. At the sight of my own withered body, the yellowed skin, the thinning hair that came out now in clumps, she had said, "Oh God, child, I thought *I* was the one who was dying."

She was leaving me the Chevy when she died, a car she had had for thirty years, a two-tone Bel-Air hardtop with a steering wheel the size of a semi tire. She'd told me, "Take her to Altheimer, see how she runs." She'd never wanted a new car, as fond of the Chevy now as of any human. It had been a life's work with her, frugality, the look of a thing never as important to her as its function—I remembered this from the way she'd refused to wear a prosthesis when she'd lost her breast to cancer decades before. "What am I supposed to do with this stupid thing?" she'd said, holding the pointed cup of foam rubber at arm's length. "It doesn't even look like a tit."

Now she was a relic. And the car was a relic, its value increased tenfold. It was the car in which I'd given up my virginity, the car I'd sat in as a grubby kid at the local beer-and-burger drive-in, the car Freda drove barefoot even in winter, and the car we'd taken to Pine Bluff Lake on those hot, still summer mornings. One summer day we had driven it to the Sanger Theatre and left all the windows rolled up. When we'd come out a few hours later the pent-up heat, five hundred degrees, like an oven, had shattered the glass in a diamond web. It was still held in place, puzzlelike, by the frames. I remember Freda's delight at this freak of nature, how she oohed and aahed over the crackled windows, calling them "festive." I had wanted one last spin in the Chevy because who knew, exactly, how long *I* was going to last? Doctors had done liver and pancreas tests on me, too, my liver enzyme levels astronomical, and I was in the home stretch, down to ninety pounds now, a fight-to-the-death weight.

I pulled into the narrow gravel parking lot outside Mac's Cafe, across from the railroad tracks where a baby had died once, years before, its body crushed beneath the wheels so that all that was left was a mass of red jelly Sheriff Pinky had scooped into a plastic bag. I remembered Pinky as I sat in the heat of the Chevy, the sun cruel as it was in midsummer, the big gun and holster on his soft hip, the way he talked of fishing all the time, never doing it, just talking, and then of how he died, on the same road he traveled every day, so quick it was easy to forget he'd ever lived. The same with Pa and Ma Mac, dead now for years. Someone had bought the cafe after they had died, kept it going for a while, and then the highway had been routed past Altheimer and business had fallen off. The old place was gutted now, the front windows broken, the red-on-white wooden sign that had said *Mac's* in simple script faded now and hanging lopsided from the roof.

I stepped from the car onto the baking gravel and peered through the jagged glass, expecting to see the old Formica counter, the red leatherette stools, Catfish's face dark through the kitchen window. I remembered how she had slid burgers afloat in grease and extra pickles through the tiny kitchen porthole, the look on her face always cranky as she yelled, "Sammich, missy!" I thought, predictably, of Thomas Wolfe, how he'd said you could never go home again, and I figured this was why, because everything was busted up and tarnished—people's lives, the things they had owned, your own frangible part in the equation. In the empty, dusty light of the cafe I saw a single red vinyl chair, tipped on its side in the rubble, and the rusted butt end of a spinning rod propped in a corner. If ghosts fished the river, this was the place they gathered afterward, here in the cool, secretive dusk. I thought of Catfish and how I had never heard what had become of her. I was hoping she had outlived them all, and that in summer she still stood swaying on the banks of the river, her jar of homegrown night crawlers cooling in the shade. I never asked around about her. Who was left to ask? I like to think she's still there, hooting each time she gets a big cat on, feet dug ankle deep into the red clay.

On the way back to Pine Bluff I stopped on the tall, narrow bridge that spans the Arkansas and watched it from above, the way it spread out broad like a plain, its steady, deliberate current eerie from up high, the solid, girdered steel upon which I stood nothing more than willow sticks in its path. I thought that if this bridge were left untended, allowed to rust as Altheimer had, the next big flood would take it easily. I wondered how fast a body could move in this water. If you jumped in at Pine Bluff at noon, could you make Vicksburg by sundown? I remembered how a man had fallen from this bridge when I was a girl, lifted by the wind and then slammed into the cresting waters, and how when they had found him, washed ashore, speared on an oak limb, there had been a smile on his blue face, and I understood now how that could be. There was so much water here, so close to home.

Back in Pine Bluff, in the high-ceilinged rooms of the old house on Sixth Street, I visited with my aunt, paying up, finally, for that time her arrow had found its mark years before. The last time I had seen her I had been a hippie girl, broke and hungry and hitchhiking my way to California. She had taken me in, fed me, clothed me, and let me sleep in the bed I had slept in as a child. It had rained hard that first night home, a gully washer so strong you could almost hear the river rising, and I remember being glad to be inside as I watched the rain flash in sheets across the windows. A black gospel church fronted the alley to Freda's property, and that night the choir was singing "Just a Closer Walk with Thee," voices belted out so loud I could see the shiver of them in the rain-streaked glass.

To me, *Freda* had been my mother, not that sad drunk whose despair I could never alter, whose life I could not fix. It is why when Freda said, "Come home, I'm dying," I came.

She lay in the old wrought-iron-backed bed, propped up high on white pillows, her hands lying still across her chest, her hands that looked like mine. We were the same height, our small, athletic builds identical when we had been healthy, our hair jet black, eyes to match. We even had the same mole, low on the right side of the back. Now we stared at the ghost forms of each other, each of us wanting to deny what we saw, each of us unsure how it had come to this.

She'd stocked the refrigerator in the butler's kitchen with cases of beer for me, the full, brown bottles lined up ten deep, six wide, so when I slammed the heavy metal door of the old Amana they rattled like a bag of dimes. Freda knew, after easing her brother H.L. out of the DTs with quarter-cup doses of bourbon every hour, exactly what I needed.

I sat drinking a beer as she talked, understanding this was one of those milestones in a life, the prodigal fuckup come home to keep vigil at the elder's bed. I loved my aunt, her undeniable beauty (even in old age, even mortally ill, she looked electric, the white halo of her hair standing on end, her skin poreless and luminous as a wax doll's), the pure eccentricity of her life, and the way she apologized for nothing. If there was something she wanted to say to me, I would listen.

"You look worse than I do," she said, her eyes steady on mine. She was the only person I have ever known who never seemed to blink. It was why she had taken that cottonmouth with an arrow. It was why she could size me up better than I could myself.

And what she said was true. Freda's skin, always smooth and translucent, unlined even now, far outshone my own. I touched my fingers to my face, felt the papery skin, remembered how it looked now in the mirror, yellow as a busted yolk. I felt a tidal wave of shame at coming to her like this. I wanted her to remember me as that mud-caked, mouthy kid in the lake, swimming for her life. But what stalked me now she could not undo. It had plagued me for a good eight months now, figuring out how not to drink. I'd heard that if you really wanted to change something badly enough you had to write the objective one hundred times on a piece of paper—with your left hand. I had tried it, scrawling, "I will drink less," in loopy, backward script until a page was filled. When I was done I still wanted a drink. There was no way left to hide it. People knew, watched me with an odd mix of regret and fear, as if somehow what I had might be catching. What was worse, *I* knew. I'd tried cutting back. It didn't work. I might as well have tried breathing underwater. And stopping now—*slam-bam*—in the middle of the tracks was as deadly as keeping at it. Convulsions. DTs. Heart failure. It seemed safer to stay liquefied.

"You have anything to say to that?" she asked, shifting in the bed, the pain clear on her face. She'd refused to take anything for it, but the doctors had stocked her up anyway. Vials of morphine lay unused on the bedside dresser. "I want to know I'm dying," she'd said when I'd asked her why she didn't take it. I thought of popping the vials in my mouth and crunching down hard. What was there to say?

"I drink too much," I told her lamely, knowing it would piss her off, curious to see her anger. "Family history."

Had I really believed this? I caught myself wondering how much blame you could lay on heritage. It was a coward's way out.

"So that's where you'll point the finger, will you? Convenient, isn't it?"

Here it came, that rage that flooded her every time I fed her bullshit.

She sat straight up in bed, her eyes wild looking, arms rigid at her sides, ready to blow.

"So what is it, then?" I asked her, honestly curious. I'd finished off one beer and was opening another. Dr. Engle had said no more beer in his house. Freda's was an open bar.

"You're a drunk, Lorian. Goddamnit, what do you think? That's all there is to it. You want a fancy reason, you want an easy reason, then go ahead and think yourself right to death. Explaining it won't help one degree. Do you hear me? Not one degree. You have to *do* something, child."

"I tried," I said, thinking for one brief, soul-ripping moment that I was the biggest liar who had ever lived. Tried? my head said in that quick blast of clarity. Like fun you tried.

"Bullshit, you tried!" It was like an echo in me, right where my ribs met my gut. No fooling the dying. They have a bead on you like nobody else.

She reached to the dresser where a picture lay facedown, one of her paintings. All her life Freda had painted, primitivist oils of her house, the river, her adopted son, a lover, her mother as a young woman, cotton print dress clinging to her full hips. I would wander through the huge old house, my gaze moving from wall to wall, studying them, this chronicle of her life. Years ago she had painted a black-and-white Fellini sea, telling my mother she could have it for her living room, but once it was done Freda kept it for herself, saying it was the closest she'd come to painting philosophy. My mother had never understood this and Freda had said, simply, "Too bad." An eerie portrait of the Manson family hung in the living room next to a portrait of Jesus—the dark force face-to-face with the light, she had explained to me once, and I had nodded, pretending to understand. The picture she turned face-up now was one I remembered her painting when I was a kid, quickly, with a butter knife.

"You remember this?" she asked, holding the small, framed portrait out so I could see. "You were there when I did it."

I nodded.

In the painting a man sat across Sixth Street on the curb, in front of a big white house. The house was still there, but the boards were peeled free of paint, just bare gray wood. When I was young it had been pristinely whitewashed, the brightest house on the block. In the picture the man was dressed in filthy clothes, his shirt torn, his shoulders hunched over, and at his feet lay a broken bottle, liquid flowing in a pale brown stream into the sewer drain.

"He came out of the liquor store that day," Freda said, "and I watched him from the window. He sat down on the curb to drink his bottle and his hands were shaking so bad he dropped it. I could hear him start to cry—sob, really—right over all the racket of the traffic, over the noise of the washing machine going. That's when I went to get the paints. What do you think of that?"

"What?" I asked. It was another trick question, a theme puzzle Freda had a piece for. It seemed to be the only way people talked to me anymore, in riddles, and if I'd gotten even one of the answers right, they might have left me alone.

"Him starting to cry," Freda was saying, "just because he broke his bottle. I want to know if you know how that feels, Lorian, to cry about some liquor spilt in the gutter."

I knew all right. I knew by now that I would kill to have it. I remember when it had come to me that, yes, I could murder for it. Eight hours without a drink once, I had torn the doors from the cabinets looking for rubbing alcohol, vanilla extract, antifreeze, anything with *that* smell, that promise of a cure for the crawling skin, the shakes, the sweats, the dry heaves, the sensation that with the intrusion of one single sound just a little bit off, one note just a little too loud, a little too sharp, I would lose my mind. I had thought then in this rage of ramming a gun up hard against someone's temple—it didn't really matter who—and saying, "Get me what I need. Now!" and if they said, "No, I won't get it, I won't do it," I would blow a hole straight through their brain. I told her, "Yes, I know."

"I went and bought him another bottle," she said. "And he thanked me like I'd given him absolution. Knowing what I know now, it's what I did, absolved him right there on an ordinary street curb."

"Why'd you do it?"

"Because I've seen enough of you to know how bad it is. I try to imagine it, what it's like, and the closest I've got is when I dreamed I'd die, and I couldn't get out of the dream, and when I finally did, being awake didn't make it any different. I panicked. For the first time in my life I panicked. And I've seen it all over this family like dirt. Your uncle, your granddaddy—both of them—your mama, all the ones on your daddy's side, and now you. There's a reason for it. You'll find out if you want to. Look at me here, Lorian. Look at me. I'm dying. You want me to die knowing you're on my ass, ready to do the same? *Do* something, child, *quick,* before it's too late. This boat you're on is sinking."

Ah, the euphemism. Your boat is sinking. Not your liver is the size and consistency of an intake manifold, but *your boat is sinking.* I thought about how corny the phrase sounded, but still, it was true. Portholes were busted out, the hull was cracked, the sails were jammed up high on the mast, and I was about to run aground. No yacht to stop me now, but a mile-high concrete wall instead, where I wouldn't even make a dent.

That night I slept in my old bed in back. I stared for a long time at the portrait of the drunk Freda had conveniently hung at the foot of the bed. She had never been subtle. I got up and took it down, drank a couple of beers, and hung it up again. Back in bed, I crossed my arms up against my chest and looked at it some more. It had to have been a Saturday night because the voices in the church by the alley were tuning up, and I remembered how they used to make me feel electric all over, the dark skin on my arms pricking up in points, all that fitful hollering about salvation, of Jesus as the road to mercy. Mercy would not be so bad now, so high-flown a concept. I would take a shot of it right in the veins.

Freda had told me once that people always tried to make it home before they died. So here I was. Shored up in Pine Bluff in a dry season. In the other room lay Freda, surrounded by her paintings. I thought about her and how she had looked those mornings when we'd gone to Pine Bluff Lake, shot through with strength and youth and this idea of herself as an Indian warrior, quiver at her back, bow pulled tight, arrow aimed on its mark. She had been a wonder. It seemed so long ago, someone else's memory locked in my head. I looked up at the wino again. The bottle in the gutter was my life, broken by my own hand, smashed, and what was leaking out was all the rage of all those years, and I didn't want to die that way. I was sure of it.

I heard the train coming on the nearby tracks, louder, low and hollow, and I thought of the gospel singers I had seen once, down by the Arkansas when I was a girl, baptized in their slick, pearly robes in that water so heavy with clay you could see the pools of red swirl up in it where their bodies went down. I had wanted to walk in with them and take the cure, turn my life over to that thing that made their voices rise up so strong and certain. What was it they so believed in that they would trust their lives to it, walk into that dark, deepening water wearing virgin white, and be redeemed? It didn't matter, I figured, as long as it was something. I had believed in Freda, but she had told me once no one person could change your life. I remembered what she'd said, only differently now: it had to be something greater, more mysterious than you. It could have been the river, I thought when I was younger, or the way its red clay felt in my hands, as if I held the flesh and tissue of a living thing. Whatever it was, maybe I could pull it to me, cast my line into that dark water, and heave.

Before I left, Freda took me to the butler's kitchen in back, her white-socked feet slipping along the polished mahogany floors I used to run and slide on when I was a kid.

When she wasn't barefoot she wore white socks, the thin, Mary Jane kind that folded down at the ankles. She wore them even with sandals in summer, and when she'd seen my bare, dirty feet she had said, "My God, child, put these on," and handed me a fresh pair just like hers. It occurred to me how we might look, institutional, shuffling along beside each other.

"Here's the light socket you stuck the tweezers in," she said as we passed a blackened hole in the wall. I remembered how the lights all over the house had shot out in one big *pop* when I'd pushed the tweezers in, and the fizzing ball of fire that had leapt from the wall and run up my arm.

"You were a blessed child," she reminded me. "Nine lives, like a cat. And here's where you kept your toys, in this window seat. And here, look here, the bullet hole when I shot at Bimicain and missed."

There was regret in her voice. I could hear it. I looked to where her finger pointed at the small hole bored through the flowered paper, still visible after all these years, a thin cobwebbing of dust around the edges, and remembered how I had crossed my fingers when Freda had aimed the gun at Bill's forehead, praying she would not miss. The house, too, was scarred, exactly as our lives had been. The difference between us was how we looked at scars. Freda regarded hers openly, in the light, and I in a dark corner, pretending they were still fresh.

In the butler's kitchen there were still small, dried patches of yellowed flour from the time I'd poured a ten-pound sack of it onto the kitchen tiles and rubbed it in with water, concocting a cementlike paste that had to be chipped up with a screwdriver. I had raised hell in this house, and Freda had let me. That had been part of the charm of her all these years, the way she looked the other way when you were being bad. I had leapt from the roof once, a bedsheet looped around my waist, pretending I could fly, and I'd tied a swing of rope and wood high up in the pecan tree and had buried treasures—all of her cooking utensils—deep in the sandbox in the backyard. When I was older I had made love with the neighbor boy on New Year's Eve in the alley by the church, my body covered in leaves when we were done, and Freda had never said a word when she found leaves in my bed, except to ask, "Was it good?" One summer I'd tossed a banana peel into the path of the cranky mailman as he made his way up Freda's walk, and then howled with her from behind the blinds when he went into a heel spin, the letters in his mailbag scattering on the hot, dusty wind.

We had root beer floats each night after supper, and when I was older we talked late into the night in the living room lit by candles. Freda was fond of candles. She'd given me Carl Jung to read when I was fourteen, explaining to me when I would stare up from a page, puzzled, "Every answer you'll ever need, you'll find in these books. Everything fits, so don't you worry about it."

"Look here," she was saying. She waved me over to the double-wide standing freezer that sat next to my refrigerator of beer and held the door open wide. Inside were stacks of bagged greens, a six-foot-high, three-foot-deep compartment of them, fingers of lacy frost at their edges.

"See all this?" she said grandly, gesturing like Vanna White, her pride obvious.

"Sure," I said, puzzled. What was the deal? "I see."

"You know what this is?" The delight on her face was clear.

I had a few choices, none of them exciting. Collard greens. Mustard greens. Maybe spinach, maybe turnip. I settled on turnip.

"Turnip," I said, decisively.

"Fool!" she hollered so loud I jumped back. "You think I brought you here to show you turnip greens? You know what turnip greens look like, don't you?"

Yeah, I thought, exactly like that stuff in the bags. Another trick question.

"Sure," I said, jabbing my finger at the greens, testy now. "They look like *that,* for Christ's sake."

If it crossed my mind to wonder why we were talking about turnip greens at seven in the morning and wearing stupid-looking socks, I do not remember.

"I just can *not* believe you," she was saying. "Am I standing here dying showing you turnip greens? Is this what I'm doing?"

"Yeah."

"Do you think I'm crazy?"

I regarded the opportunity for what it was, a chance to tell the truth.

"I do," I said mildly.

She stomped her socked feet on the bare floor like a kid.

"No, no, no, no, no." She fussed, her voice rising. "This ain't no goddamned turnip greens, you fool. This is mare-ee-wah-nuh, child."

My head snapped back in the direction of the freezer.

"I grew it myself." Her words came at me slow and funny sounding, like she was talking through a kazoo. Had she said "marijuana"? Nah.

"In the backyard, for the nausea, the pain. Who wants to die addicted to morphine?"

Who has to? I thought.

"So I make tea with it. Mare-ee-wah-nuh tea." I loved the way she said it, like I had trouble hearing.

"Those stupid boys in the neighborhood pulled up my fig plant, thinking it was this, so I had to harvest quick. Before, I could just wander out and snip off a few leaves. Now I have to chip it with a pick."

I think my mouth was still hanging open. I know I was staring at her.

"How can I use all this? I can't. But you can. You can set yourself up real nice. I die, you get this and the Chevy."

Then she told me the exact street value of her stash. It hadn't been that long that I didn't realize I was staring at the down payment on a Ferrari.

"Whoa," I said. It was the only word that came out.

She eyed me, expecting more.

"I thought you wanted me to quit drinking?" I said lamely. My mind steamrolled ahead with the possibilities.

"Well, sure," she said, frustrated by my lack of enthusiasm. "Of course I do. And here's your ticket." She did the Vanna White thing again with her hand. "I don't want you to smoke it, honey. I want you to *sell* it, to the right people. This is money, child, green, frozen, pretty little bags of money." She grabbed a frosty Baggie and held it out to me. "This is your legacy, right here in this freezer. You can pay for your alcohol treatment with this."

I was still considering who the "right" people might be. The Tyson chicken family, maybe, someone local.

She was beaming, proud of herself. It pleased me to see her happy, her eyes bright, crazy white hair standing straight up, bag of dope in her skinny fingers, my aunt the drug pusher. It struck me then how the two of us must have looked, a couple of scrawny crazies dressed in men's cotton pajamas and Mary Jane socks, me with a beer in my fist at seven in the morning, Freda with the freezer door flung wide, standing in front of the best *Let's Make a Deal* door ever.

I laughed. Not the everyday chuckle, but the kind of laugh that sucks your sinuses flat, makes that vein stick out on your forehead and the muscles behind your ears hurt. I doubled over, slobbering.

"What's so funny?" I heard her through the din I was making and looked up to see her eyes wide with hurt. She meant it.

I couldn't breathe. I pounded my fist on the kitchen table, upsetting the beer. I didn't care. I tried to take a deep breath and then thought of Freda rolling a joint.

"Quit laughing!"

I couldn't breathe out. I tried. "You want me..." And then there was a sound like the scream from a grown man being beaten with a hammer.

"Say it," she said, huffy.

I tried again.

"You want me..."

I couldn't do it.

"Say it!" She stood with her hands on her hips, freezer door slammed shut, her face as red as if it had been boiled.

I took a deep breath. I concentrated on something tragic, like pancreatic cancer, like alcoholism. It didn't help.

"You want me..." I started off slowly, trying not to lose it, staring at the spilled beer on the table, picturing the wino in the painting. "You want me...to pay for detox with dope money. Is this what you're saying to me?"

"Well, sure." She looked relieved.

I crumpled to the floor. She was like nobody else.

"It's expensive, you know, alcohol treatment. I checked."

"Yeah," I said in between chokes. "Worth about twenty years in the state pen."

She looked worried and I felt instantly sorry for her.

"You'll go, won't you, honey? You'll go, right?"

I told her I would, meaning it. I'd never have an offer this good.

• • •

MY AUNT died that November, her ashes buried in the backyard, not far from the empty holes where her fig and marijuana plants had grown, close to the alley near the gospel church, where they still sing on Saturday night, their voices full as bellows with the wind of God Almighty. It's the way Freda put it once as she sat in the dark on the back stoop, listening, so I quote her here in remembrance, in honor. I remember her the way in which I remember certain moments of childhood, days at the river and the lake, bright, glazed, hard-as-diamond days when everything in the world looked absolutely right and there was not one single thing you could not do: swim, fly, ascend to the sun in an unbroken path because that is where you felt you belonged on those days, swallowed up in the very heart of all that brightness.

• • •

I DIDN'T use the drug money to get sober (numbered account, Switzerland), but that January, 1988, my best friend, Julie Rosten, took me to a hospital. There is no trick to how I got there, there was no Pollyana epiphany, no intervention by well-meaning souls, nothing more, really, than a deal struck with God at three in the morning on what St. John of the Cross called "the dark night of the soul," when some sort of divine spotlight was aimed at my life and I saw it the way they say you see it before you die; and in that quick, kaleidoscopic burn of images there appeared one that had lain waiting, biding its time, all those years, the one only a psychotic could conjure, the one that put me in the league of the criminally insane, and it was this: murder.

I would murder to drink, kill to quiet the panic, put a knife to the throat of anyone who kept me from it, and thrust.

Murder wearing the infinitely logical mask of self-preservation, and I knew I could do it as certainly as I knew my own name. Just like that I knew it, and there was no looking past what it was because there was not one thing beyond it. And in that same instant of knowing, there appeared the sliver of some bright thing, the barely audible beating of a hope that I could live some other way, and then the elusive but quickening belief that I could be borne across this deepening river.

There are ministers of grace for such occasions, an army of them who patrol even those darkest nights, waiting for that one moment when it all breaks apart and a soul is offered up for grabs. And they can smell surrender and they can take you past it. Call them angels of mercy. Call mine Julie. This infinitely polite, bordering-on-the-meek friend of mine who has been closer to me than my own family for over twenty years dragged me to the threshold of the gates of hell and pushed. I came to, to stark-raving consciousness, in the detox unit of a local hospital, where I took the cure, something that at first seems far nastier than the disease.

The bare truth of withdrawal is an ugly one. Lucky for me. Where once I had walked through the world lubricated and confident, I now retched and trembled. I had convulsions my second night in. On my fourth day in the special care ward I was given some broth, and I remember a nurse propping me up in front of the tray and working a spoon into my locked-down fist, her eyes averted as I shot the spoon out at the bowl and missed. I remember her feeding me. I remember bits of barley floating in the broth. I remember how it looked on the sheets when she rolled me over to change them. I remember my red flannel robe bleeding pink all over my body, through the sweats. I remember a card from Julie someone showed me. It read: "Dearest Original Lorian. Congratulations on 24 hours without a drink!" I remember weeping. I am not proud of this, of what I became, but I am not ashamed either. I see it all now as a matter of humbling, of falling so low, so hard, so deep you hold your head up once again merely because you can.

I have seen a black wind pour from the walls and streak into my lungs, strangling me. I have seen snakes drop from holes in the ceiling, watched scorpions clatter across tile floors, venom falling like yellow pearls from their stingers, and believed in the throes of alcoholic psychosis that I was Jesus Christ. I have felt my body rise up in convulsions and slam back down, limp and wet and ordinary. I have stared at my face in the mirror and seen the yellow eyes of a cat stare back, rabid, full of poison. I have heard the splitting timbre of hell and known it is a concoction of the mind, the nervous system gone haywire, and of the soul, riddled with holes. I have wanted to replace my blood with the pure fever that bore me up for fifteen years, and one day in a moment of absolute grace and clarity, I begged to be rid of it. Not timidly, but with the kind of full-throated rage that can kill—"Come on and save me, you fucking bastard," screamed in an empty room at three in the morning. When the doctor at the hospital asked if I wanted to be sober, I looked him in the eye and said, "Yes," meaning it more than I have ever meant anything. He told me when I came in I had maybe two weeks to live, and I said, "Wanna bet?"

The horrors of detox? There is no horror but what owned me when I walked through those doors. I arrived there possessed, and it was a nice, safe place but for the boiling hell of me. At one point my blood pressure was 210/200. The vessels in my eyes ruptured, my right arm went dead. Once, when no one was watching, I made it to a pay phone and called a man I had been seeing. I told him they were trying to kill me. They gave me little pills to ease the withdrawal. I thought they were poison. Someone said the food was good. I never kept it down. When they gave me clothes to wear instead of the green, institutional pajamas, I thought of creeping into the snowy January night, of begging for a drink at a bar whose red-and-green neon sign I could see from the window of my room. And if begging didn't work, I knew exactly what I could do. And knowing, I waited, trusted a little, tried to breathe.

It took them fourteen days to detox me—average time, three days—and after that I did a two-month stint in a women's facility. The truth is, I did this to myself. What's more, had I the power to reorder my life, obliterate any fiber of the past, touch the magic wand of absolution to my history, I would not. Had I not come to understand, in time, that pain exists to make you stronger, then I would have understood nothing at all. Had I been a woman immune to darkness I might never have fully appreciated the blood-quickening, bone-baking heat of a Southern summer day. It is the way I feel now: sober, alive, and warm, washed in possibilities.

For a year and a half my hands trembled and my heart raced and skipped beats, the yellow tide slowly receding from my face and eyes, but I did not have to pour a drink when I woke. I did not have to pour a drink at noon. I did not have to pour a drink before I slept. I did not have to pour a drink thirty-two times a day. That is the reality of it. Being free.

Chapter

SEVENTEEN

I PREFER THE confessional to the cross, figuring if I own to enough treachery I will be spared in a moment of mercy, like that bass in the ravine years before. When I quit drinking—finally—after years of uncommon buoyancy on sea as well as land, my liver shot, my eyes yellowed as the fish the alchemists used for insight—I quit the gonzo lifestyle. "Blind drunk" is not a phrase without meaning. To me it came to mean that I had been blind, almost irreparably, not only to the damage leveled in my own life, but to the life beneath those waters that had once come so frequently in dreams.

Dead cold sober now, I took up fly-fishing. Not on the same day, certainly, because the shakes rack you for a while and all you're really good for is mixing paint. It took me months—years, actually—to recover physically, a daily regimen of liquid B vitamins and massive carbohydrates my therapy.

It felt as if I hadn't eaten in years, and within a few months I was scarfing three full meals an evening. I recall eating a friend's entire pepperoni pizza while he was in the bathroom. I drank gallons of apple juice, craving the sugar, scores of hot turkey sandwiches piled high with mashed potatoes and stuffing, whole pies. My body seemed to burn the calories as quickly as I took them in, and it was a year before I gained twenty pounds. Muscles that had atrophied began to grow smooth and firm again. I had hair and fingernails now and a hunger for fresh air and water.

I'd held a fly rod only briefly during my fish-killing days, once to pass one to Jimmie Albright that day we fished for tarpon, and once or twice as I'd packed my own cheap fly rod, pointlessly, for a fishing trip. I had not tried, even once, to cast with the absurdly long pole, but I had watched people in the exercise. All that whipping and hauling and peering into the distance just reminded me of bad westerns.

But something happens when you get purified, take the cure, lob your body onto another plane of perception. Without a beer in hand, fly-fishing seemed far more appealing than it had when I'd been trolling with bait big enough to eat. And less exertion, yeah, than being chained and belted to a five-hundred-pound marlin. Back then I'd called the sport effete, elitist, prissy, pussy, wussy, wimpy. Get me going on the subject and I'd shoot back to my redneck roots, expound on the value of split shot and 1-aught hooks, plastic bobbers. If bait fishermen were bank maggots—I had been referred to as such, once, by a pod of white-water rafters—I theorized, then fly fishermen were wading wimps, the entire state of Montana wimp heaven, everybody there hefting custom fly rods, tiptoeing through the water.

Now in a completely altered state of mind, I began to notice the grace involved in a simple cast, how the arm of a good angler was merely an extension of the fly rod. I studied the art a little, secretly, feeling disloyal.

About the time I was reading Izaak Walton's *The Compleat Angler,* I got a call from Florida writer and fly-fishing guide Randy Wayne White asking me to fly-fish on his PBS fishing show, *On the Water.* Randy had yet to have a woman on his show and mentioned this to his friend Jeffrey Cardenas, who, in a gesture of forgiveness for the Michigan trip, suggested me. I didn't tell the man I couldn't cast spare change into the hand of a willing

Hare Krishna, much less fly cast for tarpon, which was what he had in mind.

"Sure," I told him, eager, as always, for a new opportunity to humiliate myself, "I've caught tarpon before," neglecting to mention it was with an orange Day-Glo bobber and a live mullet when I was ten sheets to the wind. Could I fish sober? I wanted to be prepared and figured with all I'd read recently on the subject I could learn the basics in half an hour of hands-on practice. Les Johnson, fish book author and a gifted angler, offered me a lesson in a downtown Seattle park. I confess to being impressed by the distance he achieved with his wet noodle line, but the physics behind it eluded me. I remember Les, who looks a little like a fleshed-out Wally Cox (similar falsetto), watching me with a sinking look on his face as I bullwhipped the rod back and forth, huffing and straining, producing nothing but nasty little BB-sized knots in the delicate tippet.

"You'd be murder with a hook on there," he said grimly. I thrashed and looped some more, snapping the line across his forehead. Ten minutes into my lesson I felt hopeless, the same way I had back in gym class when everyone could stand on their head but me.

"It just takes some practice," Les said, trying to reassure me. I imagined him rolling his eyes when he turned his head, mumbling to himself, "Yeah, right. Sure."

"But you can't go on TV like this, Lorian. Absolutely not."

I was soon sitting anchored off a mangrove island on Florida's Gulf coast with Randy. Randy Wayne White is what you would call a burly man, built like a fireplug, with forearms the girth of oak saplings, an image that belies his physical grace, and particularly his ability with a fly rod. He is also a humble and infinitely kind man who would never think of pointing out your inadequacies.

"Where'd you learn to cast, Lorian?" he was asking politely as he grinned into the sun and the PBS camera, while I whizzed a live pilchard past his head. He hadn't seen me fly cast yet because I'd begged off after watching Randy sail his line eighty feet toward a school of feeding redfish. The man was grace in motion, his massive arm snapping the rod and line back with calculated precision, then dropping it just right on the follow-through. Nah, I told myself after watching a redfish pounce the fly, this won't do. I was out of my element entirely, beerless, baitless, naked.

"I never did learn," I told him, my back to the camera as I slung another pilchard into the mangroves. "Amazing, isn't it," I said, "what you can teach yourself?" Randy nodded, his eyes losing hope. This exchange never survived the edited version of the show's tape, and in subsequent shots the camera gently panned away into the mangroves, or to the pelicans flying above, as I cast upside down and reeled backwards, dragging whole mangrove tubers boatside.

I should mention that the show did not have a whopping budget. The first sign of this was when the cameraman, aka the producer, aka the sound guy, to spare the expense of an additional boat, rode along with us on *our* tiny boat. We were jammed in together, hips to camera lens, poles poking ribs, ice chest as intrusive as a sectional sofa, and the guy was able to get shots of Randy and me only from the rear of the boat, featuring precisely that portion of our anatomy. Randy and I carried on whole conversations with our butts to the audience.

"Turn around so I can see you," the producer would instruct us every now and then, the same thing fathers say when they're filming really stupid home movies. And we'd turn around, flinching at the Hiroshimalike flash of sunlight off the camera lens, grinning idiotically, our poles clasped in front of us, line trailing over our shoulders.

Another bonus was that each day out on the boat I had to wear the exact same clothes as I'd worn the day before, to give the illusion of this being one long unbroken day on the water.

By day two my shorts were crusty with bait juice and my tank top sweat stained as we headed out in Randy's flats boat for the coast of Boca Grande, where scores of tarpon were rolling on the surface of the water. The seas were choppy that day, the wind steady. I felt a little queasy without the beer that had eased my stomach for years. As I stood tipping in the boat, trying to get my bearings, Randy slapped a custom saltwater fly rod into my hand and said, "Go for it, Lorian!"

Go for what? I remember thinking. For what, for Christ's sake? It was enough in a ten-foot chop on a three-foot-wide boat to merely right myself and stand there lurching starboard, portside, fore, and aft, like one of those sand-weighted plastic clowns that lean *wa-ay* over but never quite go down. I viewed the wallowing tarpon at eye level and imagined offering my lunch as chum into the churning water.

"There're hundreds of them, Lorian. Go ahead and cast," Randy called from the stern.

I think I pulled maybe six inches of line from the reel, prepared—what the hell?—to show my ineptitude, before I noticed the particular leaden quality of the sky just north, south, east, and west of us, as Randy yelled, "Two o'clock. Tarpon at two o'-clock!"

The sky at two o'clock looked like midnight, with the occasional atomically bright lightning bolt shearing the blackness.

I'm no fan of lightning while in an open boat, no fan of lightning while wearing a rubber suit in a six-foot-deep cellar. It's a phobia of mine—call it silly—one that's rampant, unchecked, paralyzing. I've been shocked more times than a career lineman—once by a ball of St. Elmo's fire as I drove with my elbow out the window down Florida's Turnpike. If electricity is nearby, it will find me. If it is in Australia, it will find me. Put me in an orchestra pit with a dead car battery and I am, instantly, the conductor. There are people, I've heard, whose electrons are aligned just so, electric eels in human bodies, who give off a faint smell of ozone. I am one of these.

Graphite, my head said, you're holding a goddamned graphite rod. *Put it down.*

What they don't tell you about fly rods is that they're superb electrical conductors, right up there with copper. I chucked the rod in Randy's direction, hit the deck, and yelled "Drive!" about the time a bolt struck just off the bow and the air turned crispy crackly with electricity. I could feel the hair on my neck and arms rise up.

I spent the beat-your-kidneys-to-Jell-O ride back to shore face down in the boat, my nails dug deep into Randy's calf, hissing Hail Marys as lightning popped in the water around us.

"Tomorrow I'll give you a casting lesson," Randy told me after we docked safely at Cedar Key and I wandered around randomly kissing the ground, his hand, the cheeks of strangers, stunned to be alive.

"Like fun," I said.

Day three. I had spent the night before on Cedar Key, refusing to make the long boat ride back to Fort Myers in the dark, a flashlight our only beacon. As I sat in the boat that day, wearing the same bait-juice shorts, which could probably walk without me in them, same once-black tank top, gray now with sweat and salt water and reeking of pilchard, I worried that I'd blown the show for Randy. This day, Randy said, we'd take it easy, stay in close to the mangroves, go for snook and redfish. I did catch a snook after an unbelievable, within-a-hair's-breadth cast tight up along the mangroves, forgetting in a moment of "fish on" psychosis how to reel. I didn't pump and pull, but stood with my legs locked at the knees, spinning the handle on the reel while the line whined out, *scree! scree!* and Randy said, "Here, darlin', let me help you." Something clicked then, a remembered talent from my soggy days, and I snapped to and began to fight the fish the way I'd always fought fish, just an inch, no more, half an inch will do, lowering the rod as I reeled, pulling to get some slack on him. As I eased him alongside the boat I noticed the beautiful black barred flanks of the snook. My first fish sober. On bait, what else?

I watched the sky like a scout for the National Hurricane Center, sneakers braced against the bow of the boat while the cameraman got different angles on my butt. Randy asked a few probing questions about my life, and for reasons still unknown to me I decided to answer them, waxing eloquent on fishing, writing, alcoholism—you name it. There was no shutting me up. As I stood with my back to the camera, mouth moving at a gallop, the wire of the mini microphone clipped to my crusty shirt, I waved my arms wildly and gestured with the passion of what I was saying. In my gut I knew this was great material and felt vaguely redeemed, as if this monologue from the pulpit of a boat bow made up for my so-so angling. And I liked Randy. I wanted to do well for him.

When I was done the cameraman yelled, "Great. Terrific. I got it all. This'll make a great show."

That afternoon Randy, the cameraman, and I parted with some backslapping and sighs of gratitude that we would never have to see one another again before we died, and I returned to my motel to pack.

That night I got a call from the cameraman/producer/sound guy/editor, who informed me that the audio portion of my righteous fish-imitates-life speech was lost. They'd gotten my butt on tape, but not what I'd said.

"Would you," came the timid voice, "consider coming to the studio tomorrow morning and trying to recreate what you said?"

"I'd rather drive nails through my feet," I told him.

"Well sure," he said, "but would you wear the same clothes." He hung up before I got my mouth to work.

The result of this voice-over is something that makes the dubbed version of *Godzilla* look in sync. In the final tape I stand at the bow of the boat, mute, arms flailing wildly. But as my lips begin to move real quick and my head tosses from side to side, there is silence. I look like someone in the cruel, final throes of St. Vitus's dance.

As I watched the tape in the studio room with Randy I slid down the wall I leaned against, limp with hysteria, my eyes watering as I watched a scene of me diving for the bottom of the boat as lightning cracked Fellinilike over the water. "Shit! Are we hit?" comes an unidentified voice. Fade to black and then a shot of me with a fifty-pound mangrove tuber on. Then a close-up of a big, oily stain on the seat of my shorts. Then the final serious, thoughtful moments, my shirt gray and nasty looking as the sky, my erratic, impassioned movements accompanied now by the calm, bored, I-don't-give-a-shit voice they'd gotten on tape that morning.

"Yeah," I say, stifling a yawn, "I . . . like . . . fishing," and my arm shoots out, arrowlike, toward the horizon. "It's . . . cool."

"What'd you do," Randy asked, eyeing me, "take a Valium before you came in?"

This was my television debut. My fishing career finally portrayed in all its seedy glory. My one shot at the front page of the *Pine Bluff Commercial*. "We're calling it *How's Fishing in Hell?"* Randy said as he handed me a copy of the video. They never did get the tape in sync.

Chapter

EIGHTEEN

IT TOOK A while before I could look at a fly rod again without itching to buy life insurance. But my old dreams had begun to return, coming with the frequency they had in youth, this time of pink speckled trout in blue streams, less threatening than tarpon in boiling black water, and I thought, Sure, that's where I belong, in a trout stream wearing waders and a nifty vest displaying hand-tied flies, maybe a telescoping depth wand strapped at my hip, Swiss army knife dangling from that ring on the vest pocket. That's me all right, the Orvis girl. And since I figured you don't have to be a ballerina to dance, I took up casting again, practicing in my backyard—and a one, and a two—secretive and clumsy, the cat my only witness. Even early on, when I was first learning, the rhythm of the cast matched up with the rhythm my life had taken on. Don't ask me why, but fly-fishing just fit being sober. It was steady. It was even. You had to breathe through it. You had to be aware.

I had married again, after a ten-year break from the sport, and would divorce again in seven years, to another man whose name began with *J*—a Jeff this time, last name Fischer, ahem—and whose tether to a sober life was of the same fiber as my own. Ten years younger than I, he was, people said, a nice "catch," and I pictured him sometimes, wiggling, a 1-aught hook snagged in his pouty lower lip. Somewhere around my fortieth birthday he gave me a fly rod and reel, complete with weight-forward line, and I took to the business of learning to cast as earnestly as I take to anything, which means if I don't master it on the second or third try, I quit, cross my arms over my chest, and glare. I had achieved midbeginner status (capable of placing the fly on the water by wadding the line in my fist and chucking it hard) when Jeff and I took a trip to the Salmon River in Idaho. I had taken fish there years before, six-pack in hand, spinning gear in the other, dragging the rocks—twenty-four trout in half a day, one of my finest hours, but drunk when I did it, so maybe the count's off by half. I wanted to return to make amends, to take a trout clean and easy without the heavy artillery.

I also wanted to show this brave new world to Jeff, a man I'd met after I'd quit drinking, who had reminded me, with his boyishness and irrational optimism, of Les. He enjoyed the outdoors in the same way I did, and his tilt on life was a lot less fatalistic. Before we met he had not fished since he was fourteen years old, a pathetic circumstance I remedied by taking him on a trout outing on one of our first dates, a big fat mistake that left me fishless and cranky and Jeff weighted down with a stringerful as we made our way back to camp. I understand now, with a sometimes powerful resentment, that from the very first time together on the water, the man stole my fish luck.

Jeff's new passion for fishing metamorphosed quickly from pastime to a when-do-we-go, when-do-we-go frenzy that frequently woke me from a dead sleep at three in the morning and had me on the water, yawning, by five. He mastered the intricacies of fly casting in an afternoon while I continued to belly out line like a rube, ripping the occasional body part, and once putting the fly dead center through a hoop earring and snagging my armpit. And my casts, if they made it past my nose, always landed in a limp pool a mere foot or two in front of me. This criminal lack of grace had no place in my new life, and I quickly developed a seething competitiveness with Jeff, occasionally filing down the points on his hooks.

"Lost that one," he'd say, walking up wet from the river, bummed.

"Huh," I'd say. "That's tough."

The Salmon is a beautiful stretch of water, clear, relatively shallow, and fast, unlike the slow, clay-weighted waters of Mississippi. When I first moved to the Northwest I had been amazed you could see so deeply into water and would sit for hours on a river shore staring at the rocks beneath. Jeff, on the other hand, a Washington State native, grew up with this purity, which may explain why it seems to be in his blood to fish these waters, and fish them well, in fact better than anyone has a right to. He has the sort of luck with a fly rod that I used to have with bait.

Our first day on the river I'd waded in bare legged and was fishing generally the same area of water as Jeff, but politely upstream so the fish would get to me first, when his luck (he calls it skill) kicked in. He had released six fish before I'd even gotten my fly damp. Normally I handled such flagrant displays with stoicism, wanting to keep my image as a good sport intact, but this day was different. I had returned to waters that, in my mind, belonged to *me* and that had blessed me with uncanny luck, waters that had kindly not swallowed me whole as I staggered through them, and all I wanted was that brief, immortal contact with aliens, the way I'd known it when I was a kid, new and simple. I thought of nothing else that day but taking a fish on a fly. I'd read A. J. and Norman. I'd gone to the outdoor shows. Nothing seemed more perfect or vital than the feel of a trout on the end of that nerve-sensitive line. I'd felt how mere water current could electrify the line, transforming it to a buzzing high-voltage wire, and I wanted some of that magic.

"Yee-ha!" I heard Jeff yell from downriver as he released another flashing form into the water.

I false-cast and hooked my chin.

I could feel them all around me, the sense of them, fish moving the current in swirls around my bare ankles, fish swimming between my thighs. I inched my way in Jeff's direction, uncertain on the slippery rocks, watching his fly thread out before him and then drop like a whisper onto the water.

I got within twenty feet of the man and flung my line in an awkward side cast—to date the only cast that wasn't life-threatening—right where I had seen his last fish surface. I waited. I prayed. I watched. I peered. Nothing.

Jeff was always someone who took athletic grace for granted, figuring it's something we all can achieve in time.

"Your presentation's wrong," he told me.

Had I read about this? I searched my memory.

"My what?" I said, coming up blank.

"The way you're putting the fly down. It's wrong."

Well, what the hell? It was enough, I thought, to get the fly on the water. Who could resist after that? And when did fish get so picky, worrying about presentation, the particular color of a hackle? With worms there had been no guesswork. Eat this tasty sucker, you cretin, I was thinking as I fingered a rubber worm I'd stashed in my vest pocket.

"Fish are color-blind," I said with some authority, apropos of nothing.

"So?" he said in that way he has that tells he's already written a book about it.

To illustrate presentation, Jeff whipped off another perfect cast. A trout rose to his fly, and bingo, the water around us was alive. I hated him.

"Maybe it's my fly," I said.

I waded over to him and switched rods, thinking, OK, you, give me that magic wand. We'll see who catches fish.

"Yours casts so easily," he said as he set the line in motion.

Snap. Wham. The fish shot up out of the water like a barracuda and hit the fly in midair.

"Nothing's wrong with your fly," he told me as he released the biggest trout of the day.

"That's it," I said, stomping toward shore as gracefully as possible in four feet of water. I'd snatched my rod from him and I threw it on the bank when I emerged, soaked and cold, as pissed as I'd ever been.

"I thought you were a good sport," I heard him calling from the river.

There, I'd blown it. Years of cultivating an image, gone.

"Go to hell," I yelled. "You go straight to hell, you and your stupid fly rod, you jinx. Put a worm on there, asshole, we'll see who the fish like, huh, won't we? Bet you couldn't catch a catfish on stink bait. Huh? Bet you couldn't. Jinx! Ever since I've fished with you I've caught nothing. Not one goddamned thing. You took all my luck and now you flit around like you *own* the river. Well, you don't. It's *my* river. *Mine,* you hear? I'll never fish with you again. I swear to God. Never!"

I sat down on the bank and stomped my feet, hands clenched into fists at my sides, my heartbeat clearly audible in my forehead. I'd heard about people like me. Lousy sports. Whiners. Lunatics.

"It's just your *technique."* The wind carried his words so that "technique" seemed to be underlined, and I shouted back, "Eat your technique. Eat it, you hear!"—the comeback of a five-year-old, but it felt good anyway.

It was then I saw the naked man in the raft drifting past, fly rod poised in midair. Ordinarily naked would have been enough—and it was *strange* enough—but as I watched more closely I noticed he was throwing his rod tip *up* to twelve o'clock and then waiting a beat before following through with the forward cast. During that beat the line straightened out behind him, unfurling slowly as he brought the rod forward. Again he cast, my own personal naked instructor, oblivious to me on the bank, and again with the same hesitation. Some technique, I thought, peering in Jeff's direction to see if he'd noticed the man. Nah. Naked women could have been skydiving into a bull's-eye on his head and he'd have kept on casting. I watched the man spin out another perfect length of line and discovered my arm moving involuntarily, following his motions.

I watched his wrist. Hardly a bend in it as he pointed the rod arrow-straight in the direction of the unfurling line. At that moment something settled into place, the way it did that one time I bowled a strike, and I saw the whole process, not as frantic thrashing and whipping, but as one liquid motion, seamless and intact. It was the way, I thought, I should have always fished, naked, tethered to the water by a floating umbilicus, aware.

I spent the rest of the day practicing on a dirt back road, heaving that line at first as if it were a shotput. When it would drop in a dead puddle at the end of my rod I'd try again, remembering the vision of that man in the raft, his perfect rhythm, the way he seemed to notice nothing but his line as it spun out above the water. I kept trying against what I considered rather hefty odds until I had my line singing in the air and pulling out the slack around my feet as if it were ribbon shot from a rifle. I grew calm from the effort, a way I'd not remembered being for years. I looked at my hands, steady as rocks, as they rose above my head, left hand experimenting with a double haul. Hey, I thought, I might get good at this.

That evening at dusk I caught my first fish on a fly, a beauty I watched rise in a quick thrash, greedily, as if he'd been waiting all day for my one ratty fly, frayed and battered from the day's practice, but oddly noble. It's all I wanted, that one fish, electric on the end of my line, and, God, how I could feel him, his jumpy on-and-off current carrying all the way up my arm. How do you do? I felt like saying; it's been a long time. I wet my hand and cradled his girth in my palm. Such a nice feeling. Moist, alive, not slimy the way we're taught to think. I pulled some water through his gills and released the fly from his lip, delicately, no sweat, and watched as he fluttered and then dove in a quick zigzag, deep into the stream. For an instant I remembered the delicate feel of the baby bass as I slopped him into the jar of river water, then the fish gods, white and huge, circling the perimeter of the pond, aware, perhaps, of nothing more than the rhythm their movement created; and in that instant, I too, here in the clear water of an Idaho stream, understood rhythm, but as if it were the steady beat of childhood fascination returned.

In my new dream there is the same dark pool from childhood but its expanse reaches from the very tip of my feet to the horizon in all directions, its surface flat as undisturbed bathwater, the shapes beneath it perfectly formed now, truly fishlike and sharply defined, the tails like so many geisha fans slapping left and then right in unison, a metronomic rhythm setting forth visible currents beneath the water that never break the calm glassiness above. I marvel at the dance, watch the fish line up, nose to tail, in a perfect circle, swimming faster and faster. I look to my empty hands and realize my ex-husband stands to my left ready to make a cast with my new white lightning rod. I say, "Give it to me. Now," and cast a Royal Coachman out to Jesus. "Come on, boy," I call across the pond, "walk on water for me." The fly taps the skin of the water, and the circle of fish shatters like beads in a kaleidoscope, bathing me in light.

Chapter

NINETEEN

THOSE WHO observe your life often have the keenest insight. Where you cannot, through guilt or treachery or both, strip back the bark to the smooth, resilient fiber beneath, they can. And they can name what's good in you still, even though you'd deny it, and what's vital. In a letter Jeffrey Cardenas wrote to me after I got sober, he said, "You can go into the mountains now with your daughter, Lorian, you can fish with her and teach her what you know. There's nothing holding you back any longer. You can do this again. It's all possible now."

I have fished with my daughter on a stretch of the Alsea River in Oregon that runs through vine maple forest where moon dollar beams of light spot the forest floor, the pattern shifting with the wind. In autumn the leaves bleed scarlet and the air is tinted pink with the refraction of all that red. High in the trees pileated woodpeckers knock out a beat and red-tailed hawks glide above the canopy. I have watched them snatch sparrows from their roosts and dive to earth with the tiny birds cinched in their talons, shielding them from jailbreak with their enormous, outspread wings. The death tent, I call it. It is, as David James Duncan put it, bird-watching as blood sport.

There are flat boulders in the Alsea, low, smooth tables of rock from which you can cast in all directions, pockmarked like the deep ravine in Mississippi after the floods. Where the river spills over the rocks, clear as springwater, it settles in the gullies, miniature lakes where tiny fry zip from side to side, relieved for a moment, it seems, to be borne into this calm place. I have lain upon these cool rocks with my daughter, our eyes aimed at the sky, and understood how a refuge, however brief, is the bedrock upon which lives are shored. I have also understood, in these moments, that the young woman who lies beside me could well have been lost to me and that I owe her the respect I would owe one who has been through a war and come out with an *understanding* not only for her mother, but for the white flag waved at daybreak.

Cristen took her first camping trip when she was two years old, outfitted in tiny hiking boots and bib overalls, her long hair done up in pigtails to keep it from catching in the branches as she tipped and toddled through the brush, head aimed half a foot ahead of her feet. She was a true outdoors girl, her senses saturated by the humid green of the woods, the thick, pliant overlay of the forest floor, thinking of it all as one great rural toilet, dropping her pants and squatting whenever it suited her, and when we returned to the city, never quite comprehending that you were not free to do in Safeway parking lots what you so freely did in the woods. She caught her first fish when she was four or five, a Dolly Varden big enough to fill two skillets. We cooked it over a campfire on the lakeshore and I picked the carcass clean for her, tossing the bones into the fire. I remember Cris and her friend Michael on that trip, a black boy her same age with skin the color of oil-stained walnut, the two of them running shirtless by the lake, drunk on the light air of summer, the blazing sticks they'd held to the fire raised high in their fists like torches, the circles they made with them cutting neon *O*s in the night.

There was the fishing trip we took when her Donald Duck sandal slipped from her foot into the fast, eddying waters of the Stillaguamish and bounced downstream in a wreath of foam as

Cris stood purple-faced on the rocky shore, howling. Faced with the loss of a favorite possession, she became a foghorn of inconsolability. Unwavering and relentless in her demands that the thing be found or repaired, she turned into a sawed-off version of Joe E. Lewis, her mouth working like a horror movie rubber mask. Buying a new thing just like the old thing would not do. I stalked the sandal the way I now stalk trout, but faster, diving deep into the brambles body first whenever I spotted the blue-and-yellow Day-Glo shoe jet-skiing past. I remember a small brown bear on the far riverbank eyeing me curiously as I crashed past, wondering maybe if this was the way wild humans stalked their prey, cursing and lunging for the water only to come up empty handed. A mile or so downriver I spotted the inscrutable face of Donald Duck snagged on a low branch that hung above the bulldozing water. I returned by a wood's path, scratched, bloodied, and exhausted, to my now-pacified kid, who said, simply, ignoring my open wounds, "Thanks, Mom. I knew you'd find it."

We camped by the glacial runoff of the Carbon River once, my friend Mary, her son Michael, Cris, and I, roasting hot dogs over a fire built on the riverbed, watching meteors streak the dark sky. Past midnight we bedded down, the kids snoring the minute they hit their sleeping bags. Not long after, Mary and I heard the distinct crunch of boots near our camp and peered through the tent flap to spy four men with shotguns creeping through the woods by the beam of a single flashlight. "Poachers," Mary whispered, and in ten minutes we had the kids packed up, shoving them in the backseat of the car like sacks of groceries, still fast asleep, and our headlights aimed north toward Seattle. On the way we talked about how pissed they'd be to wake up in their own beds, cheated out of a camping trip they'd looked forward to for weeks. So we pitched the tent in my backyard and slipped them in, two thirty-pound sacks of flour, unaware. The next morning Mary and I sat on the back stoop and watched as Cris crawled from the tent and stood bewildered, blinking in the early morning sun. "Hey, Mike," she called into the tent, "the river's gone."

When we moved to Little Torch Key we fished each day in

the pond while the swaggering, never-say-no-to-bait white heron edged in closer to our bag of pilchard, stabbing the sandy ground angrily with its sharp-pointed bill, the same thief who'd ripped off my Swiss army knife. I told Cris once, fed up with the heron stalking us, that it would be the star of a new Disney movie.

"What's it called?" she asked as she cast across the pond, close in to the seawall where snapper hovered.

That Goddamned Bird, I told her.

I have pictures of Cris on Little Torch, dressed in a print sundress, her cheeks the color of autumn leaves by the Alsea, holding two hefty mangrove snapper, one in each splay-fingered hand, grinning. Bored at times with the fishing, she would make tiny, intricate villages of shells glued to pieces of driftwood, street markers affixed with toothpicks to the wood, colored bits of paper attached with Key West street names: Caroline, Whitehead, Petronia, Duval. She was a busy kid, rarely without big plans. Each night after the fish supper she never grew tired of, we would play radio talk show, a game she'd dreamed up in which she was the talk show host, dressed in an ascot and Groucho Marx glasses—her disguise, she called it—and I was her guest, the world-renowned fishing expert.

"So tell me, Miss Hemingway," she would ask in her professional-sounding peep of a voice, "just why do you fish?"

She'd fix me with a penetrating stare, chin cupped in her palm, cobalt blue eyes unblinking, and I'd try not to giggle at how she looked in the glasses, her lower lip covered in mustache.

"Well. Because it's there," I'd say, rattled a little by her intensity, forgetting for a moment that I was talking to my kid.

"And why, *exactly,* is it there, Miss Hemingway? I have to ask."

"I don't know. You tell me."

"Because," she'd begin, drawing herself up to her full height of three and a half feet, her palms turned up in a you-got-me gesture, "it's *there.* What else can I say?"

Or there were hours of magic shows, Cristen wearing her tall, Abe Lincoln hat with the wide black brim, shuffling cards with her tiny hands, saying, "Pick a card, any card." She had flash paper in her box of magic tricks that she would light under my nose while I slept. I'd wake to a blaze like a grenade gone off and bolt screaming from the bed, hands covering my eyes.

"Gotcha," I'd hear her say in the quick, purple-dotted blackness that followed.

Or she'd leave little yellow Post-it notes with the message BEWARE 666—THE MARK OF THE BEAST! stuck to the back of my pillow, the cradle of the phone receiver, inside the refrigerator, stuck to a bottle of beer. Nothing distilled the nature of the poison more than Cris's damp, crinkle-edged warning, and nothing told me more clearly that my kid knew her mother was a drunk. But we didn't talk about it. I pretended she didn't notice. She pretended she didn't notice, except for once when I said I was going to the store for beer and cigarettes, and her response—"Just the necessities, huh, Mom"—made me realize that my denial had an expiration date, and that to take this child down with me was not only cruel, but punishable by a different, less forgiving God.

In Idaho she learned to let a cast run with the current and to retrieve, smoothly, with steady, even pressure, the wild trout that ran thick in the river in spring. She knew the names of the lures she used by heart and would recite them in a redneck litany as I pointed to them in the tackle box: Buzz Bomb, Rooster Tail, Crocodile, Spinning Devil, Flat Fish, Blue Fox. She liked the names of them and the images they gave her and sometimes lectured me on my own tackle, shaking her head no at a particular spoon, a certain-sized hook. There are pictures of her then, too, Cris with a string of fourteen trout, the fast, shallow river behind her, pole and fish held high, a look of sheer triumph on her young face.

On a trip to a Northwest river once we foraged for crickets in the tall grass and used them as bait, Cris flinching as she drove the hook point through the hard body. After that we kept them as pets, Cris mortified when they sometimes ate their own. Every evening, as dusk came on, their jumpy song would rise from the jar and we'd pretend we were camping, the moon rising high above the water as the crickets sang.

We had fine times, but there came a time when I grew steadily sicker, and Cris suffered then, too. I have tried to imagine her confusion, her sense of betrayal at having had a mother who each year was missing another piece and who had slipped so far away she couldn't help but believe that, soon, I would die. And not die in the ordinary way, with some fiber of dignity, but used up, wasted, and pathetic. Once I was sober it was not so hard to understand. I had known these same things; fear, worry, anger, shame, the late-night praying for my mother's life, and eventually, a consuming hatred for the fact that she had never truly lived. That was the tragedy of it, for her to have dissolved into nothing, the breath, the blood still in her. But you couldn't tell. It was this legacy I finally saw for what it was, the black still-beating heart of it; and all the things I had sworn I would never be, I had become. When I told my daughter I was an alcoholic—not that I had the flu, not that there was something wrong with my blood that they could not fix, not all the lies I had told to keep myself floating just one more hour, but the truth in its irredeemable shame, that I was a drunk (a word I could not speak for years because the starkness of it was too ugly, too real), knowing I had to own up to her of all people—she had said, "No. I don't believe you." And I knew then there had been no other way for her to answer. I ask her now if it was true that she did not believe, and she tells me no, looking back on it she can see it clearly. I ask for this clarity daily, that I, too, should not forget it as it was.

When I was six months sober and Cris had just turned seventeen, we were in Key West together, pushing down Duval Street with the rest of the tourists, trying to ignore the snorkeling-trip hawkers on every corner, the guys who want to get you out in twelve-foot seas and strap a suction cup to your face. We passed a bench where a dirty, sun-blistered man lay, shoeless, shirtless, chest sunk in, belly protruding, his hand outstretched for change. His arms trembled, the sign of the full-time drinker drying up. I glanced at the man, knew why he wanted money, and kept on walking. A moment passed and I felt Cris pulling at my arm.

"What?" I said, catching the look in her eyes, a searching of mine that made me uncomfortable.

"That man," she said. "He needs money."

"He'll just use it to drink," I told her, the arrogance of what I was saying coming up on me quick, so I felt like ducking and running.

"Don't you remember, Mom?" she said, still looking down. "He *needs* it. You remember what it was like, don't you? He needs it."

There was only one way she could have known a truth this dark.

I looked at the man, at his hand twitching as it hung off the bench, and burst into tears there on Duval Street as people pushed past us, looked back for a moment, and then moved on.

"What the fuck are you staring at?" Cris asked them, moving in close to me.

I walked back to the man, knelt beside him, and felt the heat from the pavement hit me like a furnace blast. I folded a wad of bills into his hand, felt the current running through him, that electric zap of nerves gone haywire. He looked up at me, eyes red and yellow, the flesh of his cheeks a clot of broken veins, and there was relief in his look because he knew the reprieve was coming, those few hours when everything would seem right again, and he'd think it had been someone else's skin that had been crawling, someone else's body that had jerked and thrashed, someone else's nightmare. I told him what I knew about it. "I quit," I said. "You won't believe this, but if I can, anyone can." He looked doubtful, in fact he looked on the verge of being pissed with me, maybe handing the money back. I gave him the number of a place in town anyway, said, "Call if you want help. I mean it." He never did, but I've learned some do. You take chances.

I walked back to Cris, who stood there smiling, people in Hawaiian-print shirts flanking her in a moving stream, and for a moment we saw each other for what we could become.

I tell this young, beautiful woman, whom I cannot believe was born of me, the names of trees and plants when we are out together in the woods. She nods dutifully, pretending to listen, far more interested in the rocks at her feet, slipping them into her pockets until there are so many she rattles when she walks. For her frequent journeys—six months in Europe, countless train, plane, and bus trips across the country (she is a traveler)—I give her a rock to keep in her pocket, and once a sweet gum ball from a tree in Freda's yard and a boll of cotton from a field outside Altheimer. Once, when she returned a coat she had borrowed, the sweet gum ball and rock were still there, worn and smooth as the cotton.

She asks me the names of rocks, expecting me to know.

"I don't know," I tell her, "but they're cool."

She nods as if this is elemental wisdom.

She is a natural fly caster, my girl, graced with the gazelle limbs of her father, the quick eye that adjusts a mistake immediately. When I gave her her first casting lesson, by the Alsea, confident enough now in my own ability to pass along the basics, I was faced with another Jeff, an athletic wizard who studied every move I made and then improved on it.

"Look at this," I had called to Jeff as he trudged up wet from the river, pointing to Cris arcing her line with unmistakable talent. "Look at what she's learned in half an hour. It took me a year to do this."

"Means you're a good teacher," Jeff said, being kind.

Eventually Cris and I decided to plan a trip across the country. I will take her to the ravine in Jackson, show her the baby bass that have come back thirty years after a tornado tore the length of the tributary. I will open this one unbroken window of my childhood and watch her gaze into it, imagining her mother as she once was, caught in the quickening pulse of wind and light and the brimming life of a mud hole. We will go on a hunt for the albino catfish pond, where the fish gods must be monsters now, white as alabaster, tracing circles, one upon the other, that by their unbroken paths are familiar, comforting.

Chapter  TWENTY

A FEW YEARS ago I wrote a novel that began with a scene in that Mississippi ravine. The book had nothing to do with fishing, but in it was the legacy of rivers that had moved through my life. I titled the novel *Walking into the River,* completely ignorant at the time of the nationwide fly-fishing mania that had arrived on the heels of the film version of *A River Runs Through It*. I had even chosen my book's epigraph from Norman Maclean's work—"Eventually all things merge into one, and a river runs through it"—long before the film was on the horizon.

After publication, I went on a small book tour. To the uninitiated this stumbling blindly into the realm of Stephen King and Anne Rice fans is the ultimate test of ego. If you emerge from the experience with even a shred of self-worth, you are in the wrong business. For first-timers, like myself—the unknowns who must carry a stun gun to get an audience's attention—it can be the definitive humbling experience of a lifetime.

My publisher had set up some signings for me, most in the Seattle area, where I live, and I came to know quickly that at signings normal rules of modesty do not apply. You have to be "out there," as my agent put it, which for me feels a little like having a root canal on the Oprah show, all former, socially accepted patterns of behavior now of no use at all. Forget you were taught not to say, on a whim, "I am the greatest living writer since Faulkner." You learn not only that you can do this, but that people expect you to be a self-absorbed asshole. While I am not exactly retiring, I do tend to keep my mouth shut in large crowds, but could be found at one point during the tour, on a particularly dismal sales day, outside a bookstore in New Orleans, shouting to passersby, "Goddamn! Buy this book!" I wish I were making this up. At the beginning of a tour you start out strong, feeling, for the most part, that what you've written is right up there with the Bible, and then you fizzle down to nothing, the will to sell, sell, sell the only remaining honorable instinct.

It is painfully obvious to anyone who enters the bookstore or mall in which you sit at some pathetic card table, books stacked twenty deep at your elbows, that you are there to push something. Normal human reaction to this is for them to put about two hundred yards between them and you. They have a sixth sense that you see them, not as an attractive blonde in a red jacket, not as a tall, handsome European, but as twenty bucks with feet. This is true. You spend your time at the table—and you have lots of it, requests that you sign your book about as frequent as locust plagues—figuring in your head, or on a calculator you slip from your purse, how much every single goddamned book in print, if each and every American buys one, will bring you, come royalty time—*after* you pay off the publisher's advance, the agent, the IRS, the likelihood of all three occurring in your lifetime negligible. The incentive for writing the book, which had once been lofty and spiritual, has now turned the color of money. After hours of sitting at the table, books unbought, back muscles locked into a fist, nicotine levels at an all-time low, mood foul, you don't give a flying rat's ass if anyone cares if you can write. You hope to God by then that they will buy the book simply because they like your shoes.

There is, however, one particular signing that I have, for no other reason than for its sheer bizarreness, committed to memory. It took place at a snooty Brentano's (read: *book hell*) in Seattle. In the bookstore window was taped an index card announcing my arrival at high noon, reminding me vaguely of shoot-out time. The card could have come straight from the microfiche files at the local library, so cramped and tiny was the print. Inside the store a card table was set up, its top scarred by cigarette burns, coffee stains, newspaper ink, a similar index card taped flat to it with my name and the book title written in teeny-weeny letters. To have deciphered who I was and why I was here you would have had to possess powers of horizontal levitation and the retinal gifts of Superman.

A few books lay unstacked on the table. The first time I had seen my book on a bookstore shelf, I had wept, partly out of relief that I had seen this thing through to the end, but mainly because it looked so alone, just a simple, dark-looking book swallowed up by all the bright, attention-grabbing covers.

I remember one of the clerks at the bookstore saying to another clerk, after I'd been lashed to the table for half an hour or so, idle, the decision to pick my nose in public a distinct possibility, as I watched wary customers file past: "Oh. So she's here to sell herself, is she?" I had the definite sense then of my blood heating up, my face going red, and something as dangerous as pride kicked in. I sat up straighter, tossed my head back, snorted once like a horse, and glared at the woman. She would have no clue who she's messing with, I thought as I eyed her. In my drinking prime I'd gone after people with broken bottles for cracks like this. "Bitch," I said loud enough for her to hear. A few customers snapped their heads around. I smiled.

Once in a while someone would stop and pick up the book, look at the jacket, flip it over, look to me, then back to the dust jacket photo in which I look, regrettably, like Little Richard wearing a hat. "Huh," some would say, apropos of nothing. Then, "Huh," again as they looked back to me sitting slouched at the card table, picking my nose. I'd smile and nod to the possible bearer of my mortgage payment, and then they'd drop the book as if it were radioactive and walk away.

I bought a newspaper from the snooty clerk and sat back down at the table, feigning interest in the sports section. For a full year afterward I had the Mariners' box scores memorized. As the minutes ground by I acted as if I did not give a damn that I was breaking out in a cold sweat, something comedians aptly refer to as "flop sweat." And I felt like a flop, the urge to run home to my cats, turn on a soap opera, kick back, and eat Egg McMuffins nearly overwhelming. My cousin Hilary, after publishing her first book and doing similar signings, called to tell me of her experience. "The day I puked in my plate at school might have been worse," she said.

Then, from across the store, an enthusiastic voice, a male.

"Wow!" he was saying, making a beeline for the rickety table where I slumped now, bored past existence. "I have wanted to *read* this book, man oh man. You just can't believe it. This has gotta be a great book."

My cone of silence shattered, my self-pity punctured at its core, I eyed the young man skeptically, suspecting he was making fun of me. Little bastard, I thought, go away.

"You've written a great book," he kept on. "All I've heard are good things about this book."

There was a very slim chance he wasn't kidding. The reviews had been good. Maybe he'd read them. Or maybe he'd just taken some mind-altering drug. I lowered my eyes modestly.

"Yeah," he was bubbling, "I've wanted to read it ever since I saw the movie."

I felt my ego shift gears, drop a couple of hundred stories, dive straight to the basement. Just another confused video junkie, my luck.

"Yeah, yeah," the little moron continued. "Brad Pitt was *great* in it. Man, I never knew fly-fishing could be so beautiful. And the way he kept fighting the fish all the way down the river, swimming with it. Wow!"

Should I or should I not tell him that I had about as much to do with Norman Maclean as I did with, say, Gandhi? A fleeting moment of conscience eluded me.

"Yeah," I said. "Fly-fishing's pretty goddamned cool. You want me to sign it?"

The boy looked at me as if Elvis were sitting on my lap.

"Would you? Oh, that'd be great, just *great*. You know, I kept trying to remember the title."

Don't, I thought. Just don't. May a stroke of amnesia follow you to your grave.

"River. River something. Hey! I was just looking for it and here you are. I never guessed you'd be a woman."

He and my two million other fans who think I'm really J. D. Salinger.

"I hope you enjoy it," I said as I signed "Norman Hemingway" beneath MacLean's quote.

"Oh, I will. I will," the young man said as he hurried up to the snooty clerk. "Thanks again, Miss...Miss..."

Oh, come on, I thought, call me Norm.

Chapter

TWENTY-ONE

THE PEOPLE you fish with often change more than the places you fish, although the way Eudora Welty writes of the Pearl River in Jackson, it, too, can look "old sometimes... wrinkled and deep." It is the way I think of my old friend Dr. Engle now, wrinkled and deep, his pronounced tendency to reflection these last years the part in him that runs further to the core than I could have gauged; and the wrinkles that were coming on twenty years before, when we first met, have etched paths that are indelible. But he seemed ancient even then. And wise. He has always been wise.

When I returned to south Florida sober, I could tell when I saw him that over fifty years in the medical profession had left their mark. He'd had several surgeries on his back, the pain he suffered from this constant now, a fact that never seemed to interfere with his deadeye casting or his eagerness to spend entire days at sea. And finally, after a lifetime in the sun, he had developed skin cancer. The surgery had left pale, mottled patches on his face, and the salt-and-pepper beard had gone pure white.

The brass-tipped cane he had once carried because it looked good, he now relied on.

When I walked into the cool, icebox stillness of his home on Miami Beach I was reminded of other times spent here, the early years that were good and fun, when we would sit around the coffee table in his living room, smoking cigarettes, reliving a fishing trip, looking at pictures of me strapped down in the fighting chair, of Les on Bimini holding what he called his "matching luggage"—two brown paper grocery sacks—and of Dr. Engle with his trophy catches. There was the time after I'd torn my muscles during the marlin fight when he'd fixed my arm up in a polka-dotted kerchief sling and had taken a picture of me out in the yard, my arm heavy in the sling, so, he said, twenty years later we could look at it and remember the day I'd caught two marlin. He'd let me sleep in his and Mrs. Engle's bed that time and I had felt cared for here, welcome. There was nothing strange about coming back.

As I stood in the foyer, my back to him as I closed the door, he lay his hands squarely on my shoulders, turned me around gently to face him, and stared at me as if I were magic.

"My God," he said, obviously struck by the flush of health that had come back to me, "you look absolutely wonderful. I have never, *ever* seen you look so good." He touched my cheek with his hand and I noticed the sun freckles on them, the way the veins stood out. He smiled. "Not a trace of yellow left. Just look at your skin, and your muscles." I struck a beach boy pose and he rapped a bicep with his knuckles, impressed.

There seems, at times, a singular value to rebirth—the sheer disbelief in the eyes of those who have seen you walking dead. I remembered the last time we'd met in Dr. Engle's kitchen. It was another woman who had sat there, I knew that now, conscience paralyzed by years of anesthetic, muscle tissue starved, will to live nominal.

He watched me as we moved toward the living room, both of us ignoring the pool of light from the kitchen. This time we sat on the low, deep sofa instead of hard-backed kitchen chairs. We faced each other.

"That was one of the hardest things I ever had to do," he

said. "You know that, don't you? And I think you know why I did it."

I nodded, feeling oddly secure. There was nothing he could say that I feared now, and what other reason could there be?

"Because I love you, that's why. Like my own daughter, I love you."

"Daughter." That word that to me sounds like a bell rung once.

I nodded again, felt my throat ache, took a breath, and studied his face. He looked confused, unsure what to say next.

I sat with my hands in my lap, waiting, thinking how it had always been a luxury for all of us to step from the sauna of Miami Beach into Dr. Engle's deep freeze. I remembered Les sitting on this same couch, the sweat drying on his face, a glass of ice water in his hand.

"I'd told Les," he began, still looking rattled, his fingers knotting and unknotting on his lap. "I had told him, ten years before he died, that the drinking would kill him if he didn't quit. And he quit, goddamnit, just like that. You know, all that time I thought it would be enough, that he'd shake everything. But it wasn't enough. It just wasn't."

I could see the struggle in Dr. Engle then, how he was on the edge of tears, the weight of his friend's death on him now, and I knew he wondered if suicide would ever take me, if I'd fall.

"But we both knew him," he was saying. "Those years he lived after were good, weren't they? Productive. You saw him when he was happy."

The way Les's face looked when he grinned came to me, the one eyebrow cocked. He'd looked happy, all right. Wickedly happy. Illicitly happy, like he knew the one big joke that would make us all die laughing.

"I did," I said. "He was happy."

I knew what was working in Dr. Engle. It was that guilt, that cruel, deceitful belief that he could have done something to stop it. It had come to me in bizarre dreams a few years after Les's death. I had dreamt that I had killed him and kept his body hidden so no one would know. I dreamt the gun had belonged to me and I had handed it over to him, thinking he was only going to check the safety. Then, not long after I was sober, I dreamt that Les stood on an empty plain at twilight. Beside him was a raised sundial, made of hard-cut opalescent quartz, that cast a fractured, intricate shadow of light, and in a gesture I remember well he raised his fists to the sky, and shouted once in a voice that resonated even in sleep, that one word, "great!" so I had no question who it was. It was after that dream that I felt better about where he'd gone, how he'd gotten there.

"So I had to say what I did to you," Dr. Engle was saying, his eyes focused hard on mine. "Otherwise I couldn't have lived with myself."

"I know," I told him. "I couldn't have lived with you either."

He smiled. "You keep your butt where it belongs and your elbows off the bar. You hear?"

I laughed. "Sure," I said, and it was a relief to mean it.

• • •

WE FISHED together with Glenn Smallwood one last time, in the thick of the shell mounds of the Ten Thousand Islands. Built by Indians around the time of Christ, they had offered refuge from storms and high water, and Dr. Engle and Glenn had often anchored in their lee when the winds grew too strong.

In less than a year Smallwood would be dead, and Dr. Engle would say of his friend's passing that he was "a traditional, Florida-born, Everglades-raised cracker who was impeccably honest, always on time, patient, and never complained. He was a gentleman of the old school."

They both seemed to know Glenn's death was coming and talked of it openly, Dr. Engle saying he hoped he and Glenn would die on the water together, after a good day of fishing, be struck by lightning or just pass into the ether as the boat drifted, and maybe someone would find them and maybe they wouldn't. Glenn was the only guide he knew, he said, who never once got lost in the maze of islands, who could orient himself by the particular bend of a mangrove. It was the way he wanted to go, the doctor told me again and again, borne upon the water on an outgoing tide, the sun hot on his back, Glenn steering the open boat; and I knew by his insistence that death was a thing he thought of often now, not with regret or fear that it would come, but as if it were the final statement to a life well lived.

The morning of our last trip we had headed out from Miami long before dawn, the flat, narrow stretch of the old Tamiami Trail the arrow we sped along, and as Dr. Engle turned to look at me with his hot-damn-we-get-to-go-fishing smile, I had a sense, as I always did when I fished with him, of having gotten away with something. He'd always made it possible to believe that this was the last anyone might ever see of us because who could ever understand the charge we felt when the sun broke the clouds and we could tell by their very color how the fishing would be? And who but Dr. Engle could get how the sound of a boat's motor, the smell of diesel as it pulled into the harbor, the blue haze that enveloped it, could make me tremble because *this* boat was for us, and this day fishing belonged to no one else?

It was a pale day with low, thin clouds riding the horizon, cool and windy. We were fishing the edge of winter, no other boats in sight. Glenn ran the boat out quick along the channel of the Barron River, picking up speed early to break the thick cloud of mosquitoes that hatched and bred along the banks. It was a nuisance to breathe them in, but other than that we didn't complain, all three of us immune to the insect's bite.

Smallwood, wide and big boned, missing a finger on one hand from a slip with a filet knife, his skin the color of cured tobacco, teased Dr. Engle about his newly pale skin and the sunblock he lathered on his face.

"You're so white," he said, "you'll scare the fish."

"Well, then, you'd have to work to find them, wouldn't you?"

Dr. Engle had often said that his friendship with Glenn Smallwood was the best marriage he'd ever had, "although Mrs. Engle is much better looking."

"You know, when I met her," he was telling us as we drifted among the mangroves, our rods set for redfish, "I had never seen such a delicate, beautiful woman. And it's still so. All these years."

I thought then of Mrs. Engle, her delicate, perfect features, her jingly little-girl voice. She is a woman I have respected, not only for her talent—she is an accomplished painter—but for her compassion and guts. It was she, this sparrow-boned, fragile-looking woman, not five feet tall, who had cleaned up the bloodbath of Les's suicide, mopping the floor with a sponge so her friend Doris, Les's widow, would not see it. It was she who had said, "Stay outside," to Hilary when she had wanted to see her father one last time. And it was she who had let me drink beer at her breakfast table at nine in the morning, never criticizing, never looking at me as if I were the self-destructive slob I was, but instead with veiled concern, as if she could not bear to watch me hurt myself.

And she has a true screwball's sense of humor that, given her toney New England demeanor, can rattle you.

Once, when Dr. Engle and I were getting ready for a trip to Islamorada, he was showing us the gadgets on his new car. Ever the believer in technology, he has bought more lemons than Carmen Miranda.

"See here," he was saying, as Mrs. Engle and I stood outside the car in the cool April night, "this is the computer readout for the interior temperature of the vehicle." He punched a little button and the car cabin temp was displayed. Seventy-two degrees, it read.

We smiled politely.

"Now," he said, "just watch this. Want to know the air temperature *outdoors?*"

I shrugged. Mrs. Engle said, "Sure, Howard," in her breathy little voice. "And I want to know the humidity, too, while you're at it."

He gave us both a dark look and pushed another button. One hundred ten degrees, the display read.

"Hah! Look at that," the doctor said, excited. "It's one hundred and ten degrees outside."

Mrs. Engle and I looked at each other, eyebrows raised, and she whispered in my ear, "You'd think he'd *sweat* in that heat." I giggled, shot a look at Dr. Engle behind the wheel of his new toy, beaming. "How about that?" he was saying, oblivious. "How about *that* for accuracy?"

"Now, Howard," Mrs. Engle said, the tone of her voice parentlike, "that can't be right. It is *not* one hundred ten degrees out here. Your computer is off by at least fifty degrees."

"Computers don't lie, Brooke."

"Well," she said after a long moment, slipping her arm around my waist and pulling me close, "then it must be these two *red hot* girls standing beside the car."

It was only fair to think of Mrs. Engle when we were on a boat because it was she who'd sanctioned our fishing marriage, telling me once, "The way I look at it, Lorian, if you fish with him, I don't have to."

We rode the lip of the open mouth of the Gulf, close along the protective cove of the mangrove and shell islands, casting little chunks of pilchard, scouting for redfish, once in a while trading the bait rods for fly rods, listening to Glenn talk about how everything out here was just as good as it had ever been; and I was struck for a moment by the simple acceptance of his life, the way he talked of how this bounty of water had blessed him, not of how he had been shortchanged. Nearing the end of his life, he seemed reflective, grateful.

"I've been given every good thing," he was saying. "For me, right here, right now, there's as many fish as there's ever been. I been out here sixty years. This is all I know, and I'd know if it was different."

There was a philosophical tilt to this day, each of us a little subdued, a little edgy, the way you are when you can't just talk the ordinary bullshit, so we were quiet at first, reading the water, reading one another.

Dr. Engle caught a small redfish right before lunch. I remember standing in the bow of the boat, ready to make my cast, when he elbowed me aside and lay his line out smooth, right alongside the fish's eye. There was no way I could have matched his quickness, and he knew it.

"Better to catch a fish, young lady, than to lose it," he said as he reeled the redfish to the boat. "You've got to be fast, girl."

"Not much chance of that," I said, "with you shoving me out of the boat."

I looked at the redfish with its fancy tail spot, like a big, black eye, its soft, dark salmon color, and blunt, fanlike tail. They'd had to stop the hunt for them off Texas when the blackened redfish craze had threatened their numbers.

"So what's so special about blackened redfish?" I asked Dr. Engle as he slipped the fish into the water.

"Not a goddamned thing," he said. "It's so damned hot and charred you might as well be eating surgical gloves. Blackened pork rinds would taste the same."

Dr. Engle had always packed terrific lunches when we fished, but this day he'd gone all out. And I noticed food these days, planning meals the way I had once planned drinking.

We anchored off some mangroves, beneath a bright break in the clouds, and the doctor passed around the gourmet eats. First course was a bronzed cornish game hen filled with spicy sweet potato stuffing. The notion of Thanksgiving occurred to me, and I wondered, idly, if Dr. Engle had thought of this when he'd planned the meal.

"You spoil me, Doc," Glenn was saying as he bit off whole chunks of the hen, digging his fingers into the body cavity and pulling out great orange globs of stuffing.

"Only way to eat on a boat," Engle said, doing the same.

The drink, instead of beer, was fresh, cold apricot nectar from the cooler; exotic, multicolored vegetable chips were a side dish. Then crisp, whole stalks of Florida celery.

"Nothing better than this," I said, looking around at our protected cove, the sun bright on the water, mangroves stirring a little in the wind. A huge nurse shark glided below the boat, a few feet down, and I watched it burrow in the sand and grass of the shallow water. I had seen one up close once when I'd been diving for lobster, its big, flat head and harmless mouth mucking in the sand, stirring up little puffs of it as I floated above.

There's always something that's vaguely illicit about being on a boat. That morning when we'd put in on the Barron River, I felt as if I'd pulled a fast one. Nature never dictated that I be at ease here. I don't have the buoyancy of an otter. My feathers are not oiled, my toes webbed. The truth is, I sink quick and deep, without props, so each time I find myself floating, with nothing but sun and water and the dark green of the mangroves as reference points, I run up hard against something that approaches outright awe, and it is the greatest trick of all how this never gets old.

"Cool," I said, apropos of nothing.

Engle was looking down at his hands a lot while he ate, reminding me of the way he'd been back in Miami. He glanced up at me, then out to the water. It spooked me, the way he looked, as if he might cry.

"Ever have any regrets, Lorian?" he asked. He flung the game hen carcass into the water then and wiped his hands on an old rag in the bottom of Glenn's boat.

The question fit his mood of the last few days. He'd been contemplative, almost downright sorrowful, not loud and bossy as usual. I could tell by the look on his face he didn't want a toss-away answer. If he'd asked me the question two years before, I'd have told him yes, there would be no mathematical way to calculate the enormity of my regret, but now, in this place of sun and light and salt-scented air, I scanned the history of my life, and thought, No, there is not one thing I can recall that I regret. All the bad things seemed like monumental lessons now, blunders and treacheries and a life that had hung in the balance that had, rather than the power to embitter and shame, the unique ability to teach. I was lucky, and in these new, bright, hard-as-diamond days I felt sometimes, almost giddily, as if I had walked away from murder. But I knew this for what it was, no more than a childlike sense of relief at being alive, and that what had changed in me went deeper.

"No," I told him. "I don't. I can't honestly say that I do."

A white pelican sailed near our boat, its heavy, pouched jaw opening wide as it neared the water.

"Not a one?" he asked.

"If I had," I told him, "what would be the point?"

He looked at me hard, gauging me.

"You're a lucky woman, then. You get to be my age, you have regrets." "You have any regrets? Glenn." He turned to Smallwood, who was rigging a line, his thick, bloated fingers calm and steady as I remember Jimmie Albright's.

"Can't say I do, Doc." He winked at me. "What would be the point?"

"Guess I'm outnumbered," the doctor said, standing to brush the crumbs from his khaki pants. "Guess I'm the only one here too serious to fish." He smiled at me, leaned down to kiss my cheek.

"Love those long pants," I said, teasing him.

All these years, until the skin cancer, he had always worn shorts, his strong, wiry legs bronzed to where his white socks began. My daughter was the only person who'd ever gotten him to take his socks off in public, to swim with her once in Key West when she was six years old. She said it looked as if he still had them on, the skin beneath that had been covered for years a fish-belly white.

"None of us have any regrets today, do we?" He stood to cast then to a nearby school of tarpon. I watched them do their barrel rolls, spinning cocoons of air that seemed to trap and fossilize them for a moment, like ants trapped in amber. If I could have done the same for the three of us, I would have. I'd have put the brakes on hard, kept Glenn timeless in the bow of his old boat, his arms extended wide as he measured out line, his eyes following the plane of his outstretched arm to the horizon. I'd have freeze-framed Dr. Engle, his khaki pants rolled up at the ankles, his lucky fishing hat tipped back on his head as he cast low and straight for the tarpon. And I'd have kept fast and tight in the hold of friendship I felt with these two old men, these two ancient, I've-seen-it-all guys who said, by their very actions: this is it. This is what it's all about, this day, right here, right now, with every goddamn good thing in it you could ever want.

"It's how I want to go," Dr. Engle said again, his back to us as he cast. "Right here. On this boat with Glenn. Something prophetic, like lightning."

• • •

DR. ENGLE called a few months later to tell me of the death of his friend, and I was touched to be included among the few he talked to of his loss. "Best times of my life," he kept saying. "The very best times." A few days later, while on a trip, I found a card with a painting of an empty boat adrift, and sent it to Dr. Engle. It was such a peaceful painting, the water a liquid, sulfurous expanse, the wake of the drift barely visible. There could have been someone lying in the bottom of the boat, unseen, borne upon the current, safe.

Chapter

TWENTY-TWO

FROM THE mountains of the north Cascade Range in Washington State the White Chuck River flows, a glacial artery, milky white during spring runoff. It meets with the olive green of the slower-moving Sauk, the mixture of waters a stunning, subdued lime that stirs up fractured particles of light, a liquid Ireland, chilled as deep well water.

Along the Sauk dippers bob and dive from the worn boulders anchored in midstream, the rocks creating slow, backwash pools of swirling water, perfect deep, cool pockets where rainbows and Dolly Varden hide. The dippers are silly birds, their stumpy tails ducklike, their jerky up-and-down dance suggesting impatience, and it is hard to keep a straight face around them. After a day of watching them I imitate their quick dip and bob, imagining the instinct of this, what purpose it could serve. They dive as deep and fast as cormorants, then pop to the surface like plastic bobbers, their slate gray feathers water darkened and sleek.

Their cry is a sharp *zeet* as they fly low over the water, banking quickly and lighting on a rock when the territory looks interesting. Along the shoreline where the water runs thin over pebbly gravel, they move so low they look as if they're water-skiing, their chicken yellow feet threading the shallows.

The forest that makes a damp cove of the Sauk and White Chuck is dense with cedar, pine, spruce, hemlock, and vine maple. In the nearby town of Darrington loggers and their families live, many of them relocated from the Carolinas. It is my favorite part of Washington, this area. It has a Southern feel to it, slow and lazy and unbound by time. I go here to fish, sure, but more for the sound of the rivers, the way the light plays on the stirred-up water, the weighty lumps of granite and basalt beneath it, and the quirky wildlife.

In the late afternoon, when the sun edges the foothills and the light changes from sparkle-dazzle to a deep subterranean green, I have seen cedar waxwings perch on the low branches of cedars, their punk, swept-back-feather do and black face mask startling against the field of green. They are exotic, made-up-looking birds, colorful street hoods who frequently arrive with a crowd of their friends, manic and adept in their fly catching. I have stood a mere foot from one, watching the bird watch me from behind his Zorro mask, belligerently almost, seeming to dare me to move closer.

I have camped and spent long days on the Sauk, pitching my tent in tight against the river's edge, so in the morning I wake to the sound of water and the cathedral of trees along the bank. I have read by flashlight in this tent pitched by the Sauk of Carl Jung's final years, of the rock dams he built along the lakeshore near his home in Bolligen, of how this simple rearranging of stones, to him, lay his finger along the pulse of the infinite. At night, atop an old bridge that spans the two rivers, I have stared with my head thrown back at the sky unpolluted by the lights of cities, a sky inexhaustible in its depth, the Milky Way a diorama of cosmic dust, Pegasus, Andromeda, Cepheus, Hercules, Cygnus, Sagittarius—all clear as water droplets frozen on dark earth—and I have remembered when I was a kid in Mississippi, peering from my bedroom window into the platinum wash of light, imagining the meaning of light years, how a star I gazed upon might have winked out eons before, so that what I witnessed then was nothing more than the afterglow of death.

Since then I have come to suspect that death is that last star on the curve of the infinite, pulsing with the urgency of a quasar, beckoning. All my life I have haunted the darkest nights, waiting for the molten-glass drop of meteors into the dark ditch of sky. At the Sauk I have seen the Perseid shower in August, hundreds of shooting stars cutting neon paths in the textured darkness, laying it wide open for an instant, the trailing shaft of light burned diamond white on my retina. I have seen the shooting stars glow green and red all the way to the horizon, tight balls of fire that seem to fizzle out inches from the silhouette of trees that rise up by the river. For first-time ownership of a meteorite I would forfeit my house and car, take a lien on my soul, and wander the earth in search of more. Here is the fascination of this strange visitor from another planet: to hold in my hand a galactic stone, its journey from there to here dark and immeasurable, its history unrecordable. I would sleep with it under my pillow, travel with it gripped tightly in my fist. I would charge you to view it. I saw a sign once at a burger joint in the desert of eastern Washington. It read: WANTED: METEORITES. Fool, I thought, of the person who had penned the sign, like I'd give you mine if I had one.

From that same bridge I have seen the comet Hyakutake, its fuzzy tennis ball head trailing an expansive, fully formed tail of ice, 93 million miles close on its once-every-ten-thousand-years journey to the sun. And the comet Hale-Bopp, its two tails split in a perfect chevron, one blue, one white, frozen in an arc low in the northwest sky. Return date: two thousand years. I cannot say, like Mark Twain, that I will be around for the next one.

I have watched the stuttering pulse of satellites in this same sky, the dim, man-made orb sailing the edge of gravity's sea, its course unbroken. I always imagine they are UFOs and that some dazzling, star-strewn night one will lower itself in a rush of wind and atomic light, feet from my tent. "How do you do?" I will say when they step, gleaming and poreless, from the craft. "What kept you?"

In the morning juncos grub on seeds and berries, their dark

executioner's hoods making them seem serious and important. Flocks of them spread wide and deep within a territory, calling to one another as they fly, never out of touch. It is their sense of community I marvel at and the full-throated panic they screech out when a hawk soars nearby. I have seen red-tailed hawks rip them from their roost and hover with their broad wings shielding the trilling prey and cutting off their breath in the lock grip of their talons. To my own wild yard a red-tail returns each season, circling the house, on the hunt for sparrows. The cry of warning that rises from the bushes is deafening, the resounding screech of communal fear. To be predator and not prey would seem the best bet, but when the predator develops a conscience, what then?

It is on the Sauk that I have often slid back to consciousness, to a heightened sense of my surroundings, and in that altered state conscience surfaces. I do not stalk and bellow and make a big noise about the fact that I'm out here. I am quieter now, I watch more, I keep my mouth shut, I try to learn. This is a river I have fished only sober, and for that reason alone I respect it. I have taken Dolly Varden here, a nineteen-incher on a mudler minnow, fat and heavy in the belly as a catfish, and rainbow fry, jittery and electric at the end of the fly hook, but not much else. I let them all go. I have a friend who catches whitefish and fries them up for breakfast, wrapped in bacon, telling me it's a fine fish, I should try it.

"Mouth's too small," I tell him. "No one should eat a fish with such a small mouth."

There must be something in the Bible that says small-mouthed fish are sacrilege. According to a friend I invited to a catfish supper, "Scaleless fish are an abomination" in the eyes of God, catfish the lowliest, most vile of all. The logic of this eludes me and I have nothing to say to it except the less this guy eats, the more there is for me.

Along the smoothly defined shoreline where the water bellies in during spring runoff I dig through the aftermath of glaciers, plunge my hands into the cool deep bed of fire-forged rock. Rocks, like stars, have ancient, invisible histories. When I was a kid I would hold them in my palm and smell them with my eyes closed, able to tell an iron-rich chunk from a piece of smooth obsidian. And I will still smell a rock the moment I palm it, expecting, I guess, a whiff of creation, the scent of centuries. Every trip I've taken I've come home with the floorboard of the car paved in rock; speckled pink granite from Michigan, agates and quartz from Arkansas, shale, jasper, turquoise, bloodstone, pumice light as Styrofoam, oxidized rocks in the shapes of heads, hearts, kidneys, and torsos, and each one speaks with its own peculiar science. There have been gifts of rocks; a hard, flat chip of flint from England, a lump of anthracite coal from Alabama, a sugar stone from Agate Beach. There are good rocks and bad rocks, sacred and common. This affinity I have for them comes as instinct, locked up tight in me long before the woo-woo New Age of pseudoscience, where polished, generic-looking stones are supposed to heal, bring love and fortune, keep the wolf from your door. What's missing here is the chance for nature to cough up a rock on its own, exactly when you need it. I have never bought a rock. That is to me, like scaleless fish to my friend, an abomination.

Carl Jung was a rock lover who built, both in childhood and when he was grown, fortresses of stone, one of which, eventually, he lived in. In the dream I have had of him he stands atop his stone tower, fishing.

I have spent hours in the green water of the Sauk, gathering stones, dumping them in mounds at the shoreline, making secure and intricate dams to divert the flow of water from the White Chuck that trickles along the shore. And I have built these dams, not in defiance of nature, but to observe its habits. Water has a strange tension as it builds and waits, anxious to flow as water before it has flowed, along a familiar path, keeping pace. Sometimes it scares me and I sense that it would bulldoze me in a fist of fury were I to mess with it too long. I watch as it accommodates itself to this fork in the road, a breath of liquid seeping through the rocks, and then it bends, avoiding the roadblock of my dam, forming a new, strengthened rivulet. Here is where water has consciousness, makes an abrupt decision. It could wait, its slow, even friction against the stones turning them to dust in a thousand years, but it is a mover, a doer, an energy-packed skein of molecules linked ankle to foot, and does it cruise. I have felt the force of rivers deep at their heart. I have felt that force slam into my belly and carry me weightless into its dominion. I have dived into it naked, unafraid, watched snakes glide on its surface, seen it rise in fury tall as trees, watched waterspouts drink it deep into the funnel and then wilt before its vastness. I have seen it baptize, drown, and resurrect. It is the resurrection I want.

There is a huge, ancient cedar at my favorite spot along the Sauk. In autumn spiders spin their webs between the branches, iridescent threads of disgorged filament that billow out like soap bubbles in the wind. I do not like spiders, but I leave them alone. In autumn it is their tree. In spring the waxwings and juncos jump from branch to branch and the chipmunks climb high to the crow's-nest limbs. I have slept beneath this tree in summer, drowsy from the sun and the river, the sand beneath it cool as the underside of a pillow.

I have felt whole here, curiously undamaged, as if all the gonzo years before were someone else's history. I am idle here. I hold my palm to the sun and trace the outline of veins in my hand; twirl tree branches as if they were batons; build fires within the circle of rocks from my broken dams; return the birds' calls, tunelessly, but with the conviction that I am, momentarily, family; skip flat stones along the river's changing current; hoot across the water at fishermen along the bank. And sometimes I fish, practicing my cast, loving the feel of the rod as it loads the line, the unfurling loop that snaps so hard at the tip it drags the fly back in midair. It delights me I can do this, and that even though I no longer cast like a child, I feel like one, fed from the hand of these waters, washed clean in it, wrapped tight in a cape of starlight, a believer, once again, in mothers.

Chapter

TWENTY-THREE

ON THE SHORES of Gitche Gumee, on Michigan's Upper Peninsula, agates rattle on the incoming tide, tumble among the plainer rocks, deflect sunlight more subtly than the blue-diamond water. It is a trick to tell an agate by the way it catches light. I have not mastered this, nor do I have the same calibre of luck as the Agate Lady, whose cabin in the woods was once filled with the bounty of her daily expeditions to the shore: chunks of ruby agate, snowflake agate, plume agate, flame agate, crazy lace, lavender lace, fire, and snakeskin agate, their names as varied as their colors and irregular banding, all of these in jars and boxes and crates, lying mosaiclike on tables, mounds of them propping open doors, their waxy opalescence casting a light of their own, like foxfire in the woods. The Agate Lady has died since I first heard of her, my loss, too, because I had imagined walking the beach with her, watching her keen eyes search where the water meets the shore so I might steal the trick of her good fortune. I think sometimes about taking over where she left off, dumping everything and living in this place, where dark behind me would rise the forest, where by these shining deep sea waters I would become a daughter of the moon, searching for its stolen light trapped in these stones. I wonder if there should be an heiress to the agate throne, and if by mere eccentricity, by the value of my curiosity, I might make myself worthy.

I like the ancient history of them. I like the word "Precambrian," at the close of whose age these rocks were formed, a billion years ago when lava rolled out in a boiling sea over this area now covered by Lake Superior, forming bubbles of hot gas that cooled and hardened near the top of the flow. Then, *boom,* all this was paved over in another veneer of lava, the land layered now like a casserole. Superheated water pushed from beneath the carapace and seeped along the contact points of these flows, dumping minerals in the gas bubble cavities, and so were born these stone witnesses to the dawning of an age. It is the iron, manganese, titanium, and other metals that give agates their patchwork colors—blue, red, gray, green, white, purple, pumpkin—arranged in fine, delicate parallel bands. The glacial advance of the Ice Age into the heart of this continent scraped agate-containing rock and carried agates as far away as Iowa. I imagine this miracle of discovery in an Iowa cornfield, a child kneeling in the harvested field, poking around for any old rock, a pocketful of them to pass the day with, and what he gets is this time capsule lit up like Christmas. How could he ever believe it wasn't magic that brought it to him, that somehow upon him has been conferred the elemental blessing of the universe?

It's why I came back to Michigan. For the agates, and to find Travlin' Gravlin.

The last time I'd seen him we had cooked the steelhead I had caught over a campfire we'd built outside his slide-on camper, there in the woods near the mouth of the Big Two-Hearted, where it feeds into Superior. Jeffrey Cardenas had taken pictures of the fish laid out on the moss of the forest floor, and as dusk fell, all around us had floated the blue-and-white spirit moths of the Chippewa. A man named Jack had joined us at the campsite for supper, pulling from his deep pockets a trove of agates he'd found on the shore that day. I remember in particular a fire-plume ruby agate, its flame of translucent red distinct in the center, and had reached out my hand to touch it, envious. Travlin' had watched me, his face lit by firelight, a curious expression on it as he poked the coals of the fire with a stick.

"You're blood, girl," he'd said, looking down at the fire. "It's in your nature to want those stones. You'll find your own when it's time."

"I want them now," I'd said, pouty. I eyed the rich-colored stones resting in Jack's huge palm, the distinct banding of colors that made them look like rock candy.

"Patience," Travlin' had said, looking up at me again, and I had remembered that word as a promise.

When I returned to the Upper Peninsula in the late summer of 1993, before the legions of black flies had died off, I packed my fly rod along with an empty canvas bag I planned to fill with agates. I knew that Travlin' came in autumn, that I was perhaps too early.

I camped on a sandy rise that overlooked a sunlit, pine-flanked bend in the Big Two-Hearted, near the old bridge where I had first seen Travlin', the bridge repaired now, reinforced at the tether ends with heavy steel supports. I remembered how the bridge had swung with his side-to-side gait, how the red ball on his stocking cap had appeared before he did, and how with his first hard look he had assessed me. "You need help," he'd said, simply. I wanted to let him know how right he'd been, because when people have a bead on you that sharp, that focused, they deserve to know.

Rainbow Lodge is the hub of a spoke of campsites on the Big Two-Hearted, a rustic place with a few cabins, a small store, and a restaurant, open only in season, reached by way of a fourteen-mile track of sand and dirt that snakes and bumps through a thick canopy of maples. The undergrowth of the forest is low and thin, so the deer that roam here are spotted quickly and will turn in midromp to eye the intruder. As I plowed the track on my way in I read their looks as "How dare you?" and slowed the rental car to a crawl, letting my eyes adjust to the underwater cast of pure green light that turns to stark raving orange in autumn. Ravens light high in the limbs of the maples, then drop in a dead dive to the forest floor, where they strut like linebackers, shoulders forward. Hawks shadow-glide into the airy protection of the canopy, looking for prey, and the head raven calls his squad of bullies to drive the enemy back into the leafless sky.

I like what goes on in these woods. I like the feel of the place. It has that edge-of-a-dream quality, light and shadow overlain, sounds absorbed back into themselves. You cannot see the sky in these woods, only the shadow of the sky. It is cool as stream water here, even in the wind-fueled heat of summer. The sand along the track is pink, centuries of erosion of pink granite, and farther up the track stands of birch rise up out of the pink sand, white and polished looking, sentinels at the juncture of the road and the river. It is magic here, and I do not just imagine it, do not just wish it were so. I have seen things here that I do not expect ever to tell, and some that I do, less from a wish to prove them than to simply make them indelible. There is a certain power in this, a heeding to of the elusive character of all variables, this force that takes rein when I come here and won't unhand me until I hit the interstate.

I am an admitted believer in the odd coincidence, a proponent of the powers of synchronicity, an armchair mystic who revels in the bizarre, so I became eerily accustomed, in time, to the fact that the song "Cherokee People" came on the car radio each time I entered the forest on that fourteen-mile track to the Big Two-Hearted. The station, with the exception of this one glitch, played strictly instrumental music and would crackle in and out of range until, *bam,* I slipped into the woods. The native rhythm of the drumbeat would start up and I'd feel my skin gathering up in gooseflesh, hair pricking up on the back of my neck as Mark Lindsay wailed out, "Cherokee people, Cherokee tri-ibe," and I'd substitute the word "Chippewa," idiotically, as if the name of the local tribe would make sense of this warp in the air waves.

Once, a murder of ravens sailed from their perch in the maples and flanked my car for a full two miles, cruising low right at the edge of the windows, a wildly flapping blue-black nimbostratus of wings, the sound of them like a gloved fist hit square against a punching bag, over and over. Yes, I thought of the movie *The Birds,* remembered Tippi Hedren cowering helpless in a bolted phone booth while crows crashed against the glass. This wasn't the same. I have always dreamt of crows, ravens, blackbirds, their appearance an arrow straight into the unconscious. The meaning of them? Who knows. I leave this territory to dream theorists or to chance.

The schizoid radio fuzzed in and out while the ravens banked and wheeled in front of the car, leading me now in a mad chariot spin down the soft sand track, and I heard a voice come over the waves, loud and clear, speaking once and once only, two words, "It's magic," and then the voice was gone. I've heard about people who claim to pick up radio stations through their fillings. I know about auditory hallucinations. I have stared with test-pattern eyes into the howling face of the DTs. None of these has a lick to do with what goes on in these woods. It is a place where clarity lit upon me even when I was dumb and blind, and when I returned clear eyed and scrubbed clean, the strength of it hit me like a fist. I *do* believe in spooks.

It had been six years since I had walked the low sandy banks of the Big Two-Hearted, six years since I had ridden with Travlin' against a frozen wind in his wobbly two-tone canoe, six years since I had heard him say, "Daughter, those pines are talking to you." Like all other places of potent memory, where the ragged and the sublime are fused so as to become indiscernible, I believed of this place in Michigan that I had returned to an essential fork in the road, the place at which my life might have slammed, eternally, in reverse.

I did not fish the Big Two-Hearted. I cast with my hookless line, remembering the very edge of winter I had fished before, my crude rig of salmon roe and lead weight, the way I had cast upside down and backwards—like a child, Jeffrey Cardenas had said—and how I took this not as instruction but as offense. I remembered, too, the way he and Travlin' had hooted when I'd gotten the steelhead on and the embarrassed looks on their faces when I had cried at the sight of the bloodied fish in the boat. It had been another girl on this river six years before, and as I watched my line unfurl clear to the other bank I imagined her here, bound by the delicate filament of my line, caught across time by this umbilicus, happy for me.

That day I gave a casting lesson to a grumpy man who had a cabin at Rainbow Lodge. I'd watched him from my spot on the bank, the way he snapped his rod back and forth like a riding crop, the line puddling limp with each release. I remember the look in his eyes when I asked if I could help, one of perceived lunacy that I, a five-foot-five-inch-tall woman could know anything worth teaching him, a six-foot-ten gargantuan whose biceps were the size of my cranium. There is a good deal of truth in the often-repeated notion that men will resist being taught a sport by a woman, and as I approached this man it was the first thing I addressed.

"Forget I'm a woman," I told him as I put into motion my modified hammer cast, explaining how I stopped abruptly, as if hitting a wall, and how the line responded to this action, my special take on the theory of perpetual motion. "Forget everything except the fact that you want to learn how to do this. Forget you're embarrassed. Forget the fact that I'm a girl. Forget that I might think you look stupid."

The look in his eyes said, *Bitch*.

"You sure want me to forget a lot" were the only words he spoke. The lesson did not go well. After ten minutes of resisting everything, and of making a less-than-feeble attempt to learn my name, he turned his back to me and walked away. I spotted him later, by the mouth of the Big Two-Hearted, on his knees on a sandbar where the water of the river and the water of the lake meet headlong. He was filling an empty gallon jug with river water, his bent form massive and hulking, and I was struck, for the moment, with the image of a baboon at the watering hole. The liquid looked like tea inside the milky plastic container. I squatted down beside him, bold, determined to make him notice me, and asked what he planned to do with the water.

"You won't go away, will you?" he said, clearly annoyed.

"Odds are not good," I told him, hoping for a smile, a grimace, anything.

He sighed, resigned to the fact of me as a blight on his day.

"Not that it would mean anything to you," he said, standing up and stretching to his full Paul Bunyan height, "but Hemingway fished here."

There have been times in my life when I've wanted to say, "Who?" This was one of them.

"That so?" I said politely, thinking to correct him, but changing my mind. Often it is the lie that matters more.

"Well. It means something to *me,*" he said, turning to walk away again, one huge finger looped through the jug handle, the water sloshing in it.

I could see the defensiveness in his posture and wished that by my very sex I had not offended him.

"Hey. Hey!" I called to him. "Hey, wait a minute."

He turned to me, his face impassive now. "What's that?"

I bit down hard on the one thought I had in my head and spit it out.

"I bet he'd like it. Hemingway. You taking water from here. I bet he would."

The mask of his face strained a little at the edges and I could see something working in him, a thought, maybe, that I might be right.

"Nah," he said finally. "He'd just think I'm nuts."

My head said, Not half as nuts as *he* was, but I didn't mean it. I knew differently now.

"No," I told the man, certain now of what I was saying, "I think he'd say it was a form of honor, like the way they float the dead down the river to set them free. Like that."

At my words the man's eyes brightened perceptibly, one corner of his mouth pulled up in a half smile, and he fixed his eyes on mine for the first time.

"You know," he said, "I like that. I really do." He turned his back again, but waved this time, his huge paw of a left hand held in the air a moment before he dropped it to his side.

I found an agate this time as I sat with the sun at my back in the cool, speckled water along the shore, a mound of stones heaped before me, oval paperweights of granite, pale pink like Easter eggs, others green as moss. I didn't have to dig too deep or look too long—it lay in the water to the left of my pyramid of overturned rocks, a perfect triangle of quartz giving it away. I palmed it, turned it over to examine the perfect striated layers of caramel interspersed with clear bands of quartz. It looked like a tiny chunk of rock pie, dense and rich, no more than an inch in length. I smelled it, licked it to bring out the color, thought of my imaginary boy in the Iowa cornfield kneeling to palm this same treasure, and I knew that he, like me, would keep it safe, pocket it when he traveled for good luck, this chip of stone that would say he alone had been granted something real, and hold it tight in his fist to feel it heat up like the sand in summer. I looked back over my shoulder expecting to see Travlin' on the bridge, its new, strong supports giving with the weight of him, but instead I caught the wind full in my face and saw the spindly pines along the bank bend and spin wildly with the force of it.

Old fishermen are the most elusive, able to cover their tracks in all seasons, vanishing and reappearing along the length of a stream like wind-spotted water. I was convinced I would never find him again, that my being here alone in this place he had known first was the coda to that clear moment of coincidence when his life had slammed into mine. ACCEPTANCE, the pamphlet he had given me had read. What more was there to know?

I asked at Rainbow Lodge about him, was told he didn't camp there anymore. Remembering his reference to "two-tracks," man-created woods' paths, I moved away from the river and the lake and deeper into the forest, following the tree-shrouded sand and dirt track that grew narrower and bumpier and spit me out, finally, at a small store at Pike's Lake. There I found the female proprietor, someone who knew of him.

"Oh sure," she told me. "He comes each year, early spring, early autumn, when the flies are gone. He'll be back October."

I handed her a brown paper bag with a copy of my novel inside. On the fly leaf I had written a letter, thanking him.

"Please see he gets this," I said to the woman, wondering how many seasons would pass before she would remember that she had slipped the bag onto a shelf below the cash register, how much dust would collect before she decided to take inventory.

I pocketed the agate, packed my fly rod, and took the sand and dirt track out to the unreal highway, heading home.

In the early spring of 1996 I received a thick blue envelope in the mail. In the sender's address corner it said, simply, "Travlin' Gravlin."

Inside were pictures, a long letter, a card, and on the front of the card an etching of an Indian woman, camouflaged in a snow-filled birch woods by the running forms of Appaloosas. Behind her runs an Indian brave, a wolf skin draped about his shoulders. Seeing this, I remembered Travlin's respect for Native Americans. I remembered that his wife was Indian.

He wrote that it was good to have heard from me, good to know I had written a book, "but most of all that you are clean and sober. And as you mention in your note you wrote in the book you sent, you are telling how I recognized your alcoholism, which as you said is not so easy to miss. My heart truly went out to you, specially the time you and I stood on the top of the hill looking down a steep two-track going toward the river. Remember?"

Sure, I thought, as I read the line, I remember, but how could this man ever know how precisely I remembered, how often I had laid out that scene, inspected it the way I do my face in the mirror now, getting reacquainted with the new look of an old girl, called it up to test the perimeters of its truth, seen clearly the headlong precipice above the river, heard that running water sound of wind in the pines, and decided that, yes, I owed this man a footnote in my life for what he had done?

"And I said a prayer for you, and a few since then. You seemed like a lost girl. But I believe that God works through people, and that perhaps God put us together to help each other. If you remember the place you caught the steelhead? If you think back you caught that fish on the second cast, and later that day you, the photographer, Harry, Harry's friend Jack, and myself had a cookout and ate the fish at my slide-on camper I kept at Richard's. Good times."

I remembered, all right. I remembered the kerosene smell of the small camper, and how it was dark and warm inside at the end of our day on the river. I remembered drinking in that camper, alone, while Travlin' beached his boat and Jeffrey went off to fish another part of the river. I remembered how I could not comprehend at the time that this place was sanctuary and that for me to have been drinking here was sacrilege. And then there was that night when we cooked my steelhead over the low fire and I had asked Jeffrey, sarcasm in my voice, why he wasn't drinking, and he had told me it was out of respect for Travlin', for his sobriety. I had responded defiantly, not quite believing my words when I had said, "He doesn't care," and had cracked another beer.

"Anyway," Travlin' continued, "the hole where you caught the steelhead we named 'Hemingway's Hole.'" Jesus, I thought, and laughed out loud at the unfortunate choice, wondering at the kind of fame to be had from being the inspiration for Hemingway's Hole. I imagined other, equally suggestive names, and gave it up. I could hear the jokes already.

"And many of the true fishermen know that hole as such," Travlin' went on, "men with nicknames like Ranger, Tight Lines, Indiana, and of course, yours truly, Travlin' Gravlin. And you know what? We are still catching fish there—not as many, but still catching. When I paddle up the river I think of you, and often wonder how you are. Now I know. And as I said, I am so very, very happy for you. You made my year. Only thing left for a perfect year is catching a steelhead at Hemingway's Hole. With Love, Travlin' Gravlin."

In the picture Travlin' sent he stands outside his cabin in the Michigan woods, his arms extended in a Les Hemingway gesture of welcome, a cockeyed grin on his face, and in the photo he wears the same red knit stocking cap he wore the day I met him on the Big Two-Hearted. I have taped the picture above my writing desk, next to a picture of Dr. Engle holding a trophy-sized snook. I tell myself I have found a new fishing buddy for the doctor, and that the two of them look good together.

The day Travlin's letter came a crow flew hard against the glass of my front window, believing it was air, and in that moment of contact when his wing snapped, a clean break, and the glass bowed, unseen in this ordinary light, but visible, I suspect, at a point in space and time infinitely more forgiving, there broke free in that fractured second the tone and very timbre of mercy.

Chapter

TWENTY-FOUR

THE ALBINO catfish pond is gone, the woods that once held its secret paved over in houses now, a sprawling extension of the suburb that had begun when I was a girl. In the gauzy warmth of a Mississippi May I looked for its deep cool well of water, its white-bodied sorcerers linked nose to tail in an exotic, orchestrated dance, the cracked sign looped over the barbwire that read WARNING: SNAKES, but found instead a labyrinth of lanes and cul-de-sacs, concrete and blacktop and brick erasing the world as I had known it thirty years before: the huge sweet gum tree that had marked the beginning of the woods gone; the buttercup-flecked grazing fields that had once flanked those woods gone. The girl who had climbed that tree and stalked those woods in the wet heat of summer and the red blaze of autumn and stood with her fingers pressed cautiously against the barbwire was gone now, too.

It is the smell of this place that pulls me back—earth and fire and water that bring up a longing sharp enough to taste and a need to belong again to this land. I pledge allegiance to its soil, its waters, and to the exalted sense of needing it as I have needed no other time or place.

Up the road, about a mile from where the pond once stood, was the house where I had lived. The facade had been blasted down to the original old brick, and the silver-leafed maple I had planted outside my bedroom window when I was nine years old—my mother insisting it was only a stick—was now over three decades old, its shade beyond the window where I had once stood at night, watching the stars, long and deep. The massive oak that had loomed beyond the picture window in front had been blown to pulp by lightning the year we had moved.

I dream about the house often. Sometimes my mother is in the dreams, in the kitchen, drinking, and I am comforted not by her presence, but by the very house itself, the rooms shadowy and warm, cast always in the light of dusk. In these dreams the doors are always open, the windows flung wide, and I can smell the heavy red clay scent of the ravine across the street, the place where I first comprehended form and substance, and where I separated myself, irrevocably, from the bonds of maternal blood. This is where I first observed, in a jar of algae and clay-flecked water, the depths from which I came.

It is this place to which I belong by unspoken oath. I understand the pull of it, my lifelong marriage to its mysteries, as I stand on the lip of the ravine, its chasm choked thick with poison ivy and saw grass, and further up, threaded with honeysuckle. I knocked first at the door of the house that fronts the ravine, a house where Charles Stickler used to live, a red-haired myopic boy from Pennsylvania who had a crush on me and who I smashed in the face with a toy truck one summer day when he tried to kiss me. A black woman and her two little girls live there now, the girls answering the door, acting shy at the sight of me, calling out, "Mama! Someone here." I told the mama I used to live across the street, used to play in the ravine when I was a kid. She had a handsome face, wickedly beautiful eyes like Freda's, and she looked at me as if this information were worth something. I said to her, "Can I walk out back and look?" and she grinned big, nodded her head as if she were in on a secret, saying, "Go ahead, girl. Knock yourself out."

It's what I did, knocked myself out with the smell and sight and sense of memory. But this was more than memory. This was the apex of memory, the light-blasted pinnacle of recollection where I stood at an earthly junction, timeless in my experience of it. Everything looked the same. It was grown over, choked thick with weeds, but I knew what lay beneath all the window dressing, saw it as clearly as if I had just stepped out the front door thirty years before.

Walking through the high grass in the backyard I felt chiggers burrowing beneath the skin of my legs and I reached down to scratch, idly, taken back to my girlhood and evenings spent examining chigger bites, scrapes and cuts and scabs, my battle wounds from days spent in this trench. I spotted a pair of cardinals perched in a sweet gum tree, the bright red of the male's feathers a gash in the canopy. I remembered nursing chicks fallen from the nest, and a yellow warbler, whose wing I'd mended, flying from the perch of my open palm one summer morning in my tenth year. I remembered the smooth feel of garter snakes cool in my hands and the black anvil base of storm clouds moving in from the southwest, and how when the sun shone full on them the clouds grew darker, so dark sometimes I would panic. It always reminded me of death, that kind of sky, and I figured later on this was pretty much the deal with life, that when something was bright and infinitely clear its shadow always followed, the sky split open, and there you stood in the deluge. I remember being baptized in the street, waist deep in water, by this ravine in flood season, when the waters swelled over the lip, bearing snakes and turtles and frogs on its rampage. I remembered walking across the narrow tarred pipe that spanned the ravine, on a dare, and how when I reached the middle, my bare feet slippery on the pipe, the water a moving wall beneath me, I thought of free-falling, like the man who fell from the bridge that spanned the Arkansas, and I thought of how it would feel to be held by all that water.

There is a sign posted farther up the ravine now that says you cannot enter, by penalty of law. I ignored it, but wondered what had come to pass here—a child swept away again in the gully-washing floods? Someone bitten by a cottonmouth, maybe, or a boy's leg broken when he fell from the hot tar pipe? All the dangers that had bloomed at every turn in childhood had called out to me once here, and I had heeded them as I had the WARNING: SNAKES sign, defiantly.

I sat down on a cleared-out patch of clay, halfway down the bank of the ravine, the heat trapped within its steep walls wet and steaming, and took my socks off, inspecting a half-moon scar on the bottom of my right foot where a broken bottle had, in this same place years before, cut clear through to the tendon. That afternoon I had limped home, trailing blood, not crying, because even then I considered it a show of weakness. I remembered thinking idiotically of Hansel and Gretel and their bread crumb trail. When I had stood in the carport of our house, watching the blood pool and seep into the concrete, banging hard on the door so my mother and stepfather would let me in, trying the knob and finding it locked, I had understood in that single moment the strength to be had in being absolutely alone. I'd followed the blood trail back to the ravine, gathering oak and maple leaves along the way, and had rinsed the wound in a deep pothole, the free-flowing blood mixing with the red-orange water, and I had thought then of how this blood could nourish, that if I were to trap a bass in a jar of my own blood, what a monster it might become. I had wrapped the cut then in the leaves, tied them on with a thin whipcord of honeysuckle vine, and had thought myself to be infinitely able.

It is here I came to sovereignty, where it greeted me with the stern face of the elder, and why I say with certainty it is of this one place I am born, and that had it not been for the drumroll beat of summer, a message pounded out from my heritage of this land, then I would have never known that all these years—quiet, steady, aware—the memory of it walked with me. And had I not been given the memory, indelible, of grace and redemption, that tiny bass trapped in a jar of river water, then would I have ever understood the same grace might be given me. I doubt it. The older I get, the more I understand it is the land that nurtures orphans.

As I made my way along the ravine, across a patch of briars that trailed thick and tangled in the mud, I felt my feet grow damp inside my shoes, which reminded me of how I would steal into the thick wet night air, pulled by an arrow of moonlight behind the clouds and the sense that all things worth knowing belonged to the night and would rise up in chorus on the voices of frogs. There had been a jagged skin of ice once, in late autumn, along the edge of the water, and I had poked it with my fingers, watched it crack like the dried clay in summer, and had thought then of my mother's face, oddly, how so often it seemed thin and fragile, about to break. She is in a nursing home in Memphis now, brain damaged from a head-on car crash twelve years ago, safe, finally. I knew now as I stood barefoot in the ravine, the feel of the mud cool and familiar, that I had not outwitted, had not escaped, but had instead put a twist on her sad legacy and the similar legacy of others bound to me by blood. Who would have been fool enough to say I would be the lucky one—the ravine girl, the snake girl, the fish girl, the drug addict, the drunk, the girl who had said, without equivocation, "I want to be a hermit?" Who would have guessed I would survive, not merely, but with some blood left in me?

As I knelt with the sun in my eyes and tried to make out the shapes of stones that littered the ravine bed, I remembered the feel of rocks in my palm, the smell of them, and how I had found once an oval of obsidian. I had rubbed it for good luck, believed then, as I have come to again, in fortune.

I looked down the clogged channel of the tributary, at the sedge broom, wild holly, and saw grass, brambles knotted up like barbwire, and watched the clean red feather of a cardinal drift from the open limbs of a sweet gum tree, spin like a maple seed caught on a draft of wind, and land just short of my outstretched palm, an invitation home.

Chapter TWENTY-FIVE

DOWN THE street from where I live now is an authentic barbeque joint—an anomaly in these parts—called the O.K. Corral, run by a big black ex-boxer named Otis. Otis came to Seattle from Georgia years ago, and I first spotted him strolling out the front door of the local Safeway with a twenty-five-pound sack of pinto beans slung over his shoulder. Since they know precious little about pintos in Seattle, except maybe they're cars, maybe they're horses, it was a fair guess this man was from my part of the world.

"Hey, mister," I called to him. "Where you going with those pintos?"

He told me, across the street to this new soul food joint he was opening up, and thus began a weekly pig-out of mine on the best Southern food not only in Seattle, but in the South as well.

You can smell the sizzle of sauce-basted ribs a full mile away, and when Otis doesn't have anything on the grill he just burns wood, "to entice 'em," he says. The trick works. You can see people in the Safeway parking lot sniffing the air like empty-bellied hounds and then wandering zombielike in the direction of Otis's smoke. As far as I know, Otis has not patented his spicy, aromatic, real-deal sauce, but its ingredients are a fairly well guarded secret. The one slipup Otis made was giving the recipe to a girlfriend, who eventually became an ex, and who took to the streets with his prized recipe, handing out the Xeroxed list to passersby.

The smell hits me like a memory locomotive when I walk in the front door, and I'm back at Freda's after a sun-baked day at Pine Bluff Lake, the smell of frying catfish saturating the already steaming air, or waiting outside the porthole window at Mac's Cafe for Catfish to slide my lunch onto the narrow pickup counter. I smell the river at Otis's, too, even though it's just a mixed-up smell from Puget Sound, salt air pretending to be river-bottom air. Otis serves ribs and chicken, pintos and greens, corn bread, Big Otis's Sweet Potato Pie (I kid him about a franchise), peach cobbler, and a special he calls the Hook-Up, which includes more or less all of the above. I asked him once why the name Hook-Up, and he said, "'Cause once we hook you up to this, you ain't gettin' loose." There's also the plainly stated "slab of ribs" dinner, approximately the whole hind section of the hog. And Otis has catfish, bags and boxes and crates of catfish, sweet and white and firm, fresh from Mississippi catfish farms.

I get the catfish. Always. I have, in a traitorous moment, had a bite off the ribs, a bite off the chicken, but it's the catfish I crave the way I crave beets dug fresh from the ground. I want it for breakfast, lunch, supper, dessert. For my birthday, Cristen's birthday, Halloween, Election Day, Christmas, I go to Otis's to celebrate. I figure if I am going to indulge abomination, this is the way to go.

Otis hires catfish wizards to cook for him, none of these "lightly breaded and pan-fried" chefs who present you with a "medallion of fish" and a sprig of parsley, but down-home, deep-fry cooks who *know* that the major part of the catfish ritual is cornmeal and that a magic incantation mumbled at the exact moment of immersion—something like "Bee-bop a lu-la, she's my baby"—evokes the true catfish soul.

Tooz was Otis's first cook, a lanky whipcord of a man, black, my age, and raised in Jackson, Mississippi, where he grew up poverty stricken while I grew up at least well fed. I remembered, listening to him when we first met, the incalculable distance that would have been between us had we met some thirty years before. Tooz pointed it out himself one day when he said to me, "I couldn't know you then, but hey, I can know you now." His words underlined what I often so conveniently overlook in memory—racism, final and unyielding as the hilt of a bayonet—and I was reminded not of the nobility of being Southern, but of the shame. Eventually Tooz tired of Seattle and its mild, stupor-producing weather and returned to his family in New Orleans. "I want to be able to walk down the block and have people call out my name, friendly, like they care how I'm doing," he told me before he left. "I don't get that here."

After Tooz came Nelson, who still cooks for Otis. Nelson, too, looks like a prizefighter, low to the ground, compact, and tightly built, his face handsome and open. As some peculiar quirk of fate would have it, Nelson is from Pine Bluff. At my delight in learning this not-so-cosmic tie, and asking, stupidly, as it turned out, if he missed the place, Nelson made a face and said, "Hell, no. Who'd miss that place? You know it's on the list of the ten most *un*livable cities, huh? Bet you didn't know that."

I told him I did know, but you had to be born somewhere.

"Then you be born there, then," Nelson said, cranky as Catfish used to be. "Not me though, uh-uh. Not me."

Nelson's the one who always throws on an extra piece of fish for me, and when I come to the window to order, he stops what he's doing to give me a hug.

"Let me guess," he says, looking me in the eye like he knows something real important. "You probably want the catfish."

"No salt," I tell him, like he hasn't heard it a hundred times, and he rolls his eyes each time and says, "You and salt. What you telling me you don't want no salt? You can eat *all* the damned salt you want. You're young."

When the order's ready I walk up to the warped, wooden three-quarter door that swings out from the kitchen and stand up on my toes so I can see in. There's the deep-fat fryer with catfish bubbling in it, a mammoth pot of greens simmering on the small stove, the corn bread kept warm over a tray of steaming water, and out the backdoor, which is cracked open, I can see a patch of dirt and weeds and imagine for a long, timeless moment that it is the beginning of the path Catfish beat to the Arkansas each day. I expect to see a pole propped against the heat-thickened door, her strong, pink-palmed hand reaching for it. I expect to see her take off running. I expect to see her face, maybe, in Nelson's.

"Order's up, missy," Nelson calls to me. "You hungry?"

As I head out the door to Freda's '56 Chevy parked at the curb, the paper bag of fish warm against me, I hear Otis call out, using the name he remembers me by.

"Hey, Catfish," he says. "You have a good night, now."